India's Emerging Economy

India's Emerging Economy
Performance and Prospects
in the 1990s and Beyond

Edited by Kaushik Basu

The MIT Press
Cambridge, Massachusetts
London, England

This book was set in Palatino on 3B2 by Asco Typesetters, Hong Kong.
Printed and bound in the United States of America.

Library of Congress Cataloging-in-Publication Data

India's emerging economy : performance and prospects in the 1990s and beyond /
  edited by Kaushik Basu.
      p.   cm.
  Papers with revisions influenced by discussions held at a conference organized by the
editor.
  Includes bibliographical references and index.
  ISBN 0-262-02556-6 (alk. paper)
  1. India—Economic conditions—20th century—Congresses. 2. India—Economic
conditions—21st century—Congresses. 3. India—Economic policy—20th century—
Congresses. 4. India—Economic policy—21st century—Congresses. I. Basu, Kaushik.
HC435.2.I62324   2004
330.954—dc22   2003061409

10 9 8 7 6 5 4 3 2 1

To Dr. Manmohan Singh,
scholar, parliamentarian, senior economist, and friend

Contents

Acknowledgments

This book is the product of a long period of planning and intellectual spadework. Apart from the efforts of the authors, which will be evident to the reader, several people were involved in the making of this final product whose imprint the book bears, though not their names.

After the authors had written a first draft of the papers a conference was organized, in which a number of people participated in the capacity of discussants and chairs. Their comments and criticisms contributed immensely to improving the book. Among them were Swaminathan Aiyar, Iwan Azis, Alaka Basu, Luis-Felipe Lopez-Calva, Purnendu Chatterjee, Mrinal Datta Chaudhuri, Nancy Chau, Gary Fields, Maitreesh Ghatak, Ron Herring, Devesh Kapur, Mary Katzenstein, Mukul Majumdar, A. Prasad, Mahesh Rangarajan, Hunter Rawlings, David Sahn, Anand Swamy, Erik Thorbecke, Miguel Urquiola, and Henry Wan.

In organizing The Indian Economy Conference at Cornell University (April 19–20, 2002), I was greatly helped by my students, Vidhi Chhaochharia, Leonid Fedorov, and Akshay Murthy. I am indebted also to the chief administrator of my department, Dan Wszolek, for smart help, as always. Various Cornell University officials were very supportive of the effort and, at the risk of omission, I want to express special thanks to Provost Biddy Martin, Dean Phil Lewis, Tapan Mitra, who was then department chair, and the president of the university, Hunter Rawlings.

In the final stages of the editorial work, I was helped by Amanda Felkey and Gayatri Koolwal, without whose painstaking effort the book would not be what it is.

And finally, I must thank my editor at The MIT Press, Elizabeth Murry, for her great interest in the project, from the time of its inception to now. It was very useful to be able to call on her for advice and comments at various stages of this work.

Contributors

Abhijit V. Banerjee Ford Foundation International Professor of Economics, Massachusetts Institute of Technology, Cambridge, MA

Pranab Bardhan Professor of Economics, University of California, Berkeley, CA

Kaushik Basu Professor of Economics and C. Marks Professor, Cornell University, Ithaca, NY

Manuela Ferro Lead Economist, World Bank, Washington, DC

Barbara Harriss-White Professor of Development Studies, Queen Elizabeth House, Oxford University, UK

Renana Jhabvala Chairperson, SEWA Bank, Ahmedabad, India

Ravi Kanbur T. H. Lee Professor of World Affairs and Professor of Economics, Cornell University, Ithaca, NY

N. R. Narayana Murthy Chairman of the Board, Infosys Technologies Limited, Bangalore, India

Mihir Rakshit Director, Monetary Research Project, Investment Information and Credit Rating Agency, Calcutta, India

M. Govinda Rao Director, National Institute of Public Finance and Policy, New Delhi, India

Y. V. Reddy Governor, Reserve Bank of India, Mumbai, India

David Rosenblatt Senior Economist, World Bank, Washington, DC

Amartya Sen Master of Trinity College, Cambridge, UK (From January 2004, Lamont University Professor, Harvard University)

Nirvikar Singh Professor of Economics, University of California, Santa Cruz, CA

Nicholas Stern Second Permanent Secretary at the UK Treasury, Head of the Government Economic Service and Managing Director of the Budget and Public Finances, London, UK

I Introduction

1

The Indian Economy: Up to 1991 and Since

Kaushik Basu

1.1

With the exception, perhaps, of the years immediately following India's independence, never before has there been as much optimism about the Indian economy as in the last decade. But India is notorious for blowing its chances, not only in cricket, but also vis-à-vis the economy. The hope, in the immediate wake of this country's independence, was firmly belied. In the late 1970s, with foreign exchange reserves beginning to build up, the savings rate crossing 20 percent for the first time, and the economy running a food surplus, many felt that the time for India's economic takeoff had come. But India remained stubbornly rooted to the tarmac. Hence, there is reason to view the current buzz with caution. Is the recent growth spurt of the 1990s sustainable? How has the growth been shared among India's different regions and different people? Is the optimism founded too excessively and exclusively on India's celebrated success in information technology? How successful, in fact, has India been in information technology? Given the surge of interest in the Indian economy, it is natural for such questions to arise. This book is an attempt to provide answers to some of these issues and to offer perspectives on India's recent performance and future prospects from a group of people who have been on the cutting edge of research, policymaking, and industry building in India.

In this introductory chapter I cover some of the ground addressed in the subsequent chapters but do not confine myself to those issues. Subsequent chapters are written by independent and prominent commentators, with their own distinctive views. Hence, while on some of the most fundamental policy matters they share a common approach —remarkably so—the chapters have different foci and, often, different perspectives. Hence, one purpose of this introductory chapter is to give a general, overarching account of India's economic performance, recounting not only what happened in the 1990s but also filling in some of the background story leading up to the past decade. I hope this overview helps readers better appreciate the essays that follow, which have their own themes and, with a few exceptions, are concerned with India's post-1991 economic experience.

But I cannot resist going beyond this editorial task to put on record my own views on the Indian experience and, in particular, to argue that, as soon as one takes a slightly longer view of an economy's performance it becomes important to understand the social and cultural setting in which this occurs.[1] I argue that economic performances, good and bad, may owe a lot to the cultural underpinnings of the economy in question.[2] There is also reason to study the social, cultural, and political environment in itself. As Amartya Sen argues in chapter 2, economics is not the only yardstick with which to evaluate a nation's performance. And, on the political and social front there is much concern about India's recent experience,[3] even though its *economic* prospects look encouraging. Democracy and secularism were two basic tenets behind the vision of an independent India. Sen assesses how India has figured in terms of these two larger political and cultural aims and alerts us to the possibility of these being endangered. Moreover, it is arguable that economic success in the long run may depend on such political and cultural factors.

In explaining the economic success or failure of a nation, economists and others study the kind of macroeconomic policies in effect—openness to trade, the size of the fiscal deficit, and the nature of the exchange rate regime—and the hard structural features of the nation in question—such as its geography, topography, and natural resources. However, it will be argued that the roots of India's prolonged economic stagnation and the glimmer of hope that one notices today cannot be fully understood if one ignores the variables that conventional economic analysis has taught the public to ignore—the social norms, culture, beliefs, and fabric of social interaction.

To say that the cause of a nation's overall stagnation lies in its culture or its collective beliefs does not mean to deny the importance of its economic policy, just as the assertion that the spilled fuel on the floor caused the fire does not exonerate the smoldering cigarette stub thrown carelessly into it. Also, culture and social norms must not be taken as immutable features of society. These norms evolve and change, often responding mechanically to the altering global environment and the inexorable advance of technology, but also at times consciously, through the will of the people to adopt a norm that may seem valuable or to discard values that may have become an anachronism.[4] Public intellectuals, writers, and Keynes's academic scribblers of yesteryear play a crucial role in this.

One can find many historical accounts of a nation's changing culture and norms. In 1950, Alec Adams, the British Charge d'Affaires in Korea, described Koreans as follows: "[Foreigners] who live here mostly entertain the lowest opinion of Korean intelligence, mores, ability and industry. It is hard to believe, I gather, that [Koreans] will ever be able to successfully govern themselves." (qtd. in Clifford 1994, 29). It seems impossible to square this perspective with our contemporary view of Koreans, who are known for their intelligence and industry. It is possible that Adams's opinion was shaped in part by racism, but he was not the only one to hold such a view (see Clifford 1994). It also seems possible to argue that Korean mores have changed during these last fifty years; while Adams's perspective may have had some validity then, it has no validity now.

Thus, an understanding of the role of culture and collective beliefs in the life of a nation can help analysts and policymakers design better and more appropriate economic policy. In the case of Russia it is now recognized that standard economic policies designed to speed transition did poorly because they amounted to a change that Russian society was not prepared to accept—the requisite culture and norms for the market economy were not in place. But this is true not just for Russia. When economists propose their favored economic policy agendas and fret that they are not immediately adopted, or get aborted, after adoption, because of social instability, one reason for the policy failure and economists' frustration is the lack of understanding of the social and political context in which the policy was implemented (Platteau 1994, 2000). Hence, the focus on the politico-cultural underbelly of an economy does not have to be founded in skepticism of economic policy, but in recognition of the fact that this is a complement of it and so should assist in the design of better and more appropriate economic policy.

But before going to that it is convenient to begin with a brief recounting of the statistical context of the subject matter of this chapter and also the book. Both occur in the next section.

1.2

A broad picture of where India stands today in cross-sectional terms is captured in table 1.1. The numbers tell a lot. It is a country that remains

Kaushik Basu

Table 1.1
Selected cross-country development indicators, 2000–2001

	Average annual % growth in GDP (1990–2001)	Gross national income (GNI), per capita dollars (2001)	PPP Gross national income (GNI), per capita dollars (2001)	Gross capital formation, % of GDP (2001)	Life expectancy at birth, years (2000)	Under-5 mortality rate, per 1,000 (2000)	Adult literacy rate, % of people 15 and older (2000)
China	10.0	890	4,260	39	70	39	84
India	5.9	460	2,450	24	63	88	57
Mexico	3.1	5,540	8,770	21	73	36	91
Pakistan	3.7	420	1,920	15	63	110	43
South Africa	2.1	2,900	9,510	15	48	79	85

Source: The World Bank, *World Development Report 2003.*

crushingly poor but has had a decade of fast growth. As is evident from tables 1.2 and 1.3, in terms of pure growth the 1990s was India's best decade since gaining its independence, and, from what little one knows of her earlier experience, perhaps the best performance of the last century. In per capita income terms, with or without purchasing power parity (ppp) correction, India has now outperformed Pakistan, where political turmoil has taken its toll on economic performance. On the other hand, China, whose economic performance even a decade ago was very close to India's, has now surged ahead and has nearly double India's per capita income. Arguably, India's growth performance in the last decade has been second only to China's, but the gap between the two nations is, nevertheless, substantial.

On an examination of indicators that reflect the standard of living, such as life expectancy at birth or literacy or under-5 mortality, India does poorly but perhaps not quite as poorly as one might expect from her per capita income. South Africa, for instance, is several folds richer than India but has a life expectancy of 48 years, way below that of India's 63. It has a mortality rate close to India's. India's literacy rate of 57 percent, as reported in table 1.1, is bad by any standards, though it must be pointed out that, one year later (i.e., in 2001), the national census showed that literacy had actually risen to 65 percent.

As far as performance over time goes, these are summarized in tables 1.2 and 1.3, which show that, going by pure growth rates, there is some reason for optimism for the Indian economy. India's average growth rate, which was close to 3.5 percent in the fifties and sixties, went up to over 5 percent in the late seventies and stayed that way for a decade. After the economic depression of 1991, growth picked up even more, clearing the 6 percent mark on average and actually seeing a GDP growth rate of over 7 percent for three consecutive years starting from 1994.

With this brief statistical sketch in the background, we are now in a position to go into the causes of the Indian economy's poor performance for so many decades after independence and its seeming improvement in the last decade.

1.3

One of the most celebrated battles in Indian history was fought between Robert Clive and Siraj ud Daula in June 1757 in Plassey, West Bengal. Siraj's defeat would be a milestone in the establishment of

Table 1.2
Gross domestic saving (GDS) and growth rate in India, 1950–2001

	Rate of gross domestic saving (GDS)	Annual growth rate of GDP at factor cost		Rate of gross domestic saving (GDS)	Annual growth rate of GDP at factor cost
50–51	8.9	.	76–77	19.4	1.2
51–52	9.3	2.3	77–78	19.8	7.5
52–53	8.3	2.8	78–79	21.5	5.5
53–54	7.9	6.1	79–80	20.1	−5.2
54–55	9.4	4.2	80–81	18.9	7.2
55–56	12.6	2.6	81–82	18.6	6
56–57	12.2	5.7	82–83	18.3	3.1
57–58	10.4	−1.2	83–84	17.6	7.7
58–59	9.5	7.6	84–85	18.8	4.3
59–60	11.2	2.2	85–86	19.5	4.5
60–61	11.6	7.1	86–87	18.9	4.3
61–62	11.7	3.1	87–88	20.6	3.8
62–63	12.7	2.1	88–89	20.9	10.5
63–64	12.3	5.1	89–90	22	6.7
64–65	11.9	7.6	90–91	23.1	5.6
65–66	14	−3.7	91–92	22	1.3
66–67	14	1	92–93	21.8	5.1
67–68	11.9	8.1	93–94	22.5	5.9
68–69	12.2	2.6	94–95	24.8	7.3
69–70	14.3	6.5	95–96	25.1	7.3
70–71	14.6	5	96–97	23.2	7.8
71–72	15.1	1	97–98	23.5	4.8
72–73	14.6	−0.3	98–99	22	6.6
73–74	16.8	4.6	99–00	22.3	6.4
74–75	16	1.2	00–01	.	5.2
75–76	17.2	9			

Source: Reserve Bank of India (2001).

Table 1.3
Annual average growth rate in India across plan periods

		GNP at factor cost, 1993–1994 prices
First plan	1951–1956	3.7
Second plan	1956–1961	4.2
Third plan	1961–1966	2.8
Fourth plan	1969–1974	3.4
Fifth plan	1974–1979	5.0
Sixth plan	1980–1985	5.5
Seventh plan	1985–1990	5.8
Eighth plan	1992–1997	6.8
Average	1951–2000	4.4

Source: National Accounts Statistics 2001, Ministry of Statistics, Government of India.

the British Empire in India. The battle was bizarre and brief. Siraj ud Daula's force was some 60,000 strong. This included close to 20,000 cavalry and 40,000 infantry. Clive, on the other hand, commanded an impossibly small force of 3,000 soldiers. Even the firepower was mismatched. Siraj's army had nearly fifty guns, most of them 24- or 32-pounders. Clive's men had eight field guns and one howitzer. The balance of resources was overwhelmingly in favor of India.[5] But within moments of the start of the battle, the Indian side was in disarray.[6] Panic, lack of coordination, and betrayal made the forces look not so much like a defending army as a wild rioting mob. The battle was won by Clive, within hours of its start. The defeat cannot be understood in terms of the balance of resources or individual human capital. It was essentially a failure of organizational capital or what in business schools today would be called a failure of managerial coordination.[7]

Consider an economy where some people control all the water, some all the food, and some all the energy. Even though the total amount of water, food, and energy may be very large, if this society does not learn how to exchange and trade, it will be a very poor society—indeed so poor that all its members may die. In a modern nation, it is not enough for there to be a lot of knowledge about medicine, engineering, and information technology. If the nation does not have the organizational ability to share and exchange this knowledge and to combine each with other kinds of knowledge and harness it where it is needed, it will be a miserable and poor nation. Since one does not typically think of organizational skill and the ability for coordinated action as a resource or capital, it is easy to overlook their importance. But in the case of India, to overlook these abilities and issues is to seriously handicap thorough analysis. It may not be entirely a matter of chance that India has so much individual talent in classical music but no orchestral tradition.

This situation is, in part, a consequence of the social norm not to submit to authority, whether it be the conductor's baton or the government's order. There are not too many cities in the world, where, as in Delhi in the early eighties, bus seats with the prominently displayed label "Ladies Seat" often required another beseeching sign: "Please let ladies sit on Ladies Seat." And, based on my own limited observation (from the precarious foothold that I would have—on lucky days—on the bus, while traveling between home and the Delhi School of Economics) of passenger behavior, even this meta-order had little effect.

It is worth emphasizing here, by way of a digression, that what I am calling organization or organizational capital[8] is quite different from education or human capital. The latter resides in individuals whereas organizational ability (and coordination) is a property of *collectivities*. A society of high human capital and poor organization is like a society where lots of people have computers but no Internet exists to link the information in these computers. It is clear that the same society with the same number of computers becomes vastly more efficient if people are able to use the information in one another's computers. Likewise, the benefits of ample human capital are large, but would nevertheless be severely underutilized without a network of organization and coordination.[9]

By the same token, the "success" of the early European colonizers in India is impossible to understand without examining this mysterious resource—organizational capital. It is the development of the managerial technique, whereby a small number of Europeans could not only coordinate their own actions but use large numbers of locals to control the locals, that led to the advancement of the empires. The British Empire was the crowning example of this method of management.

The rise of the British offers another lesson in management—the importance of learning. It is arguable that this technique was not their own but that of the Portuguese, developed during the viceroyalty of Alphonso d'Albuquerque in Goa from 1509 to 1515. Albuquerque mastered the technique of using a very limited number of his own people, the Portuguese, to control masses of the local population through a carefully designed system of incentives and disincentives, instead of the age-old practice of bringing in large occupying armies from the conquering nation to establish control over the new territories. It was a managerial system par excellence, which the British emulated.

People learn most easily from those with whom they identify. It is not surprising that Albuquerque's technique was mastered by other Europeans and facilitated the spread of colonialism but had little effect on the *nawabs* and the indigenous civilians.

In the case of India the British would soon edge out the Portuguese, who were deflected from their original mission of trade and commercial plunder by their zeal to convert and kill the heathens, in particular the Muslims of India. The British, on the other hand, offered the natives protection and won over their trust; soon they were using the same method of offering small incentives and punishments to commandeer the local population against the larger interests of the local population.

1.4

While the Indians did not learn the amorphous art of control and management from their colonial rulers, they did learn one thing from the colonial experience that would get etched as a belief in the country's collective psyche.[10] The British came to India not to rule but to trade. The initial contact that India had with Britain was not with the Crown but with one of the earliest multinational corporations of the world, the East India Company. But the trading interests of the company increasingly intertwined with the ruling interest of the nation from where the company originated. Commercial interest merged with political interest and gradually, without any serious resistance, a huge subcontinent had passed into the control of the British Empire. Thenceforth, the Indians would be relieved of their resources not just through asymmetric trade and exchange but also taxation and state-sponsored extortion. The fear of multinationals and a mistrust of business and trade would become part of India's collective memory. And if their memory ever tended to fade, incidents such as the U.S. interference in Allende's Chile to make Latin America "safe" for U.S. business would restore it to vigor. Independent India would design its economic policy in the shadow of this memory.

One can see manifestations of this commercial distrust in all walks of Indian life, trivial and momentous. The mistrust of business and profit has been woven into songs and into the remonstration of parents to children who refuse to study hard that they will end up having to do business when they grow up. One can see this sentiment in advertisements. In India there is a disproportionate effort to couch business in morality, to show that the low price or the big sale is not a business stratagem but an act of honor. I have some newspaper clippings of advertisements from a 1984 price war among sellers of hosiery goods—undergarments, vests, and "baba suits" (suits for little boys, to the best of my knowledge)—who took out a series of advertisements in the *Indian Express*. These are funny because they are so blatant; but they are also significant because they illustrate the need of entrepreneurs to counter the widespread Indian mistrust of business. The first of these is an advertisement from 22 March, which shows the picture of a kindly looking man, Bal Krishan Khurana, and gives details of the sale that he is organizing, including the fact that all items are being sold at the low price of 30 rupees each. Just below Mr. Khurana's picture and above those details, a bold caption reads: "If I am asked about my last wish, I would pray to God to send me again to the great land of India, so that I can give more hosiery service to my country men."

Virtually all advertisements and commercials in every country have manufacturers and traders professing concern and care for the consumer's welfare. What is noteworthy in this advertisement is that it goes beyond pandering to the consumer. It appeals to morals beyond the marketplace; it appeals to the seller's patriotism.

A few days later, on 26 March, came a challenge to Mr. Khurana in the form of an advertisement taken out by Mr. Ramesh Arora, a person sporting a beard in a manner befitting holy men. He is selling similar hosiery items at lower prices than Mr. Khurana's, but that information is dwarfed by the moral message in bold, which reads: "Today Ramesh Arora is going to sell Hosiery items worth up to Rs. 200 [for] only 25 Rupees because I am the son of that respectable mother who did not desire Bungalows from me, but desired the service of my nation. Just imagine can any one on this divine Earth compete with me in selling Hosiery items."

Some weeks later, on 20 May, Mr. Khurana did what Bertrand competition in oligopoly would lead economists to expect of anybody who has bought a disproportionately large inventory of hosiery. He cuts the price to Rs. 5 and appeals again not to good business or concern for consumer welfare, but this time to revolutionary fervor. The advertisement has a large-font caption that reads: "The person who fights with Nations enemies is called REVOLUTIONARY. The person who sells Rs. 150 worth export quality goods [for] Rs. 5 is called BAL KRISHAN KHURANA."

The other side of this same phenomenon—namely, the consumer's apprehension that businesses are always out to cheat[11]—has had more significant consequences for India. It led to the creation of a large bureaucracy to control and monitor business and to set up barriers to foreign goods and investment. The tariffs on imports rose steadily, as successive finance ministers fell over one another to demonstrate their resolve not to allow foreigners to exploit Indians. Foreign direct investment (FDI) was discouraged, and this was done so successfully that the amount of FDI that was coming into India by the late 1980s was less than what was going to its much smaller neighbor, Bangladesh.

Growing disillusionment with the economy, a gradual drift of opinion the world over (away from planning and control to recognizing the importance of incentives and openness), and, on top of this ready soil, a major crisis in the early 1990s would shake India out of her policy stupor and make possible changes that earlier would have met with enormous popular resistance. But I come back to that shortly.

India's failure was, more than anything else, an intellectual failure. Many contemporary writers, charged by the euphoria of economic reform and the mantra of government withdrawal, have written at length about the goodness of big business and the nobility of man's acquisitive urge. This is a distortion of history and contemporary reality. And it is not as if one needs it to make a case in support of economic reforms and market liberalization. India needs to move more vigorously toward a modern, market economy. But as several of the essays in this book illustrate, this cannot be achieved through the relatively easy route of rolling back government. There is no escape from the need for purposive, intelligent action from government. Government, or good governance, is a concomitant of efficient markets, not a substitute.

It is my opinion that a suspicion of the big and the powerful (be it government, corporations, or individuals), at any time, is a sign of good judgment. The mistakes Indian policymakers made lay elsewhere. First, they failed to realize that the global business ethos had changed, not only from the mid-eighteenth century when Robert Clive had plundered India on behalf of a business concern but even through the 1970s and 1980s. Corporations are still hungry for profit, but emerging global norms do not allow them to use the kind of plundering strategy that they earlier employed. Second, the policymakers lacked pragmatism. They made the erroneous deduction that if X is interested in only his own profit, then we cannot benefit from interacting with X and so should not have any truck with X. This deduction is invalid because it presumes that, if an agent does something in his own self-interest, then that action cannot have beneficial effects on others. But "collateral benefits" in economics can be as ubiquitous as collateral damage in war. Despite this mistake the decisions of the policymakers would be fine if, other than such X's, there were Y's, who were noble and effective business partners. Maybe these Y's will come to exist in some future time, but there are few such Y's around now. So, while guarding our own interest, we must at the same time be prepared to deal with businesses that may have no interest in human welfare at large. Pragmatism requires us to decide on the course of a particular action on the basis of how good its consequences are, and not on the basis of whether it requires us to run with the hounds.

1.5

Economists keep telling the public about what is the "obviously" right policy. "If only," they say, "India had done this or that ..." it would not be a nation in such poverty. But a study of history and an open mind shows that, in crafting policy, there is virtually nothing that is *obviously* right or wrong. I do believe that India's persistence with a closed economy system—a direct byproduct of her history and beliefs—hurt her, and it is the opening up of the 1990s that has been the basis of the economic progress that has been witnessed since, providing hope for the future. But, as I demonstrate, there are counterexamples, which would make a view different from mine not outrageously wrong or obviously false. Regrettably, economics and the study of society are doomed to this innate ambiguity.

One can see the glaringly paradoxical nature of economic policy in India's most celebrated industry—information technology and software.[12] The numbers are quite stunning. The volume of India's software exports was $2.7 billion in 1998–1999, over $4 billion in 1999–2000, $6.2 billion in 2000–2001 and exceeding $8 billion in 2001–2002. This trend has been present for the last ten years—an annual growth rate of approximately 40 percent, despite the slight slowdown last year caused by the global recession. Given the compounding involved, this means that in the 1990s, India's exports virtually doubled every two years. In 1999 a study by NASSCOM and McKinsey[13] had predicted that India's exports would reach $50 billion by the year 2008. Since India's *total* current exports are less than $50 billion,[14] and nothing like this has happened in any other sector in India in anybody's living memory, these estimates and predictions have given rise to much skepticism. I was initially skeptical myself, but having checked and compared different sources I am convinced that, give or take a margin of 5 percent, the estimated volume of exports is right. No matter what one thinks of the forecast and even if one, quite reasonably, believes that it errs on the side of optimism, the sector's performance thus far has been outstanding.

What is interesting is that India's software success has resulted from policies that were commonly viewed as defective. First and foremost, it was a consequence of India's "over-investment" in higher education. For a long time Indians were used to seeing a glut of engineers in search of jobs and many economists criticized the policymakers and, more generally, government for this oversupply. Then came the admittedly unexpected breakthroughs, mainly in the United States, in the information technology (IT) sector, and suddenly the idle engineers were gone, boosting the Indian economy and sending entrepreneurs scampering to set up institutes and colleges to cope with the excess demand for higher education.

Second, brain drain had for long been criticized for many of India's ills. Yet it is arguable that it is the brain drain to Silicon Valley that made Bangalore possible. As Indian computer professionals migrated to the United States, ideas flowed back to India and the Indian industry took off. The NASSCOM-McKinsey study, mentioned earlier, has estimated that the larger the outflow of computer professionals to outside India, the greater the software exports from India. So the brain drain in this instance played greatly to India's advantage.

Third, it would be a denial of reality if one did not recognize that it was an act of closing the economy that spurred India's domestic IT sector. In 1977 the Janata government asked IBM to leave India, since they refused to dilute their ownership of 100 percent of the subsidiaries. As Infosys's CEO, Narayana Murthy, has written elsewhere, "This was in some sense a blessing in disguise," encouraging the production "of smaller, state-of-the-art but cheaper minicomputers and microcomputers" (2000, 215). But after this, the boost to this sector came, as Murthy acknowledges in the same paper and discusses in greater detail in chapter 9, from the opening up of the economy in the nineties.

One sobering experience comes from Russia. It has long been believed that privatization leads to efficiency. But as Russia privatized, it was soon recognized that, if the supporting institutions are not there, it may not be in the interest of the entrepreneurs to work to maximize the long-run value of the firms. Instead they could serve their own interest best through asset-stripping or "self-dealing." The anarchy that ensued in Russia is now well known. As Black, Kraakman, and Tarassova (2000, 1752) wrote, "The weak legal and institutional framework was no secret to the privatizers. But writing good laws can take years and building good institutions decades. The privatizers weren't willing to wait" (see also Hoff 2000). Some argued that privatization would result in a demand to reform the institutions and bring in the rule of law. But that did not happen, or happened with so much time lag that the damage to the economy in the interim period was great.

I believe that there is need now for India to move more strongly forward with the reforms, allow private firms to enter sectors earlier kept reserved for state-owned enterprises (this is more important than privatization), open the economy further, and, in particular, allow Indian companies to go for larger acquisitions abroad. But one must be aware that there are no panaceas in economic policy. One has to be prepared for flexibility, to experiment with policy but be ready to adjust, alter, and on occasion even do a U-turn, depending on the evidence coming in. To stick with one policy, unbendingly, is to make the same mistake of policy stubbornness that led India to its present predicament.

Take openness, for instance. While there is need to push ahead with this in today's India, including a further lowering of tariff barriers and even greater mobility of capital, it is not obvious that these reforms, if implemented in the 1960s, would have automatically yielded benefits for the country. There are several laws and institutional features of Indian industry that handicap our domestic producers. For example, there are some industries, such as handicrafts and toys, which are marked as belonging to the small-scale sectors. Large-scale factory production is not permitted in these industries. Imagine what would happen if India suddenly opened up the doors to all imports, without liberalizing this sector. Foreign producers would manufacture the same goods in large-scale modern factories, lower their per-unit cost of production, and outcompete the Indian producers, handicapped by the Indian laws. This would still cause gains from trade, true, but may inhibit the future development of Indian industry. Moreover, the free flow of capital could cause destabilizing currency crises. And, not surprisingly, prominent economists such as Jagdish Bhagwati have advised against full convertibility on the capital account for developing countries, observing that "the optimal speed at which one liberalizes is not necessarily the fastest" (2002, 90).[15]

The same is true for globalization, which creates great opportunities. But to maintain that it has no costs is to make the same mistake of overconfidence that served India so poorly in the past. For one, globalization is likely to bring prices of the weaker economies into alignment with prices in the industrialized nations. Given that the price of illiterate labor is close to zero in industrialized nations, this means that the illiterate population of developing nations will tend to become extremely impoverished if there is globalization without complementary government intervention.[16] In a country like India where 35 percent of the people are illiterate, globalization can contribute to increasing poverty and inequality.[17] It is important to recognize this not in order to thwart globalization but to prepare for and benefit from it.

1.6

To understand contemporary India's economic problems, I find it useful to travel back a little in time and research the roots of India's own experience. This is especially important to me because of my skepticism about history being amenable to theory or being codified in a law so that we can dispense with the details. It is a tragedy when great minds spend inordinate amounts of time to unearth the laws of history, and an even greater tragedy when they find them. This can mislead ordinary mortals into an illusion of knowledge, into a false confidence about what lies ahead, and make them shed skepticism. And skepticism is the mainspring of not just enquiry and true knowledge, but also civil society.

Many see no redeeming feature in India's performance during the first thirty or forty years of independence. But if one compares whatever data are available from pre-independence India with post-1947 data, it is clear that independence has been good for India, not just for the nation's democracy, morale, and self-respect, but for its economy and standard of living. Take literacy. Despite Britain's avowal to educate the Indians,[18] India's literacy rate in 1951 was 17 percent. In the next ten years, it would double. Thereafter the rise would be slow, reaching a level of 65 percent in the current year. But no matter how one measures it, it is clear that the performance during the first fifty years of the last century was far outstripped by the second fifty years.

The same is true for per capita income. From 1900 to 1947 India's national income grew at slightly less than 1 percent per annum, which amounted to a per capita income growth rate of 0.1 percent per annum.[19] In comparison, the notorious "Hindu rate of growth" of national income of just over 3 percent per annum, at which India was stuck from 1947 to 1975, and the 5 percent per annum that was achieved during 1976–1991 are significantly higher. And of course the period 1992–2001 with an annual growth rate of 6.5 percent looks positively bullish.[20] Indeed in terms of virtually all measures of standard of living that one can think of, independence turns out to be a dummy variable of significance, with performance clearly better after it than before it.[21]

The frustration with India is not that nothing happened since 1947, but that more did not happen, that rhetoric and achievement diverged so widely. In some sense this was inevitable because India's policy was born out of two conflicting systems of beliefs and ideas—those of Gandhi and Nehru—held together precariously, and often with the differences denied, because this was one difference that Indians found too difficult to confront.[22] The differences had roots that go back to well before 1947. They can be found in Nehru's education at Harrow and Cambridge, and his commitment to Fabian socialism and in Gandhi's grassroots struggle, experiments in alternate living, and innate convictions. As early as 1933 Nehru had confided to his diary, "I cannot understand how [Gandhi] can accept ... the present social order [and] how he can surround himself with men who are ... the beneficiaries of this social order." Nehru was more radical, in a conventional sense of the word, than Gandhi. This was clear from his diary entry: "In many ways I have far more in common with English and other non-Indian socialists than I have with non-socialists in India" (qtd. in Wolpert 1996, 150).

Gandhi lived a life with a minimum of material trappings, but did not believe in socialism—certainly not of any known variety. He viewed Nehru's difference of opinion with tolerance and understanding. Thus in 1937 he would tell some foreign visitors: "[Nehru's] enunciation of scientific socialism does not jar on me. I have been living the life since 1906 that he would have all India to live. To say that he favors Russian Communism is a travesty of truth" (qtd. in Wolpert 1996, 215). Gandhi was right in his assessment of Nehru. But the economic policies they envisaged for India were very different. In the 1930s and even the early 1940s Nehru was quite enamored by Marx and Lenin (though not by Russian Communism) and referred to their works repeatedly in his diary entries and in letters to friends. He had shed his Marxism-Leninism and even socialism by the time India attained its independence, but his faith in megaplanning, heavy industry, modern science, and technology would persist. Along with Prasanta Mahalanobis, he would try to give shape to those ideas in the form of what came to be called the Mahalanobis-Nehru strategy of development.[23]

The actual policy regime that India followed in its early days of independence was a mixture of the two competing (and almost contradictory) visions. A Soviet-style planning system was developed, but without the state having a monopoly of control over the resources. Capitalism was allowed to flourish, but a large bureaucracy was nurtured. Huge investments were made in basic industries, but at the same time several sectors were protected as belonging to the small-scale sector. Capitalism was criticized but it was also relied upon. Socialism was never practiced, but the rhetoric of socialism was the norm. A burgeoning bureaucracy became the surrogate for socialism.

Ideas played a major role, and in this case the dominant ideas were those of Nehru. Nehru was of course an outstanding intellectual, with a flair for writing that put him in the class of a very limited number of national leaders in world history. But he was not obsessive about economic growth in the way some other twentieth-century leaders have been, such as Park Chung Hee of Korea or Lee Kwan Yew of Singapore. Nehru did participate in the economic planning process; but his interest was not so much in the plans as in the prose of the plans. Not surprisingly, while Korea produced some of the most effective policy plans, India produced some of the most well-*written* policy plans.

Advisers from Washington, DC, and many economists recommend that Third World nations must have democracy and must open up their economy and privatize, oblivious to the fact that to ask for a democracy and then to insist what the democracy should choose amounts to a contradiction. Since most developing countries are not democracies, they did not face the problem, but India did. Once people's opinion had been shaped (and Nehru was instrumental in this), there was no way that policies could be easily dictated to them. Opinion would have to be molded before major policy shifts were possible. Or at least policymakers had to catch people in a moment of doubt or vacillation to usher in changes.

1.7

That is exactly what Manmohan Singh set out to remedy as the newly appointed Finance Minister in 1991. In that year India had run into its most major economic crisis. The Indian economy had always lived on the edge of a foreign exchange crisis. According to Bimal Jalan's (1992) count, for thirty out of the thirty-six years since the start of the second Five-Year Plan in 1956 the economy had faced some kind of a balance-of-payments crisis. In 1991, because of a combination of factors, including the Gulf War, a burgeoning fiscal deficit, and large international debt, a foreign exchange shortage occurred and India came closer to defaulting on its international debt commitments than ever before. Major policy initiatives were needed, and from 1991 to 1993 major and bold changes in policy were effected. An account of the basic features of the reform and the crisis that prompted it is given by Mihir Rakshit in chapter 5.

The effects of these reforms are quite apparent. The most important policy initiatives were in the international sector and the major successes have been in that sector.[24] India's foreign exchange balance has grown rapidly. Thanks to the economy's openness, the information technology sector has expanded at record rates. Of the total amount of software produced in India, two-thirds is exported. So the global trade interaction has been crucial to this sector.

The 1990s was also the time when India's draconian licensing laws were dismantled. It is easy now to forget the absurdity of the bureaucratic hurdles that had been built up in India. As Narayana Murthy, one of the architects of India's software revolution, explains in chapter 9, India's software success may not have been possible even if all the other propitious factors were present but the reforms had not occurred.[25] Despite all this, the license-raj could have been justified if it helped the disadvantaged. But as Amartya Sen (1995, 28) pointed out, "Four decades of allegedly 'interventionist' planning did little to make the country literate, provide a wide-based health service, achieve comprehensive land reforms, or end the rampant social inequalities that blight the material prospects of the underprivileged" (Dreze and Sen 1995).[26]

The economy's overall post-reform growth rate, with the partial dismantling of the license-raj, has been very good. As stated earlier, from 1994 to 1997 Indian national income grew at over 7 percent per annum, and during the entire last decade the growth rate has been around 6.5 percent. Specific sectors, such as the consumer durables industry, have done well. A study by K. V. Ramaswamy (2001) has shown that growth in the post-reform period has been significantly higher than in the pre-reform period, and, more important, firms have responded to the reforms by going in for technological improvements.

Elsewhere I have taken the view (Basu 2001a), and continue to maintain it, that an economy has to be evaluated, ultimately, in terms of what happens to the poorest and the dispossessed. Everything else, such as a nation's income growth rate, is of *instrumental* value. Not all economists concur with this view. To many, efficiency, growth, and *aggregate* welfare are the ends that they wish to pursue. Yet it is worth putting on record that Amartya Sen has consistently taken a normative stand where these are merely of instrumental value (see, e.g., Sen 1999, chap. 2). Jagdish Bhagwati has argued vigorously for free trade and raising growth, but unlike some other economists, who take such a line, he has been categorical: "As regards the *objective* of development, I should emphasize, as I always have, that growth was seen by me . . . , from the early 1960s, as simply an instrumental variable, as a means to an end, and the end was clearly the elimination of poverty" (1985, 1). Empowerment of the poor and poverty reduction also is the central concern of Manuela Ferro, David Rosenblatt, and Nicholas Stern in chapter 7. Given such a normative stand, it is important to look at indicators that relate to the lives of the poor.

On matters of basic needs and development of the most disad-vantaged, India unfortunately still has miles to go. Over the last few decades, inequality has been rising, regional disparities have been growing, and poverty and illiteracy continue to be high. Ferro, Rosen-blatt, and Stern's chapter provides a comprehensive account of what is happening to poverty and what should be done. Two other chapters that directly address what is happening to the disadvantaged, without going into matters of macro aggregates, are the ones by Renana Jhabvala and Ravi Kanbur (chapter 12) and by Barbara Harriss-White (chapter 11). Jhabvala and Kanbur look at the especially vulnera-ble, including women, from the field experience of Self Employed Women's Association, better known as SEWA. Globalization creates new vulnerability, they argue, while not denying that globalization also creates enormous potentials for advancement. Harriss-White, who is also concerned with matters of gender, looks at India's informal eco-nomic sector, in which most of the poor participate and which typi-cally gets very little attention in economic analysis.

On the overall magnitude of poverty there was, initially, a lot of very confusing data coming in and it was not clear what was happening (see Datt and Ravallion 2002, for discussion). Much of the confusion was caused by a change in the nature of the questions adopted by the National Sample Survey (NSS) of India. Regarding consumption, the NSS was trying to switch from asking people how much they had consumed in the last thirty days to the last seven days, which many believed elicited more accurate answers from people with fallible memories. This caused certain contaminations in the data that allowed analysts to make claims in keeping with their predilections, without really fussing about what the data really said, which in any case was very difficult to interpret. The most scientifically convincing study is the one by Deaton (2001), which establishes fairly clearly that poverty, after remaining steady through the early 1990s, went in for a definitive dip by 1999. Though the fall in the percentage of people below the poverty line was not as sharp as the government claimed (27.1 percent for rural areas and 23.6 percent for urban areas in 1999), it was sufficiently sharp (down to 30.2 percent and 24.7 percent in rural and urban areas, respectively) to cause the absolute number of people below the poverty line to fall.[27] This augurs well, but it must not be forgotten that the level of poverty in India continues to be unacceptably high.

Literacy has risen from 52 percent in 1991 to 65 percent in 2001. This is not so much a consequence of government policy as people's changing view of the value of education (caused by the greater exposure to the world out there), which has led to parents demanding better education for their children and often willing to pay for that at the expense of great personal hardship. Again, while this trend is heartening, it is tragic that a nation with so much policy devoted to higher education and scientific work still has 35 percent of its population unable to read and write.

On these fundamental indicators therefore there is reason to be both disappointed at where the nation stands and optimistic about the changes that have taken place. The reforms of the early 1990s, luck (as in the rise of IT in the United States) and history (such as the over-investment in higher education) seem to be going in favor of the Indian economy. One question that arises is that, if the IT sector, and more generally, services, turn out to be one of the major powerhouses of the Indian economy, will this be a reliable powerhouse and will the benefits of this sector be shared widely?

There has recently been concern expressed about this sector based on the observation that the global situation has changed since 1999 in ways that beckon economists to revise the forecast downwards. First, there is the downturn in the U.S. stock market, especially in the IT sector. This is indeed a matter of some concern, since so much of India's exports end up in North America. However, what must be realized is that the stock market tends to correlate with the *profitability* of the industry, and this need not be correlated with the *size* of the industry. And India's exports depend mainly on the size of the U.S. industry. One reason why the technology stocks are doing badly is precisely because the IT sector in the United States is such an attractive industry and growing so rapidly. As the number of firms increases, profits go down; and so the stock market does poorly—especially so since market players did not understand this and had over-invested in technology stocks. So this in itself should have only a small effect on India's exports. If, however, the U.S. economy goes into a major slump and U.S. growth stops or becomes negative, then the projections can go wrong.

The second worry pertains to the supply side in India. With the large flight of computer professionals out of India, there is going to be a supply bottleneck forming in India's software production. This problem was exacerbated by increases in the U.S. quota of H1B visas, that is, visas for professional migration, which currently stands at approximately 200,000 professionals each year. Typically, about 45 percent of these visas go to Indians (the second largest category being the Chinese, at 9 percent) and 53 percent of the ones who get H1B visas are computer professionals. This means that roughly 50,000 computer professionals have been leaving India for the United States each year. When one adds to this the (admittedly smaller) flows to Germany, Sweden, and even Japan, it is evident that the out-migration problem is quite serious for India, even though the numbers slacked off last year because of the slowdown of the U.S. economy. In chapter 10 Nirvikar Singh goes into many of these issues related to the software sector.

While this out-migration is reason for some concern, it must be recognized, as I mentioned earlier, that IT is one sector in which India has actually benefited from the brain drain. So this increased demand for Indian computer personnel should be treated as a blessing, and government should simply work hard to educate a larger numbers of Indians appropriately.

What are the consequences of this sector for the well-being of people at large in India? The concern, often expressed, is that the IT sector is not labor-intensive enough. Currently, approximately half a million people are employed in this sector. This is not a small number;

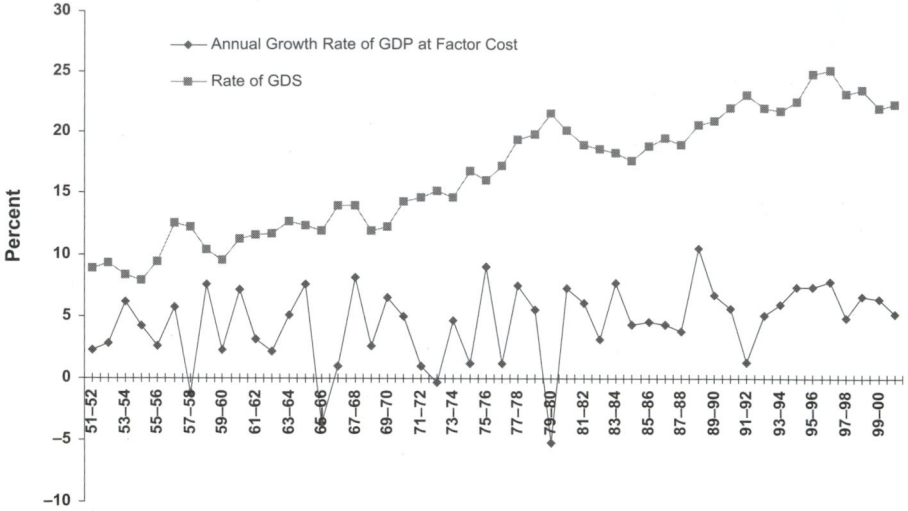

Figure 1.1
Gross domestic savings (GDS) and growth rate in India, 1950–2001. *Source:* See table 1.2.

moreover, simple projection, based on the growth of this sector as predicted by the NASSCOM-McKinsey study, suggests that employment will grow to 3 million by the year 2010. Most important, these calculations ignore the fallout on other sectors. India has an IT-enabled sector (such as call centers and data-processing units) that is growing more rapidly than the IT sector itself. The IT-enabled sector currently employs 100,000 people but has enormous potential.

Turning to more general matters, we observe that one worry for India's development prospect concerns the recent movements in the savings rate (and investment rate). After rising sharply through the 1970s, and slowly through the 1980s and early 1990s, this has declined suddenly in the late 1990s. It was 22 percent in 1998–1999, having climbed to over 24 percent in the mid-1990s (see table 1.2 and figure 1.1). While the relation between savings and investment rates and growth is a long-run one and therefore easy to overlook, reason and evidence suggest that to have sustained high growth a nation needs high investment and savings. This may not be obvious by looking at figure 1.1, but India's growth rate, averaged over a few years, has generally mirrored its savings rate, with a time lag. Until 1965, India's growth rate averaged below 4 percent per annum and the savings rate was below 14 percent—see table 1.2. Savings crossed the 20 percent mark by the late seventies, and by the early eighties India's growth

Table 1.4
Major macroeconomic indicators in India (% of GDP)

	Combined fiscal deficit of central and state governments	Gross savings	
		Private sector	Public sector
1992–1993	7.0	20.2	1.6
1993–1994	8.3	21.9	0.6
1994–1995	7.1	23.2	1.7
1995–1996	6.5	23.1	2.0
1996–1997	6.4	21.5	1.7
1997–1998	7.3	21.8	1.3
1998–1999	8.9	22.6	−1.0
1999–2000	9.4	24.0	−0.9
2000–2001	9.6	25.1	−1.7

Source: Ahluwalia (2002).

rate had moved to over 5 percent. And there were further increases in both these rates until the early nineties. Looking at cross-country experience, one sees the East Asian economies achieving growth rates of 8 percent while saving well over 30 percent. As Montek Ahluwalia (2002) points out, to have a growth rate of 8 percent it will be essential to have an investment rate of between 29 and 30 percent. Even if one achieves a part of this from foreign direct investment, India can ill afford to fall back on the savings front.

Why is India's savings rate falling? It is difficult, as yet, to tell all the reasons behind this, though it is certain that the worsening fiscal situation and declining public-sector savings are major contributory factors.[28] Ahluwalia (2002) provides some compelling numbers and argument supporting this, some of which are reproduced in table 1.4. He also points to what has been known for a while, namely, that the finances of the Indian states are in poor shape. This is the subject matter of detailed inquiry by Govinda Rao in chapter 6. He suggests reforms that can arrest this deterioration, something that is essential for the long-run health of the economy.

Much has been written about the next round of reforms, but what is not talked about enough but is important to develop is the institution of contracts, without which no modern market can function. This is one more way in which government is important: It can play the crucial role of the third party that helps enforce contracts. But contracts are partly a matter of culture. Without this culture it is difficult to develop crucial long-term markets, such as the market for mortgage and long-term investment loans, and to take full advantage of globalization. And these, in turn, are key ingredients of fast growth.

There are, fortunately, enough strengths in the Indian economy for it to be a net beneficiary of globalization. The economy has gone past that critical level where to open up is to risk being cheated and impoverished. Though there are still innumerable important reforms to undertake, the fundamentals of the Indian economy are probably strong enough for it to be able to implement and benefit from another round of market reform and further (though gradual) opening up of the economy.

Globalization and modern markets bring with them many ills. But, on balance, and given the new strengths of the Indian economy, these changes will open up rather than close windows of opportunity for India. The modern global economy is beginning to change the nature of management of Indian firms and to encourage "clean business," which, historically, used to be considered a contradiction in terms and will hopefully influence the organization of government. It is bringing in new ideas on how to organize and how to govern the market. It is changing beliefs about what is good and what is bad for the economy. These beliefs may be right or wrong, but they will have a bigger impact on the economy than most people realize. There are huge inequities and injustices in the world to remedy. It is not always clear how this can be achieved and whether this can at all be achieved by a single nation. When crafting policy, it is important for the policymaker to recognize the features of the world that must be taken as given, and try to do as much as possible *subject* to those constraints. To craft policy *assuming* that the features of the global economy and the rules of the global game that one does not like can be wished away is to court failure.

Notes

For helpful comments and criticisms, I am grateful to Alaka Basu, Gayatri Koolwal, and Elizabeth Murry.

1. In doing so, this essay draws heavily on my previous work: Basu (2001b) and Basu and Pattanaik (1998).

2. This point is compellingly made for a context that goes much beyond India in Platteau (2000). In chapter 3 of this volume, Pranab Bardhan conducts an analysis of India's economic performance that is rooted in "political sociology." See also Bardhan (1984).

3. There is, in particular, reason to be worried that plurality, secularism, and cultural openness, which were historically India's strength and distinctiveness, have witnessed threats in recent times (see Sen 1996 and chapter 2).

4. For an illuminating analysis of the general role of social and cultural norms in economic development, see Platteau (2000). For a model of how cultural norms need not be immutable, see Basu and Weibull (2003).

5. Some may argue that from Siraj's forces the 20,000 or so soldiers who were under Mir Jafar's charge and did very little to defend Siraj should be deducted. The nonfunctioning of those 20,000 soldiers or, more accurately, their betrayal, corroborates the point I am about to make.

6. Accounts of the Battle of Plassey and Robert Clive's strategies are legion. The numbers I quote here are from Chaudhuri (1975).

7. Thus Harvey writes: "To comprehend the campaign at Trichinopoly, and indeed later in Bengal, it is necessary to understand the nature of the colorful, shambling circuses that were the Indian armies of the time.... The forces of an Indian prince much more nearly resembled a travelling township than an army" (1998, 91).

8. I deliberately avoid the term *social capital* for it has been used in so many different senses in recent times, though its original meaning does have overlaps with the concept being used here. In addition, I am not confident that I fully understand what it means and fear that there are others who do.

9. Bardhan (2003) has recently made a similar observation about *contemporary* India, arguing that some of India's failures are rooted in the nation's inability to resolve "collective action problems." He maintains that China's recent retrenchment of large numbers of workers from overmanned public-sector enterprises is founded in China's relative greater skill for putting the "collective resolve" into action.

10. For a discussion of the relation between beliefs and economic progress, and a classification of growth-enhancing and growth-hindering beliefs, see Basu (2000b, chap. 4).

11. The consumers' belief is not necessarily false. I have argued in Basu (2000b) that this belief can be self-fulfilling, in the sense that, given such a collective belief, the kind of business practices that come into existence reinforce the belief, and the belief then is fully justified.

12. Two chapters in this volume, those by N. R. Narayana Murthy (chap. 9) and Nirvikar Singh (chap. 10), evaluate in detail the experience of India's IT industry and its relation to the Indian economy and polity at large.

13. See ⟨www.indianembassy.org/indiainfo/india_it.htm⟩.

14. According to the Mid-Year Review released by the Ministry of Foreign Affairs in November 2002, the April–June exports were $11,757 million. Multiplied by four this gives us $47,028 million. While it is true that the growth in exports has been high at times, it is unlikely to cross the $50 billion mark this year.

15. The role of international trade, openness, and technology transfer in the context of the East Asian economies has been recently studied and modeled by Van and Wan (1999). They construct the model specifically with an eye on how the experience can be emulated by other nations such as India. In their analysis the crucial benefit of trade is the technology transfer that results with it.

16. Research by Wood and Calandrino (2000) suggests that, as India's foreign trade increases, this raises the demand for educated workers but lowers the demand for illiterate workers.

17. The subject of inequality and poverty is an important one for global policy. I have discussed some of the measurement issues involved in Basu (2001a). I believe that, left to the market, global inequality will tend to grow. However, there is very little that a single developing country can do about this. To try to control inequality too aggressively within one's own territory is likely to drive capital away, causing greater poverty. What is needed is a concerted global plan. There is much that can be done by way of controlling inequality, without hurting incentives and entrepreneurship, but this has to be a global effort and is a subject matter that lies beyond the scope of this chapter.

18. In the case of some viceroys, the commitment to India was genuine. This was most notably so for Louis Mountbatten.

19. The figures are from Sivasubramonian (1997). For discussion and comparison of growth rates before and after independence, see Roy (2001, 2002), and Majumdar (1997). Table 1.3 gives the average annual growth rates for successive five-year plan periods and demonstrates clearly its rising trend.

20. For a discussion of this growth history and the breakup of independent India's economic history into these three periods, see Basu (2000a).

21. An interesting recent paper by Iyer (2002) investigates the more general question of whether colonial rule has desirable long-run effects. She studies this by looking at the conditions today of regions of India that were under British colonial rule and of regions that remained under Indian rulers. Given that the British did not annex regions randomly but chose them according to some criterion, Iyer's analysis is crucially sensitive to weeding out this endogeneity problem. Once this is done, she shows that there is strong evidence that colonial rule tended to significantly lower the level of public goods in the long run. Abhijit V. Banerjee's essay (chapter 8) starts from a similar framework, and then allows for the fact that history, geography, and many other variables can affect the level of public goods in different regions of India. The study is a comprehensive one conducted for a list of thirty-three public goods and across a large number of India's districts spread over sixteen states.

22. See Basu and Pattanaik (1998). Cohen (2001) discusses how the influence of Nehru and Gandhi went beyond economic policy to all dimensions of strategic thought, including foreign policy, in contemporary India.

23. See Ashok Rudra (1996), especially chapter 11 by T. N. Srinivasan.

24. What is not always noted is that there have also been significant changes in monetary policy. Since 1992 there has been a conscious effort to lower interest rates and encourage greater lending. In 1993 the minimum lending rate was lowered from 17 percent to 15 percent and the SLR was lowered from 30 percent to 25 percent, open market operations being used simultaneously to neutralize money supply increases and control inflation. For a discussion of monetary policy see Rangarajan (2001). See also Reddy (2002, chap. 4). A comprehensive account of monetary reforms, along with an account of the institutional setting for the possibility of such reform, occurs in chapters 4 (Y. V. Reddy) and 5 (Mihir Rakshit).

25. Similarly, Das (2001, chap. 13) uses the story of Dhirubhai Ambani to illustrate how Reliance may never have become a world-class enterprise under the labyrinthine laws

that controlled Indian industry between 1965 and 1991. It is noteworthy, however, that Dhirubhai Ambani had not done badly under the license-raj. As Das's own account illustrates, some of Dhirubhai's initial success was, there can be no denying, because he managed to exploit the protective system of India's bureaucratic government to his advantage. It should therefore be noted that one important contribution of the reform is that it constituted a step toward making "clean" business possible.

26. See also Dreze and Sen (1995).

27. For an analysis of inequality in India based on the same data sources, see Deaton and Dreze (2002).

28. Policymaker-analysts of the Indian economy seem quite unequivocal on this: see, for instance, Lahiri and Kannan (2001), Kelkar (2002), and Mohan (2002).

References

Ahluwalia, Montek S. 2002. "Economic Reforms in India since 1991: Has Gradualism Worked?" *Journal of Economic Perspectives* 16:67–88.

Bardhan, Pranab. 1984. *The Political Economy of Development in India*. Oxford: Blackwell.

Bardhan, Pranab. 2003. "Crouching Tiger, Lumbering Elephant." Forthcoming in *Markets and Governments*, ed. Kaushik Basu, Pulin Nayak, and Ranjan Ray. New Delhi: Oxford University Press.

Basu, Kaushik. 2000a. "Whither India? The Prospect of Prosperity." In *India: Another Millenium?*, ed. Romila Thapar, 193–211. New Delhi: Penguin Books.

Basu, Kaushik. 2000b. *Prelude to Political Economy: A Study of the Social and Political Foundations of Economics*. Oxford: Oxford University Press.

Basu, Kaushik. 2001a. "On the Goals of Development." In *Frontiers of Development Economics*, ed. Gerald Meier and Joseph Stiglitz, 61–86. Oxford: Oxford University Press.

Basu, Kaushik. 2001b. "India and the Global Economy: The Role of Culture, Norms and Beliefs." *Economic and Political Weekly* 36 (October 6):3837–3842.

Basu, Kaushik, and Prasanta Pattanaik. 1998. "India's Economy and the Reforms of the 1990s: Genesis and Prospect." *Journal of International Trade and Economic Development* 6, no. 2:123–133.

Basu, Kaushik, and Jörgen W. Weibull. 2003. "Punctuality: A Cultural Trait as Equilibrium." In *Economics for an Imperfect World*, ed. Richard Arnott, Bruce Greenwald, Ravi Kanbur, and Barry Nalebuff, 163–182. Cambridge, MA: The MIT Press.

Bhagwati, Jagdish. 1985. *Essays in Development Economics, Volume 2: Dependence and Interdependence*. Oxford: Oxford University Press.

Bhagwati, Jagdish. 2002. *Free Trade Today*. Princeton: Princeton University Press.

Black, Bernard, Reinier Kraakman, and Anna Tarassova. 2000. "Russian Privatization and Corporate Governance: What Went Wrong." *Stanford Law Review* 51:1730–1808.

Chaudhuri, Nirad. 1975. *Clive of India*. London: Barrie and Jenkins.

Clifford, Mark. 1994. *Troubled Tiger*. London: M. E. Sharpe.

Cohen, Stephen. 2001. *India: Emerging Power*. Washington, DC: Brookings Institution Press.

Das, Gurcharan. 2001. *India Unbound*. New York: Alfred Knopf.

Datt, Gaurav, and Martin Ravallion. 2002. "Is India's Economic Growth Leaving the Poor Behind?" *Journal of Economic Prespectives* 16:89–108.

Deaton, Angus. 2001. "Adjusted Indian Poverty Estimates for 1999–2000." Mimeo., Princeton Research Program in Development Studies.

Deaton, Angus, and Jean Dreze. 2002. "Poverty and Inequality in India: A Reexamination." *Economic and Political Weekly* 3 (September 7):3729–3748.

Dreze, Jean, and Amartya Sen. 1995. *India's Economic Development and Social Opportunity*. Oxford: Clarendon Press.

Government of India. 2001. *National Accounts Statistics 2001*. New Delhi: Ministry of Statistics, Government of India.

Harvey, Robert. 1998. *Clive: The Life and Death of a British Emperor*. London: Hodder and Stoughton.

Hoff, Karla. 2000. "The Logic of Political Constraints and Reform with Applications to Strategies for Privatization." Mimeo., The World Bank, Washington, DC.

Iyer, Lakshmi. 2002. "The Long-Term Impact of Colonial Rule: Evidence from India." Mimeo., Massachusetts Institute of Technology.

Jalan, Bimal. 1992. "Balance of Payments, 1956–1991." In *The Indian Economy: Problems and Prospects*, ed. Bimal Jalan, 163–194. New Delhi: Penguin.

Kelkar, Vijay. 2002. "India's Emerging Economic Challenges." In *India's Economy in the 21st Century*, ed. Raj Kapila and Uma Kapila, 83–94. New Delhi: Academic Foundation.

Lahiri, Ashok, and R. Kannan. 2001. "India's Fiscal Deficits and their Sustainability in Perspective." Mimeo., National Institute of Public Finance and Policy, New Delhi.

Majumdar, Mukul. 1997. "The East Asian Miracle and India." Satyendra Nath Memorial Lecture, Asiatic Society, Calcutta.

Mohan, Rakesh. 2002. "A Decade after 1991: New Challenges Facing the Indian Economy." *Reserve Bank of India Bulletin* 56:771–788.

Murthy, N. R. Narayana. 2000. "Making India a Significant IT Player in This Millennium." In *India: Another Millennium?*, ed. Romila Thapar. New Delhi: Penguin Books.

Platteau, Jean-Philippe. 1994. "Behind the Market Stage where Real Societies Exist." *Journal of Development Studies* 30, no. 3:533–577.

Platteau, Jean-Philippe. 2000. *Institutions, Social Norms, and Economic Development*. Amsterdam: Harwood Academic Publishers.

Ramaswamy, K. V. 2001. "Economic Reforms, Industrial Structure and Performance: The Case of Consumer Durable Goods Industry in India." In *Economic Reform and Industrial Structure in India*, ed. S. Uchikawa, 95–117. Tokyo: Institute of Developing Economies.

Rangarajan, C. 2001. "Leading Issues in Monetary Policy." Sukhamoy Chakravarty Memorial Lecture, 31 March.

Reddy, Y. V. 2002. *Lectures on Economic and Financial Sector Reforms in India*. New Delhi: Oxford University Press.

Reserve Bank of India. 2001. *Handbook of Statistics on the Indian Economy*. Mumbai: Reserve Bank of India.

Roy, Tirthankar. 2001. *The Economic History of India, 1857–1947*. New Delhi: Oxford University Press.

Roy, Tirthankar. 2002. "Economic History and Modern India: Redefining the Link." *Journal of Economic Perspectives* 16:109–130.

Rudra, Ashok. 1996. *Prasanta Chandra Mahalanobis*. New Delhi: Oxford University Press.

Sen, Amartya. 1995. "Wrongs and Rights in Development." *Prospect* (October):28–35.

Sen, Amartya. 1996. "Secularism and Its Discontents." In *Unraveling the Nation: Sectarian Conflict and India's Secular Identity*, ed. Kaushik Basu and Sanjay Subrahmanyam, 11–43. New Delhi: Penguin.

Sen, Amartya. 1999. *Development as Freedom*. New York: Knopf.

Sivasubramonian, S. 1997. "Revised Estimates of the National Income of India, 1900–1 to 1946–7." *Indian Economic and Social History Review* 34:113–169.

Van, Pham Hoang, and Henry Wan Jr. 1999. "Emulative Development through Trade Expansion: East Asian Evidence." In *International Trade Policy and the Pacific Rim*, ed. J. Piggott and A. Woodland, 348–367. Houndmills (England): Macmillan; New York: St. Martin's Press in association with International Economic Association.

Wolpert, Stanley. 1996. *Nehru: A Tryst with Destiny*. New York: Oxford University Press.

Wood, Adrian, and Michele Calandrino. 2000. "When the Other Giant Awakens: Trade and Human Resources in India." *Economic and Political Weekly* 35 (December 30):4677–4694.

World Bank. *World Development Report 2003*. Washington, DC: World Bank.

II

Political Economy of India

2   Democracy and Secularism in India

Amartya Sen

2.1   Questions and Doubts

The title of the talk, given at Cornell University in April 2002, on which this chapter is based, was: "What's Wrong with India?" The focus of this particular chapter is much narrower, and I have, therefore, given it a different name. I am, however, tempted to start with a comment on the old title, which still has a motivational role. To ask "what's wrong with India?" may appear to be a discouraging thought. I would, however, argue that this is not entirely so. Indeed, a diagnosis that we have done something wrong can be quite upbeat—perhaps even *too* buoyant.

As Alexander Pope said nearly three centuries ago, to admit that one has been wrong is to claim that one is wiser today than one was yesterday. We may well be getting wiser in India, but we must try to make sure that we are rightly diagnosing the "errors" of our past. In particular, it would be quite important not to disown, without good reason, the basic social commitments that were made as India became independent, and that reflected the aspirations of the freedom movement that had galvanized the nation.

In this chapter, I concentrate on two such commitments that were among the most important parts of the vision of an independent India as it was articulated more than half a century ago. I refer to the resolution to build an India that would be both democratic and secular. It was, of course, an ambitious resolve: There was no democratic poor country in the world at that time. It was also daring: The dream of a secular India seemed a distant one as the country was partitioned amid bloody communal riots that killed and threatened the lives of millions.[1] And yet as the decades progressed, both democracy and secularism became reasonably well established in India. The vision seemed to work, and there was something real to celebrate.

However, the basic principles underlying both democracy and secularism have received some hard knocks in recent years. The frustration that democracy has not, on its own, delivered as much as was expected has yielded some distrust and indeed some cynicism of the participatory political process. Attention is drawn to the fact that authoritarian countries (such as South Korea, Singapore, or for that matter, China) seem to have achieved much more in economic growth and enrichment than India has. The chaos of democratic politics seems obvious enough, and tensions and conflicts are more clearly visible than they would be under orderly authoritarian regimes. Expressions of deep skepticism are heard often enough in public discussions, frequently reiterating the view that democratic politics gives India many problems and rather few solutions. It would be good to examine whether this is a fair assessment.

If attacks on democracy reflect practical frustration, assaults on secularism seem to come from "high theory" of a sort, even though that theory is sometimes used to instigate and justify politically organized brutalities (most recently in Gujarat). The rejection of Indian secularism reflects an attempt to recharacterize India away from a multi-religious and multi-ethnic conception, which was dominant at the time of Indian independence, toward a manufactured notion of a largely "Hindu India." The commodious and absorptive idea of "Indianness" that characterized the Indian intellectual mainstream fifty years ago and that found a firm expression in the secular constitution of the newly independent country has been severely challenged over the recent decades. Despite attempts by the "Hindutva" advocates to square the circle by claiming continued adherence to "secularism" (combined with describing earlier secular beliefs as "pseudo-secularism"), it is difficult to see how the relative privileging of one religious tradition—and one community—over the others can be consistent with any interpretation of secularism whatsoever.

There is evidence that the hard core of "Hindutva" advocates is relatively small in number. But around them cluster a very much larger group of people who can be called "proto-Hindutva" believers. They are typically less zealous than the Hindutva champions, but they nevertheless see a basic asymmetry between the preeminence of Hinduism in India and the claims of other religions that are also present in India. While the Hindutva movement is intellectually impatient and politically compromised by its association with intolerance and occasional terrible violence against minority communities, this broader group of "proto-Hindutva" believers are far less extremist and thus have a substantially greater chance of being politically influential in the long run. One must ask whether the perspectives of Hindutva and, more broadly, of proto-Hindutva beliefs provide a plausible challenge to old-fashioned Indian secularism.

Even though I concentrate here on democracy and secularism, there are, of course, many other challenging questions that can sensibly be asked in a critical reassessment of the present Indian situation. The list includes the persistence of endemic hunger, the continuation of massive illiteracy and ill health, the enduring inequality of class, the ongoing denial of gender equity, the survival of social barriers of caste and community, the lack of development of economic opportunities, and so on. I have tried to address some of these issues elsewhere, but I will not go into them here, except when they are relevant to the discussion of the two main themes of this essay—namely, democracy and secularism.[2]

2.2 What's the Advantage of Democracy?

The first point to note in assessing Indian democracy is that democracy cannot be evaluated in primarily instrumental terms. Political freedom and civil rights have importance of their own. Their value to the society does not have to be indirectly established in terms of their contribution to economic growth or other such economic or social achievements. Politically unfree citizens are deficient in freedom even if they happen to enjoy a high level of income, or a favorable standard of living in other respects. Insofar as democracy is its own reward, it would be a mistake to treat Indian democracy as a failure on the simple ground that it has not helped generate a high rate of economic growth.

In fact, it can be argued, on the contrary, that the real problem is not that India has too much democracy, but that, in some significant ways, it has too little of it. The complaint here relates to cases of violation of civil rights and of individual liberties, frequently on the grounds of combating terrorism, or preventing separatist extremism, or other such "law and order" issues. There is, I believe, real ground for concern here (as the Indian Human Rights Commission has also pointed out). I do not, however, pursue this issue further in this essay.

How can one assess the impact of Indian democracy on economic and social matters? That complex exercise requires, among other things, that we place India's experience in a comparative perspective, including taking note of what has been happening in other countries. The difficulties of this exercise include the problem of deciding which countries to compare India with. When comparative statements are made that try to show the failure of Indian democracy, it is typically assumed that had India not been a democracy, it would have had experiences rather similar to South Korea, Singapore, or China, rather than other nondemocratic countries such as North Korea, Afghanistan, or Sudan. The proximate comparison of India with a not-always-democratic country must be with Pakistan, and somehow that does not tend to be the focus of the rosy portrayals of the nondemocratic alternative that India has missed. The casual empiricism of highly limited comparisons tends itself to be a problem in examining the critique under discussion.

However, a number of extensive intercountry comparisons have, in fact, been recently made by Robert Barro, Adam Przeworski, and others.[3] Little evidence has been found in these comparative assessments to indicate that authoritarian governance and the suppression of political and civil rights are really beneficial in encouraging economic development, or even in advancing just economic growth. As far as the latter is concerned, despite the frequently made casual generalizations about the negative impact of democracy on economic growth, the actual directional linkages are quite unclear and seem to depend on many other circumstances. While some statistical investigations note a weakly negative connection with democracy, others find a strongly positive one. On balance, the hypothesis that there is no relation between democracy and economic growth seems hard to reject. Since political freedom and democratic rights have importance of their own, the case for them remains unaffected.

No less important is the fact that the policies and circumstances that led to the economic success of Asian economies to the east of India are by now reasonably well understood. A sequence of empirical studies has identified a general list of "helpful policies," with much internal diversity, which includes openness to competition, the use of international markets, a high level of literacy and school education, successful land reforms, easier availability of credit (including microcredit), good public health care, and appropriate incentives for investment, exporting, and industrialization. At the level of these constructive strategies, there is absolutely nothing to indicate that any of these policies is inconsistent with greater democracy and actually have to be sustained by the elements of authoritarianism that happened to be present in South Korea or Singapore or China.[4] Economic growth is extremely important in removing poverty, but it is helped by a friendly economic climate rather than by a fierce political regime.

It is not adequate to look only at the growth of GNP or other such indicators of overall economic expansion. In assessing democracy and political freedoms, one must see their impact on the lives and capabilities of the citizens. In this context it is particularly important to examine the connection between political and civil rights, on the one hand, and the prevention of major disasters (such as famines), on the other. The availability and use of political and civil rights give people the opportunity to draw attention forcefully to general dangers and vulnerabilities, and to demand appropriate remedial action. Governmental response to sudden and acute suffering of people often depends on the pressure that is put on it, and this is where the exercise of political rights (such as voting, criticizing, protesting, and so on) can make a real difference. The role of democracy in preventing famines has received attention in this context, including the fact that India has not had a real famine since independence (despite continued endemic undernourishment and often precarious food situation), whereas China had the largest famine in recorded history during 1958–1961, when the ill-calculated public policies that led to the disaster were continued by the government without any substantial emendation for three years, while nearly 30 million people died.

The recent experience of the so-called "Asian economic crisis" during 1997–1999, which affected many of the economies of east and southeast Asia, bring out, among other things, the penalty of undemocratic governance. There are two particular connections here. First, the financial crisis in some of these economies (including South Korea, Thailand, Indonesia) was closely linked with the lack of transparency in business—in particular, the lack of public participation in reviewing financial arrangements. The absence of an effective democratic forum has been an important contributor to this failing. Second, once the financial crisis led to a general economic recession, the protective power of democracy—not unlike that which prevents famines in democratic countries—was badly missed in these countries. The newly dispossessed in some of these countries did not have the voice and the hearing that a democratic system would have given them.

It is worth noting here that a fall of total gross national product of, say, ten percent may not look like much, if it follows the experience of past economic growth of 5 or 10 percent *every year for some decades* (as many east and southeast Asian countries had experienced), and yet that decline can decimate lives and create misery for millions, if the burden of contraction is not shared but allowed to be heaped on those—the unemployed or the economically redundant—who can least bear it. While the vulnerable and the precarious in Indonesia or Thailand may not have missed democracy as things went up and up, when an unequally shared crisis developed, that lacuna kept their voices muffled and suppressed. Not surprisingly, the protective function of democracy is strongly missed when it is most needed.

2.3   China and India

Democracy gives an opportunity to the opposition to press for policy change even when the problem is chronic rather than acute and disastrous. So the limited reach of Indian social policies on education, basic nutrition, health care, land reform, and gender equity arises mainly from the weakness of democratic practice. It is, in fact, as much a failure of the opposition parties as of the governments in office, since the opposition need not allow those in power to get away with gross neglect. Commitments of political leaders of other countries, including Asian countries further east of India, have often achieved more in overcoming endemic problems than the working of Indian democracy seems to have. The educational and health achievements of Maoist China illustrate this well; indeed postreform China has made excellent use of this accomplishment in its market-based expansion.

Comparison of the experiences of China and India bring out some interesting lessons, which can take us well beyond the frequently repeated simple generalizations: (1) greater Chinese success in handling endemic deprivation, (2) larger Chinese success in making use of the opportunities of global trade, and (3) worse Chinese record in preventing famines. The comparative perspectives in life expectancy throw interesting light on a more complex reality.

In the middle of the twentieth century, post-revolution China and newly independent India had about the same life expectancy at birth, around 45 years or so. The Chinese leaders were immediately more successful in expanding health care and life expectancy than were their Indian counterparts. When the economic reforms were introduced in China in 1979, China had a lead of fourteen years or more over India, with the Chinese life expectancy at 68 years while the Indian was less than 54.[5]

The speed and composition of Chinese economic growth were, however, in many ways in great need of improvement in the prereform period. Radical economic reforms, which were introduced in 1979, ushered in a period of extraordinary growth in China over the last two decades. The Indian economy too has grown reasonably fast in this period, but nowhere near as fast as China. We run, however, into an odd conundrum as far as life expectancy is concerned. Despite China's much faster rate of growth since the economic reforms, the rate of expansion of life expectancy in India has been about three times as fast, on average, as that in China. China's life expectancy, which is now just about 70 years, compares with India's figure of 63 years, and the life-expectancy gap in favor of China, which was fourteen years *before* the Chinese reforms, has fallen to only seven years now.

One must, of course, take note of the fact that it gets increasingly harder to expand life expectancy further as the absolute level rises, and it could be argued that perhaps China has now reached a level where further expansion would be very difficult. But that explanation does not work very well. At the time of economic reforms, when China had a life expectancy of about 68 years, the Indian state of Kerala had a slightly lower life expectancy—around 67 years. By now, however, Kerala's life expectancy of 75 years is considerably above China's 70.

Indeed, if we look at specific points of vulnerability, the infant mortality rate in China has fallen very slowly since the economic reforms, whereas it has continued to fall very sharply in Kerala. While Kerala had roughly the same infant mortality rate as China—37 per thousand—at the time of the Chinese reforms in 1979, Kerala's present rate, below 14 per thousand, is less than half of China's 30 per thousand (where it has stagnated over the last decade).

Indeed, it is possible to argue that the state of Kerala, with its left-leaning politics and competitive democracy, has been able to combine (1) the same kind of political commitment to social objectives that have favored China over India as a whole, and (2) the benefits of public criticism—in particular more open scrutiny—that a multiparty democratic system provides. The latter, on its own, would seem to have helped India narrow the gap vis-à-vis China quite sharply, despite the failings of the Indian practice that are widely—rightly—discussed in the press. With all its inadequacies, the Indian health delivery arrangements have to be open to the sort of public criticism that a democratic system standardly fosters, and the fact that much is known about these inadequacies from criticism in the press is itself a contribution to improving things. This opportunity is forcefully seized in a state like

Kerala, with its high level of basic education and its strong tradition of political appraisal and critique.[6] This is also reflected in the lower fertility rate in Kerala than in China, and the comparative absence of gender bias against women (the female-male ratio in Kerala's population is 1.06, as in Europe and North America, not 0.94 as in China and 0.93 as in India as a whole).

If there is something wrong with India's democracy, it lies in the timidity of its practice. The road ahead for India will depend much on the integration of different concerns: preservation of democracy, much greater political focus on social progress (particularly in education, health care, land reforms, and gender equity), and democratic pursuit of poverty-reducing economic changes (consolidating the scope for competition, incentives and openness, while removing barriers to mobility, sharing, and equity among differently placed economic groups). India has suffered in the last half a century by ignoring the need for such an integration, and the tendency toward partial neglect, especially of social development, continues even today. Since changes in a democracy like India have to take place through public discussion and debate, the first step is to see the need for taking an integrated view of economic, social, and political progress.

In his famous speech on "the tryst with destiny," delivered on the eve of independence, Jawaharlal Nehru had talked about "the great triumphs and achievements that await us" in independent India.[7] They will continue to wait unless this basic interdependence between political, social, and economic progress is more forcefully seized.

2.4   Critique of Secularism

The secular commitments of India, affirmed at the time of Indian independence, have received severe criticism—explicitly or by implication—in recent decades from both the Hindutva school and what I have been calling the "proto-Hindutva" position. The Hindutva school has been so implicated in violence against minorities (as in Gujarat in 2002), and in the destruction of valued objects of other communities (such as the riotous demolition of the Babri Masjid in 1992), that it is difficult to dissociate its intellectual arguments form its participation—or complicity—in brutal and ruthless deeds. However, there are, amid all this, identifiable intellectual arguments of the Hindutva school and, of course, more broadly of the proto-Hindutva followers, which do need attention.[8]

These beliefs tend to draw on two importance reasons for taking an asymmetric view in favor of Hinduism—and of the Hindus as a group—against the kind of neutrality that secularism demands:

1. the *statistical* fact that the Hindus form an overwhelming majority of Indians (no other community comes anywhere close to it numerically), and

2. the *historical* fact that the Hindu tradition goes back more than three thousand years in Indian history (at least to the *Veda*s) and that nearly every part of the Indian culture bears the historical imprint of Hindu thoughts and practices.

So, the argument runs, Hinduism cannot be treated merely as beliefs of one community among others in a multi-religious and secular India. Indeed, it is claimed that on statistical and historical grounds, Hindus and Hinduism must have an unmatched special standing in the political and legal organization of India. These claims demand careful attention and scrutiny.

Consider the statistical argument first. Hindus do indeed form the overwhelming majority of Indians. And yet India has more Muslims than nearly every country in the world, including those that are standardly described as "Muslim countries" (the exception is Indonesia, and marginally Pakistan). Indeed, with 130 million Muslims, the Indian Muslim population outnumbers the total population of Great Britain and France put together. Questions can also be raised about the extent to which Hindus can be seen as one community, given the deep divisions of castes and sects (which is often reflected in politics as well). However, in what follows, for the sake of argument, I simply ignore these questions and concerns, and accept the premise of the statistical reasoning, in order to examine the nature of the reasoning itself. The critical issue concerns the reach and political implications of religious majoritarianism.

There are at least two serious grounds for disputing the plausibility of the statistical argument. First, political and legal fairness demand that the protection of citizen's rights (including political and civil rights) must be neutral among persons belonging to groups of different sizes. An individual's rights are peculiarly his or her own, and the largeness of the group to which the person belongs cannot, for that reason alone, bring in special privileges. This view of individual rights, which can be found in other secular constitutions as well (including the

U.S. Constitution), did have an important influence on the making of the secular constitution of India.[9] As it happens, in addition to this demand for neutrality irrespective of group size, the Indian constitution also recognized the need to make sure that the rights of minorities are not violated. While the outcome of political elections will certainly—and appropriately—depend on the force of numbers, nevertheless when it comes to individual rights and privileges, majoritarianism can yield a very deceptive perspective. Hinduism may have overwhelmingly the largest following in the country, but that is not ground enough for individual Muslims or other non-Hindus to have any fewer rights, opportunities, and protections.

The second problem with the statistical argument relates to the question as to what counts as a "majority." This depends surely on what *principle of classification* is used. The people of India can be classified on different bases, of which religion is undoubtedly one. But it is possible to categorize people also according to language, or literature, or class, or political beliefs, to mention just a few preeminent criteria of classification. What counts as an "Indian majority" depends, thus, on the categories into which the nation is divided. There is no unique way of categorizing people. For example, the status of being a majority in India can be attributed, among other groups, to

1. the set of rural residents;

2. the category of "non-rich" people;

3. the class of non-owners of much capital;

4. people who do not work in the organized sector; or

5. the category of persons who, it would appear, are committed to religious tolerance.

Each of these categories can have very substantial importance, depending on the context.

On matters of individual identity, a person's political freedom must include the freedom to determine the priority over the different systems of classification in which he or she figures, rather than people being forced into a preselected classification chosen by "theorists" of one kind or another. Of course, a voter may well decide that the membership of a religious community has the first claim on his or her loyalty (as it seems to have happened, at least to a considerable extent, in the recent Gujarat elections). But voters—even in Gujarat in *earlier* years (not to mention in the rest of the country)—can well take a very different view of their relevant identity and be moved by a different way of seeing themselves, for example, in more economic or social or cultural terms.

This is not, of course, a special issue in India. When the Bangladeshis wanted separation from Pakistan, they were moved not because their principal religious identity was any different from those in West Pakistan, but for reasons that linked firmly with language, literature, and political priorities. It was for the people of Bangladesh to decide what relative priorities to attach in their political actions and commitments. The weakness of Hindu majoritarianism lies, therefore, not only in the need for equity among individuals belonging to groups of different sizes, but also in the diverse ways in which a majority can be identified, given the competing claims of religion, class, language, culture, political convictions, and so on. The statistical argument is ultimately misconstrued and hollow.

I turn now to the *historical* argument. Again, the rights of individual Indians cannot be compromised on the ground that one belongs to a community that has had a less long history in India. The argument here is very similar to what was said earlier in the context of the statistical claim. But what about the standing of the historical diagnosis itself?

Certainly, the ancientness of the Hindu tradition cannot be disputed. But the other religions too have had a long run in India, which has been a multi-religious country for a very long time indeed. Aside from the obvious and prominent presence of Muslims in India for well over a millennium (Muslim Arab traders started settling in what is now Kerala from the eighth century), India has had sizeable Christian communities from at least the fourth century (well before there were large Christian communities in, say, Britain), Jews from the time of the fall of Jerusalem, Parsees from the eighth century, and Sikhs from the time when that religion was born.

It is also worth recognizing that even before the arrival of Islam, India was not, as is sometimes claimed, a Hindu country, since Buddhism was the dominant religion in India for nearly a millennium. Indeed, Chinese scholars interested in India regularly described India as "the Buddhist kingdom" (the other name used was "the Western kingdom"). Furthermore, Buddhism is arguably as much an inheritor of the earlier Indian traditions of the *Veda*s and the *Upanishad*s as

Hinduism is, since both the religions drew on these classics. In fact, Chinese scholars were introduced to the *Upanishads* mainly through their studies of Buddhism. Jainism too has also had a similarly long history and in fact a continuing presence today. Also, one must take note of the very long tradition of atheism and agnosticism in India, originating at least as early as the sixth century B.C. Sanskrit (including Pali) has a larger atheistic and agnostic literature than exists in any other classical language, and references to influential atheistic thinkers can be found throughout Indian history (from the *Ramayana* and the Buddhist texts to Madhavacarya's *Sarvadarsanasamgraha* in the thirteenth century and Abul Fazl's account of Akbar's multi-religious conferences in Agra in the late sixteenth century).

No less important, it would be futile to try to have an understanding of the nature and range of Indian art, literature, music, architecture, or food, without seeing the contributions of constructive efforts that have defied the alleged barriers of religious communities. India's culture does indeed bear the mark of history, but the mark is that of its interactive and multi-religious history. This is, in fact, an important part of the broader claim made by Rabindranath Tagore that the "idea of India" itself militates "against the intense consciousness of the separateness of one's own people from others."[10]

While the questions that the proto-Hindutva approaches present have some initial plausibility, they do not, on closer scrutiny, provide enough basis for dismissing the inclusive understanding of Indian identity that emerged during the independence movement. This broad national understanding does, of course, allow considerable variations in specific features within a general picture of inclusiveness. For example, there were significant differences between the ethical and political priorities that were advocated for India by Mahatma Gandhi and Rabindranath Tagore—to consider two leading and somewhat dissimilar voices that helped to teach us what we are. But in interpreting India and the Indian identity, they shared a general refusal to privilege any community over any other, and neither wavered from an inclusive view of Indianness. Both refused to see India in terms of religious majoritarianism. That shared vision, based on political reasoning as well as history, remains important in contemporary discussions.

In the foundational fields of democracy and secularism, we are, in fact, no wiser today than we were when the Indian republic was established. What we need is resoluteness of practice, not the abandonment of principles.

Notes

1. For a penetrating historical account of the violence that marked the partition of India and its memory and legacy, see Gyanendra Pandey, *Remembering Partition* (Cambridge: Cambridge University Press, 2001).

2. Some of these subjects are discussed in my joint book with Jean Dreze, *India: Development and Participation* (Delhi and Oxford: Oxford University Press, 2002).

3. See, among other studies, Adam Przeworski, *Sustainable Democracy* (Cambridge: Cambridge University Press, 1995); Robert J. Barro, *Getting It Right: Markets and Choices in a Free Society* (Cambridge, MA: The MIT Press, 1996).

4. I have tried to discuss this question in *Development as Freedom* (New York: Knopf, and Delhi and Oxford: Oxford University Press, 1999), and jointly with Jean Dreze, *India: Development and Participation* (Delhi and Oxford: Oxford University Press, 2002).

5. These statistics and others to follow, as well as their sources, are more fully presented in my book with Jean Dreze, *India: Development and Participation* (Delhi and Oxford: Oxford University Press, 2002).

6. Kerala's economic growth rate—a source of much criticism in the past—has moved up recently. However, at 5.1 percent per year, through the 1990s, Kerala's growth rate of gross domestic product *per capita*, while higher than the Indian average, is still much lower than China's 9.6 percent per year. There is something here that Kerala can clearly learn from China, particularly how to make good pragmatic use of the market mechanism, including global opportunities of trade and exchange.

7. Jawaharlal Nehru's speech at the Constituent Assembly, New Delhi, on 14 August 1947; reprinted in Sarvepalli Gopal, ed., *Jawaharlal Nehru: An Anthology* (Delhi and Oxford: Oxford University Press, 1983), 76–77.

8. I have tried to discuss the characteristics of "proto-Hindutva" claims in "What Is the Indian Nation?" *The Taj Magazine*, February 2003. See also my essay "Secularism and Its Discontents," in Kaushik Basu and S. Subramahnyam, eds., *Unravelling the Nation: Sectarian Conflict and India's Secular Identity* (New Delhi: Penguin Books, 1996).

9. Provisions of affirmative action in favor of Scheduled Castes and Scheduled Tribes did, however, give special rights, for a certain period, to underprivileged communities. The relevant distinction there focuses on the *disadvantaged backgrounds* of particular groups, rather than on their *numerical strength*.

10. This is from a letter to C. F. Andrews, dated March 13, 1921, published in Rabindranath Tagore, *Letters to a Friend*, with essays by C. F. Andrews (London: Allen & Unwin, 1928).

Disjunctures in the Indian Reform Process: Some Reflections

Pranab Bardhan

I

In the last two decades India has launched a widely heralded process of economic reform with a view to unleashing the entrepreneurial forces from the shackles of the nightmarish controls and regulations that have hobbled the economy for years. The changes introduced, particularly since the early 1990s, were dramatic by past standards in India, but actually quite unremarkable by the standards of many other developing countries, particularly in East Asia and Latin America, and even in neighboring countries in South Asia like Sri Lanka and Bangladesh. The major elements of changes in policy over the last decade include

• delicensing and deregulation of investment and production in most industries, and the introduction of a general regulatory framework in the case of monopolies (rather than case-by-case discretionary control);

• discontinuation of exclusive reservation of many key industries for the public sector and of budgetary subsidies to public-sector enterprises, with some gingerly taken steps toward privatization in more recent years;

• gradual abolition of quantitative restrictions on imports (except for some consumer goods);

• movement toward a market-determined exchange rate (within limits) and current account convertibility;

• reduction of average levels of direct and indirect taxes and some streamlining and rationalization of the tax structure;

• some reform in the financial sector (abolition of control of capital issues, more competition among banks and insurance companies, deregulation of some interest rates, insistence on capital adequacy norms, etc.).

In some sectors of the economy significant reforms have yet to be started, for example, in pricing, storage, and movement of commodities in agriculture, labor regulations, and reservation in small-scale industries (except very recently in some industries like garments). In other sectors reforms have started but the pace is sometimes erratic and slow. A recent international survey of business environment by the World Bank indicates that in India an average 16 percent of a manager's time is still spent in dealing with the bureaucracy, as compared to 5 percent in Latin America. Some of the obstructive regulations by state governments (in matters like electricity and water supply and land acquisition and registration) are still in place. Government-controlled financial institutions still dominate the financial markets. Import-weighted tariff rates are still relatively high at 30 to 35 percent on average. There is strong opposition from organized labor to privatization, and from politicians and bureaucrats to giving any genuine autonomy to public enterprises. Jenkins (1999) has pointed to some accomplishments of "reform by stealth," for example, in the matter of some state governments looking the other way as the stringent labor laws are evaded or diluted by factory owners in practice. But some of the major political blocks to reform are difficult to surmount this way and the constellation of interest groups that lock the system into a low-level equilibrium (for an elaboration of this argument see Bardhan (1984, 1998) is still quite powerful. Nowhere is this as evident as in the case of the continuing fiscal crisis of the state.

The various (implicit and explicit) fiscal subsidies of the central and state governments to a plethora of interest groups (mostly relatively rich) and the interest burden on borrowing to cover current expenditures contribute to a fiscal deficit of about 10 percent of GDP (as large as that at the time of the crisis in the early 1990s), and the more alarming feature is that the revenue deficit as percent of GDP is now much larger. Many state governments are near bankruptcy after paying the large recurring bills of salaries and pensions. The contingent liabilities of state governments (in the form of borrowing by the public enterprises under their control) are not counted in the estimates of fiscal deficits and already run to about 6 percent of GDP. The central government also has various ways of parking its additional deficits in the public financial sector. Large public dissavings (in the form of fiscal deficits and public enterprise losses) keep the interest rates high, and that cripples the credit-starved small-scale industries (who do not have much access to the equity markets).

This kind of fiscal profligacy has also its obvious adverse consequences in the form of the state governments' diminishing share in social expenditure and the central government's diminishing involvement in public investment (not adequately compensated by rise in private investment). Capital expenditure (of central and state governments together) as a percentage of GDP declined from about 6.6 percent at the end of the 1980s to 3.4 percent at the end of the 1990s. India's creaking infrastructure (ports, railways, power, irrigation, etc.) has become a crucial bottleneck to industrial and agricultural growth. The resultant high real costs for Indian business make it uncompetitive internationally in many branches of manufacturing. Even in agricultural products, it has been observed that it is cheaper in south India to import wheat from Australia than from Punjab.

The largest single contributor to fiscal deficit for the country as whole is the staggering burden of losses in the state electricity boards. The massive investments in these enterprises over the years have yielded a *negative* return of 17 percent by a current estimate. The corporatization of the state electricity boards with independent regulatory bodies has been very slow in most states. The problem of cross-subsidization of agricultural and residential users by overcharging industrial users is now being somewhat mitigated by reform in some states. But the losses due to theft and illegal connections (with complicity of electricity board employees in collaboration with politicians and criminals) keep mounting.[1] Unless and until the problem of charging market prices and user fees for infrastructural services is resolved, the chances of substantial foreign investment relieving the infrastructure bottleneck are low.

II

An analysis of many of the fundamental problems besetting Indian reform requires an exercise in political sociology. In the rest of this chapter I briefly focus on the various kinds of disjunctures that have appeared on the Indian scene between the policy of economic reform and the ongoing political and administrative processes. Economists often ignore these and are surprised when things do not proceed in the way they want. They need to have a better understanding of why reform is so halting and hesitant, why there is no substantial political constituency for reform (outside the small confines of India's "pink press" and sections of the metropolitan elite), and why even the few supporters of reform underplay it at election time.

Any process of sustained economic reform and investment requires a framework of long-term policy to which the government can credibly commit itself. But the political process in India seems to be moving in the opposite direction. While becoming more democratic and inclusive in terms of incorporating newer and hitherto subordinate groups, it is eroding most of the structures of institutional insulation of long-run economic management decisions against the wheeling and dealing of day-to-day politics. There are very few assurances that commitments made by a government (or a leader) will be kept by successive ones, or even by itself under pressure. A political party that introduces some reforms is quick to oppose them when it is no longer in power.

With the extensive deregulation of the last two decades, it was expected that corruption associated with the system of permits and licenses would decrease. There are no hard estimates, but by most anecdotal accounts corruption has, if anything, gone up in recent years. Some of the newer social groups coming to power are quite nonchalant in suggesting that all these years upper classes and castes have looted the system, so now it is their turn. This has implications for the milking of the remaining obstructive regulations, particularly at the level of state governments. As elections become more and more expensive, the demands on business from the politician-regulator are unlikely to relent.[2]

Much more than economic reform, the major economic issue that captures public imagination is that of job reservation for an increasing number of "backward" groups, which is accepted by all political parties. In the last decade of market reform, more and more of the public-sector job market has been carved up into protected niches. Cynics may even argue that the retreat of the state, implied by economic reform, is now more acceptable to the upper classes and castes, since the latter are losing their control over state power in the face of the emerging hordes of previously subordinate groups and opting for greener pastures in the private sector and abroad. As subordinate groups capture state power, they are not likely to give up easily the loaves and fishes of office and the elaborate network of patronage distribution that goes with it, whatever the rhetoric of reform they spout when they entertain visiting dignitaries from the Western countries.

This is more acutely the case at the state government level where these groups are more secure in power.

As I mentioned earlier, there have been few substantive reforms in the agricultural sector, and the nonagricultural informal sector has been hurt by the credit crunch. Yet these two sectors constitute 93 percent of the total labor force. No wonder they are not enthused by the reforms carried out so far. In fact even organized farm lobbies (with the exception of some small sections under leaders like Sharad Joshi or Bhupinder Singh Mann) are not very active in demanding reforms of agricultural controls like those on storage and on domestic and foreign trade. They may be worried that the dismantling of the existing structure of food, fertilizer, water, and electricity subsidies in exchange of receiving, say, international agricultural prices may be too complex and politically risky a deal. In any case the high administered procurement prices for grains have now eroded India's earlier (largely unexploited) competitive advantage in world grain markets.

Political power is shifting more to the regional governments and regional parties, which makes national coordination on macro policy more difficult. For example, fiscal consolidation in general and a substantial reduction in the subsidies in particular are difficult when the national government depends on the support of powerful regional parties that assiduously nurse their parochial interest lobbies with a liberal use of subsidies (implicit or explicit). As the logic of economic reform and increased competition leads to increased regional inequality, it is not clear how the Indian federal system will resolve the tension between the demands of the better-off states for more competition and those of other states (which a weaker central government can ill afford to ignore politically) for redistributive transfers. Can, for example, a shaky coalition government at the Centre, dependent for its survival on the large number of Ministers of Parliament from weak states (like Bihar or Uttar Pradesh), ignore their redistributive demands to compensate them for losing out in the interstate competition for private investment?[3] It is also the case that a large number of entry taxes on goods imposed by governments even in otherwise leading states in economic reform (e.g., Maharashtra, Tamil Nadu) are making the goal of reformers to unify an integrated all-India market that much more distant.

Another anomaly is that while the political power of regional governments is increasing, at the same time their fiscal dependence on the Centre is also increasing. (From the mid-1950s to the mid-1990s, the fraction of states' current expenditures financed by their own revenue sources declined from around 70 percent to around 55 percent). A significant part of the central transfers is discretionary (examples are the numerous central sector and centrally sponsored schemes); these and discretionary subsidized loans are often used by the Centre more for political influence in selected areas than for the cause of fiscal or financial reform or of poverty removal.

Reform would have been more popular if it were oriented to aspects of human development (education, health, child nutrition, drinking water, women's welfare and autonomy, etc.). Reformers usually are preoccupied with problems of the foreign trade regime, fiscal deficits, and the constraints on industrial investments in the factory sector, and they believe that once these are handled right, trickle-down effect will take care of the issues that concern the masses. However, according to National Sample Survey data, even in the manufacturing sector the rate of growth of employment has declined from 2.17 percent in the period from 1983 to 1993–1994 to 1.8 percent in the period from 1993–1994 to 1999–2000; the estimated elasticity of employment to GDP in the manufacturing sector declined from 0.32 in the former period to 0.2 in the latter period.[4] Equally, if not more important, the reformers have paid little attention to the crucial problems of governance in matters of achieving human development, which will be inexorably there even if trade, fiscal, and industrial policy reforms were successful.[5] If the administrative mechanism of delivery of public services in the area of human development remains seriously deficient, as it is today in most states, chances of constructing a minimum social safety net are low, and without such a safety net any large-scale program of economic reform will remain politically unsustainable, not surprisingly in a country where the lives of the overwhelming majority of the people are brutalized by the lack of economic security.

Of course, decentralization of governance that the 73rd and the 74th constitutional amendments in the early 1990s ushered in throughout most of the country (around the same time as serious economic reforms were also launched) has raised hopes for better delivery of public services, sensitive to local needs. But so far the progress in this respect has been disappointing in most states, in terms of both actual devolution of authority and funds and the outcome variables of services delivered. According to one general evaluation by Pal (2001): "With some exceptions in Kerala, Madhya Pradesh, Tripura, and West Bengal, nothing worthwhile has been devolved to the panchayats. The bureaucracy at all tiers of panchayats is holding the balance." Note also that in Kerala and West Bengal decentralization with regular panchayat elections started long before the constitutional amendments. In many states not just the bureaucracy (which often has overlapping functions with the panchayats) has been reluctant to let go; the local MLAs, in order to protect their patronage turf, have hijacked the local electoral and administrative process (even in otherwise better-run states like Tamil Nadu). In Andhra Pradesh, a state supposedly at the forefront of economic reform, the chief minister is reportedly using information technology to further centralize (and personalize) the administrative process. Even in the relatively successful case of West Bengal, the major role of panchayats has been to identify beneficiaries of government programs and to manage and implement local infrastructure projects like roads and irrigation, funded by tied grants from the central or state government. There is no serious involvement of the panchayat in the management or control of basic public services like primary education, public health, and sanitation or in raising local resources. Of course, prior land reforms in Kerala and West Bengal have made the panchayats somewhat less prone to capture by the village landed oligarchy as in large parts of north India.

Another potential link between economic reform and decentralization largely unutilized in India relates to small-scale, particularly rural, industrialization. (In fact rural nonfarm employment grew at a much slower rate in the 1990s than in the 1980s). The Chinese success in the phenomenal growth in rural industries is often ascribed to decentralization, by which the central and provincial governments gave "positive" incentives to the local government-run village and township enterprises (by allowing them residual claimancy to the money they make) and "negative" incentives to keep them on their toes (in the form of refusing to bail them out if they lose money in the intense competition with other such enterprises). In India decentralization is usually visualized only in terms of delivery of welfare services, not in terms of fostering local business development, and yet if this link could be established, economic reform would have been much more popular, as local informal-sector industries touch the lives of many more people than the corporate sector. A program of economic reform that involves curbing the petty tyranny and corruption of the small industry inspectors (who currently act as serious barriers to potential entry), encouraging micro-finance and marketing channels and providing the "positive" and "negative" incentives of Chinese-style decentralization, has the potential to open the floodgates of small-scale entrepreneurship in India. Examples of successful cooperative business development with the leadership of the local government, though rare in India, are not entirely absent. Take the case of the Manjeri municipality in the relatively backward district of Malappuram in north Kerala, with not much of a preexisting industrial culture. In this area the municipal authorities, in collaboration with some non-governmental organizations (NGOs) and bankers, have succeeded in converting it into a booming hosiery manufacturing center, after developing the necessary skills at the local level and the finance. This and other award-winning panchayats in Kerala (often controlled by the communists) dispel the common presupposition that civic bodies in the villages and small towns of India do not have the capability to take the lead in developing and facilitating skill-based small-scale and medium-scale industries.

It is anomalous to expect reform to be carried out by an administrative setup that for many years has functioned as an inert, arbitrary, heavy-handed, corrupt, and uncoordinated monolith. Economic reform is about competition and incentives, and a governmental machinery that does not itself allow them in its own internal organization is an unconvincing proponent or carrier of that message. Yet very few economists discuss the incentive and organizational issues of administrative reform as an integral part of the economic reform package. We have an administrative structure dominated by bureaucrats chosen on the basis of a generalist examination (rank in that early entry examination determines the whole career path of an officer no matter how well- or ill-suited he or she is to the various jobs to which he or she is scuttled around, each for a brief sojourn) and promotions are largely seniority-based not merit- or performance-based. There are no well-enforced norms and rules of work discipline, very few punishments for ineptitude or malfeasance, and strong disincentives to take bold, risky decisions. Whether one likes it or not, the government will remain quite important in the Indian economy for many years to come, and it is difficult to discuss the implementation of economic reform without the necessary changes in public administration including incentive reforms, accompanied by changes in information systems, organizational structure, budgeting and accounting systems, task assignments, and staffing policies. In these matters there is a lot to learn from the (successes and failures of) innovative administrative reform experiments that have been carried out in many developing countries in the last decade or so.[6]

Finally, in large parts of the country the judiciary (particularly at the lower end) is almost completely clogged by the enormous backlog of cases, the legal system is largely paralyzed by delay and corruption, and the institutional independence of the police and criminal justice system is regularly undermined by politicians of whichever is the ruling party. As a result, the rule of law, which is as much the foundation stone of a regime of market reforms as of political democracy, is often sadly missing.[7] This is also the institutional background of the recent state-abetted carnage in Gujarat, a state that is supposed to be a leader in economic reforms, indicating an alarming disjuncture between politics and economics in India today. Foreign investors are, of course, very sensitive to bad news about political instability and mayhem (and this affects even those few sectors like IT-enabled services in which India has a large market potential in the international arena), but the more serious effect of sectarian politics run amok is on the domestic investment climate in general. In large parts of India, sectarian interests are fishing in the troubled waters basically caused by a failed state, when the state cannot deliver the essential services (health, education, a minimum safety net, and the rule of law). Market reformers, instead of trying to organize the retreat of the state, should devote a large part of their energies to the cause of reform of the state machinery, to administrative and judicial reform to make the state more accountable to the common people, and to prevent the hijacking of the police and the criminal justice system by the politician-criminal nexus.

Notes

1. In Uttar Pradesh alone there are about 2 million illegal—*katia*—connections, and the total annual loss due to so-called transmission and distribution losses run to about Rs. 30 billion.

2. Some may point to many historical cases in different countries (including current cases in South Korea, Taiwan, or China) when a great deal of corruption has been associated with economic growth and the emergence of an entrepreneurial class that evolved out of a rentier class. But in India corruption is so anarchic and fragmented, apart from being pervasive and endemic, that it is unlikely not to have seriously corroded the potential for economic growth and entrepreneurship. For more on this issue in the general context of corruption and development, see Bardhan (1997).

3. There are those who believe that the imminent bankruptcy of government will be the major driving force for reforms in India. While there is no doubt that this can serve as a

wake-up call for some delinquent governments, the redistributive pressures underlying Indian fiscal federalism are also quite strong. It is not at all clear that the most bankrupt state governments have been at the forefront of reforms.

4. See Chadha and Sahu (2002).

5. Ravallion and Datt (2002) show from an analysis of household survey data across fifteen states over 1960–1994 that nonfarm growth is less effective in reducing poverty in states with poorer initial conditions in terms of rural development, human resources, and land distribution. For example, nearly two-thirds of the difference between the elasticity of headcount poverty index to nonfarm output for Bihar and Kerala is attributable to the latter's substantially higher initial literacy rate.

6. See, for example, Mookherjee (1997) for an account of reforms in tax administration in different developing countries.

7. The N. N. Vohra Committee Report of a few years back, now shelved, clearly spelled out the nexus between politicians, bureaucrats, the mafia, and even some members of the judiciary.

References

Bardhan, P. 1984. *The Political Economy of Development in India*. New Delhi: Oxford University Press. Expanded edition 1998.

Bardhan, P. 1998. "Corruption and Development: A Review of Issues." *Journal of Economic Literature* (September):1320–1346.

Chadha, G. K., and P. P. Sahu. 2002. "Post-reform Setbacks in Rural Employment." *Economic and Political Weekly* (May 25):1998–2026.

Jenkins, R. S. 1999. *Democratic Politics and Economic Reform in India*. Cambridge: Cambridge University Press.

Mookherjee, D. 1997. "Incentive Reforms in Developing Country Bureaucracies: Lessons from Tax Administration." In *Annual World Bank Conference on Development Economics*, ed. B. Pleskovic and J. E. Stiglitz, 103–125. Washington, DC: The World Bank.

Pal, M. 2001. "Documenting the Panchayat Raj." *Economic and Political Weekly* (September 8):3448–3450.

Ravallion, M., and G. Datt. 2002. "Why Has Economic Growth Been More Pro-poor in Some States of India than Others?" *Journal of Development Economics* (August):381–400.

III   Monetary and Fiscal Reforms

4

Monetary and Financial Sector Reforms in India: A Practitioner's Perspective

Y. V. Reddy

The objectives of this chapter are to review the monetary and financial-sector reforms in India, identify the emerging issues, and explore the prospects for further reform. Section 4.1 is devoted to a brief background on the need for reforms taken up in 1991–1992. Section 4.2 is devoted to the institutional aspects of the reform. Issues relating to ownership, competition, and regulation in the financial sector as a whole, but primarily in the banking sector, are analyzed. Section 4.3 relating to policy framework focuses on monetary policy and credit delivery. The fiscal policy, insofar as it impacts the financial sector, is also analyzed. Section 4.4 focuses on the managing process of reform in its various dimensions from the perspective of the Reserve Bank of India (RBI). Section 4.5 identifies the critical elements that would possibly determine the progress of reform.

4.1 Need for Reforms

The Indian financial system in the prereform period essentially catered to the needs of planned development in a mixed-economy framework where the government sector had a predominant role in economic activity. As part of planned development, the macroeconomic policy in India moved from fiscal neutrality to fiscal activism (Reddy 2000a). Such activism meant large developmental expenditures, much of it to finance long-gestation projects requiring long-term finance. The sovereign was also expected to raise funds at fine rates, and understandably at below-market rates for the private sector. In order to facilitate the large borrowing requirements of the government, interest rates on government securities were artificially pegged at low levels, which were unrelated to market conditions. The government securities market, as a result, lost its depth as the concessional rates of interest and maturity period of securities essentially reflected the needs of the issuer (government) rather than the perception of the market. The provision of fiscal accommodation through ad hoc treasury bills (issued on tap at 4.6 percent) led to high levels of monetization of fiscal deficit during the major part of the 1980s. In order to check the monetary effects of such large-scale monetization, the cash reserve ratio (CRR) was increased frequently to control liquidity.

The environment in the financial sector in these years was thus characterized by segmented and underdeveloped financial markets coupled with a paucity of instruments. The existence of a complex structure of interest rates arising from economic and social concerns of providing concessional credit to certain sectors resulted in "cross subsidization," which implied that higher rates were charged from nonconcessional borrowers. The regulation of lending rates led to regulation of deposit rates to keep the cost of funds to banks at reasonable levels, so that the spread between the cost of funds and the return on funds was maintained. The system of administered interest rates was characterized by detailed prescription on the lending and the deposit side leading to multiplicity and complexity of interest rates.

By the end of the 1980s, the financial system was considerably stretched. The directed and concessional availability of bank credit with respect to certain sectors not only distorted the interest rate mechanism, but also adversely affected the viability and profitability of banks. The lack of recognition for the importance of transparency, accountability, and prudential norms in the operations of the banking system led also to a rising burden of nonperforming assets.

In sum, a de facto joint family balance sheet of government, RBI, and commercial banks existed, with transactions between the three segments being governed by plan priorities rather than sound principles of financing interinstitutional transactions (Reddy 2000b). There was a widespread feeling that this joint family approach, which sought to enhance efficiency through coordination, actually led to loss of transparency, accountability, and an incentive to measure or seek efficiency.

The policies pursued did have many benefits, although the issue of the higher costs incurred to realize the laudable objectives remains. Thus, the postnationalization phase witnessed significant branch expansion to mobilize savings, and there was a visible increase in the flow of bank credit to important sectors like agriculture, small-scale industries, and exports. However, these achievements have to be viewed against the macroeconomic imbalances as well as gross inefficiencies at the micro level in the financial sector compounded by nontransparent accounting of intrapublic sector financial transactions.

4.2 Institutional Aspects of Reforms

4.2.1 Institutions

At present, the institutional structure of the financial system is characterized by (a) banks, either owned by the government, the RBI, or the private sector (domestic or foreign) and regulated by the RBI; (b) development financial institutions and refinancing institutions, set up by a separate statute or owned by the government, RBI, private, or other development financial institutions under the Companies Act and regulated by the RBI; and (c) nonbank financial companies (NBFCs), owned privately and regulated by the RBI.

Since the onset of reforms, there has been a change in the ownership pattern of banks. The legislative framework governing public-sector banks (PSBs) was amended in 1994 to enable them to raise capital funds from the market by way of public issue of shares. Many public-sector banks have accessed the markets since then to meet the increasing capital requirements, and until 2001–2002, the government made capital injections out of the budget to public-sector banks, totaling about 2 percent of GDP. The government has initiated a legislative process to reduce the minimum government ownership in nationalized banks from 51 to 33 percent, without altering their public-sector character. The underlying rationale of the proposal appears to be that the salutary features of public-sector banking are not lost in the transformation process.

Reforms have altered the organizational forms, ownership pattern, and domain of operations of financial institutions (FIs) on both the asset and liability fronts. Drying up of low cost funds has led to an intensification of competition for resources for both banks and FIs. At the same time, with banks entering the domain of term lending and FIs making a foray into disbursing short-term loans, the competition for supply of funds has also increased. Besides, FIs have also entered into various fee-based services like stockbroking, merchant banking, advisory services, and the like. Currently, while the Industrial Credit and Investment Corporation of India Ltd. (ICICI) is in the process of finalizing its merger with ICICI Bank, the Industrial Development Bank of India (IDBI) is also expected to be corporatized soon.[1] At present, the RBI holds shares in a number of institutions. The further reform agenda is to divest the RBI of all its ownership functions.

In the light of legal amendments in 1997, the regulatory focus of the NBFCs was redefined, both in terms of thrust as well as the focus. While NBFCs accepting public deposits have been subject to the entire gamut of regulations, those not accepting public deposits have been sought to be regulated in a limited manner. In order to consolidate the law relating to the NBFCs, regulation is being framed to cover detailed norms with regard to entry point and to regulatory and supervisory issues.

4.2.2   Competition

Steps have also been initiated to infuse competition into the financial system. The RBI issued guidelines in 1993 for the establishment of new banks in the private sector. Likewise, foreign banks have been given more liberal entry. Recently, the norms for entry of new private banks were rationalized. Two new private-sector banks have been given "in-principle" approval under these revised guidelines. The Union Budget 2002–2003 has also provided a fillip to the foreign banking segment and permitted these banks, depending on their size, strategies, and objectives, to choose to either operate as branches of their overseas parent or corporatize as domestic companies. This is expected to impart greater flexibility in their operations and provide them with a level playing field vis-à-vis their domestic counterparts.

As a group, however, the performance of PSBs in terms of profitability, spreads, nonperforming assets, and standard assets position seems to have been lower than that of the new private sector and foreign banks. There have been significant divergences in performance among the public-sector banks—some have performed on par with private and foreign banks, whereas the performance of others has been relatively unsatisfactory. Hence, although PSBs have been subject to government intervention, these do not appear to provide a complete explanation of bank performance. Bank-specific factors such as rapid expansion, higher operating costs, and differential industry focus seem to have been important considerations as well. Public-sector banks operating in the same environment with the same constraints have shown varied performance; ultimately this reflects the performance of management.

4.2.3   Regulation and Supervision

A second major element of financial-sector reforms in India has been a set of prudential measures aimed at imparting strength to the banking system as well as ensuring safety and soundness through greater transparency, accountability, and public credibility.

Capital adequacy norms for banks are in line with the Basel Committee standards and from the end of March 2000, the prescribed ratio has been raised to 9 percent.[2] While the objective has been to meet the international standards, in certain cases, fine-tuning has occurred keeping in view the unique country-specific circumstances. For instance, risk weights have been prescribed for investment in central government securities on considerations of interest rate risk. Also, while there is a degree of gradualism, there has been an intensification beyond the "best practices" in several instances over the recent period, one example being exposure norms stipulated for the banking sector with respect to investment in equity. Investments are valued and classified into appropriate categories, as per international best practices. To take into account the vagaries of interest rate risks, a prescription for meeting a targeted Investment Fluctuation Reserve out of the realized profits from sale of investments within a stipulated time frame has also been prescribed recently.

The supervisory strategy of the Board for Financial Supervision (BFS) constituted as part of reform consists of a four-pronged approach, including restructuring the system of inspection, setting up of off-site surveillance, enhancing the role of external auditors, and strengthening corporate governance, internal controls, and audit procedures. The BFS, in effect, integrates within the Reserve Bank the supervision of banks, NBFCs, and financial institutions.

Prudential regulations have had a significant impact on the banking system in terms of ensuring system stability even in the face of both external and internal uncertainties, almost throughout the second half of the 1990s. As of the end of March 2001, 95 out of 100 scheduled commercial banks had a capital adequacy ratio of 9 percent or more. There was a distinct improvement in the profitability of public-sector banks measured in terms of operating profits as well as in terms of net profits to total assets. Reflecting the efficiency of the intermediation process, there has been a decline in the spread between the borrowing and lending rates as reflected by the decline in the ratio of net interest income to total assets. The most significant improvement has been in terms of reduction in NPAs.

4.3   Policy Environment

4.3.1   Changing the Monetary Policy Framework

Since the onset of the reform process, monetary management in terms of framework and instruments has undergone significant changes, reflecting broadly the transition of the economy from a regulated to liberalized and deregulated regime.[3] While the twin objectives of monetary policy, to maintain price stability and ensure the availability of adequate credit to the productive sectors of the economy in order to support growth, have remained unchanged, the relative emphasis on either of these objectives has varied over the years depending on the circumstances. Reflecting the development of financial markets and the opening up of the economy, the use of broad money (M_3) as an intermediate target has been deemphasised, but the growth in broad money continues to be used as an important indicator of monetary policy. The composition of reserve money has also changed with net foreign exchange assets currently accounting for nearly one-half. A multiple indicator approach was adopted in 1998–1999, wherein interest rates or rates of return in different markets (money, capital, and government securities markets) along with data such as currency, credit extended by banks and financial institutions, fiscal position, trade, capital flows, inflation rate, exchange rate, refinancing, and transactions in foreign exchange available on a high frequency basis were juxtaposed with output data for drawing policy perspectives. Such a shift was gradual and a logical outcome of measures taken over the reform period since early 1990s.

The thrust of monetary policy in recent years has been to develop an array of instruments to transmit short-term liquidity and interest rate signals in a more flexible and bidirectional manner. A Liquidity Adjustment Facility (LAF) has been introduced since June 2000 to precisely modulate short-term liquidity and signal short-term interest rates. The LAF, in essence, operates through repo and reverse repo auctions, thereby setting a corridor for the short-term interest rate consistent with policy objectives. There is now greater reliance on indirect instruments of monetary policy. The RBI is able to modulate the large market borrowing program by combining strategic debt management with active open market operations. The Bank Rate has emerged as a reasonable signaling rate, while the LAF rate has emerged as both a tool for liquidity management and signaling of interest rates in the overnight market. The RBI has also been able to use open market operations effectively to manage the impact of capital flows in view of the stock of marketable government securities at its disposal and development of financial markets brought about as part of reform.

The responsibility of the RBI in undertaking reform in the financial markets has been driven mainly by the need to improve the effectiveness of the transmission channel of monetary policy. The development of financial markets has therefore encompassed regulatory and legal changes, the building up of institutional infrastructure, constant fine-tuning in market microstructure, and massive upgrading of technological infrastructure.

Since the onset of reforms, a major focus of architectural policy efforts has been on the principal components of the organized financial market spectrum: the money market, which is central to monetary policy; the credit market, which is essential for flow of resources to the productive sectors of the economy; the capital market, or the market for long-term capital funds; the government securities market, which is significant from the point of view of developing a risk-free credible yield curve; and the foreign exchange market, which is integral to external sector management. Along with the steps taken to improve the functioning of these markets, there has been a concomitant strengthening of the regulatory framework.

The medium-term objective at present is to make the call and term money market a purely interbank market for banks, while nonbank participants, who are not subject to reserve requirements, can have free access to other money market instruments and operate through repos in a variety of instruments. The Clearing Corporation of India Ltd. is expected to facilitate the development of a repo market in a risk-free environment for settlement. A phased program for moving out of the call money market has already been announced and the final phaseout will coincide with the implementation of the Real Time Gross Settlement (RTGS) system. Further reform is being contemplated in terms of reduction of CRR to the statutory minimum of 3 percent; removal of established lines of refinance, limits on call money borrowing, lending, and borrowing by banks and primary dealers (PDs), and a move over to a full-fledged LAF.

With the switchover to borrowings by the government at market-related interest rates through the auction system in 1992, and more recently, abolition of automatic monetization, it was possible to progress toward greater market orientation in government securities. Further reforms in the government securities market have resulted in the rationalization of the T-bills market, increase in instruments and participants, elongated maturity profile, greater fungibility in the secondary market, a system of delivery versus payment, a strengthened institutional framework through PDs, and more recently the Clearing Corporation and enhanced transparency in market operations. Clarity in the regulatory framework has also been established with the amendment to the Securities Contracts Regulation Act. A Negotiated Dealing System for trading in government securities is in operation. Further developments in the government securities market hinge on legislative changes consistent with modern technology and market practices: the introduction of the RTGS system, integration of the payments and settlement systems for government securities, and standardization of practices with regard to manner of quotes, conclusion of deals, and code of best practices for repo transactions.

The movement to a market-based exchange rate regime took place in 1993. Reforms in the foreign exchange market have focused on market development with prudential safeguards without destabilizing the market. Thus, authorized dealers have been given the freedom to initiate trading in overseas markets, borrow or invest funds in the overseas markets (up to 15 percent of tier I capital, unless otherwise approved), determine the interest rates (subject to a ceiling) and maturity period of Foreign Currency Non-Resident (FCNR) deposits (not exceeding three years), and use derivative products for asset-liability management. These activities are subject to net overnight position limit and gap limits, to be fixed by them. Other measures such as permitting forward cover for some participants, and the development of the rupee-forex swap markets have also provided additional instruments to hedge risks and help reduce exchange rate volatility. Alongside the introduction of new instruments (cross-currency options, interest rates, and currency swaps; caps/collars; and forward rate agreements), efforts were made to develop the forward market and ensure orderly conditions. Foreign institutional investors were allowed entry into forward markets, and exporters have been permitted to retain a progressively increasing proportion of their earnings in foreign currency accounts. The RBI conducts purchase and sale operations in the forex market to even out excess volatility.

With respect to financial markets, the linkage between the money, government securities, and forex markets has been established and is growing. The price discovery in the primary market is more credible than before, and secondary markets have acquired greater depth and liquidity. The number of instruments and participants in the markets has increased in all markets, the most impressive being the government securities market. The institutional and technological infrastructures that have been created by the RBI have enabled transparency in operations and secured settlement systems. The presence of foreign institutional investors has strengthened the integration between the domestic and international capital markets.

4.3.2   Credit Delivery

The reforms have accorded greater flexibility to banks to determine both the volume and terms of lending. The RBI has moved away from microregulation of credit to macromanagement. External constraints to the banking system in terms of the statutory preemptions have been lowered. All this has meant greater lendable resources at the disposal of banks. The movement toward a competitive and deregulated interest rate regime on the lending side has been completed with the linkage of all lending rates to Prime Lending Rate (PLR) of the concerned bank. The PLR itself has been transformed into a benchmark rate.

As a result of reforms, borrowers are able to the get credit at lower interest rates. The lending rate between 1991–1992 and 2001–2002 has declined from about 19.0 percent to current levels of 10.5–11.0 percent. The actual lending rates for top-rated borrowers could even be lower since banks are permitted to lend at below PLR. Further, since banks invest in Commercial Paper, which is more directly related to money market rates, many top-rated borrowers are able to tap bank funds at rates below the PLRs. These developments have been made possible to banks because the overall flexibility now available in the interest rate structure has enabled them to reduce their deposit rates and still improve their spreads.

In terms of priority-sector credit as well, the element of subsidization has been removed although some sort of directed lending to agriculture, small-scale industry, and the export sector have been retained. The definition of the priority sector has been gradually increased to help banks make loans on commercially viable terms. However, the actual experience has been that the credit pickup is not up to the mark and has been generally less than projected by the RBI in its monetary policies, in a number of years. Also, while in general the rates of interest have come down, they are available more to highly rated borrowers than to small and medium enterprises. There is considerable concern about the inadequate flow of resources to rural areas, and in particular agriculture, while interest rates have not been reduced to the extent they were for the corporate sector.

4.3.3   Fiscal Policy and Financial Sector

Several channels link the fiscal and financial sectors, four of which appear significant in the Indian context. These relate to (a) the governments' borrowing program; (b) guarantees extended by governments; (c) mechanisms such as "direct debits"; and (d) governments' investments in financial sector.

The market borrowing program of the central government continued to be relatively large, both in gross and net terms. Since a large part of the borrowing program has to be completed in the first half of the fiscal year, in view of seasonality for demand for credit on private account, the monthly average borrowing by the central government is around three-quarters of a percent of GDP in recent years. Further, there has been an upward revision in the borrowing program of the central government during the course of every year, usually around three-quarters of a percent of GDP. It has been possible for the RBI as a debt manager to complete the borrowing program while pursuing its interest rate objectives without jeopardizing external balance, by recourse to several initiatives in terms of institution, instruments, incentives, and tactics. At the same time, it has allowed the RBI to reduce statutory preemptions for banks to the prescribed minimum of 25 percent of their net liabilities. The banking system, in which PSBs account for about three-quarters of activity, holds a majority of the outstanding stock of government securities, and currently its holdings in excess of statutory prescriptions are far in excess of the annual borrowing program of the central and state governments. In any case, a large part of outstanding government securities are held by government-owned financial institutions, especially in the banking and insurance sectors. The RBI has so far been able to successfully reconcile the interests of the government as its debt manager and of banks as a regulator and supervisor. In this regard, recognizing the importance of containing interest rate risks and widening the participant profile, the RBI has prescribed an Investment Fluctuation Reserve for banks and is pursuing the retailing of government securities. While technological, institutional, and procedural bottlenecks for retailing are being overcome by the RBI, some of the constraints such as tax treatment and relatively high administered interest rates do persist.

The conduct of the borrowing program of state governments does, however, pose several problems. While the market borrowing program of states in aggregate is well below a quarter of the central government's market borrowings, in a liberalized environment banks cannot be compelled to subscribe to the program. It was necessary to provide investors a premium for states' paper over the central government's paper of a comparable maturity. Of late, the premium is widening and differing as it is between states, while in the case of some states, there have been some difficulties in ensuring subscriptions. In recent years, the increases in states' borrowing programs over the budgeted amounts have been large with the attendant problems of garnering subscriptions. It has, however, been possible for the RBI to conduct the program without serious disruption in the markets, since some states have also begun to take initiatives to improve their fiscal profile and discharge their liabilities, especially to banks, in a timely fashion. It is necessary to recognize that size of government borrowings is only one element in public debt management, since there are other liabilities also, especially the ballooning of pension liabilities.

In this regard, extra-budgetary transactions are also emerging, which impinge on the balance sheets of banks and other financial institutions that leave them vulnerable to risk. For example, "oil bonds" to settle the government's dues to public-sector oil companies and "power bonds" to settle dues from state electricity boards to national level power utilities fall in this category. Banks' exposure to food credit, which is in the nature of funding buffer stock operations, is also relatively large at over 2.0 percent of gross domestic product (GDP). The RBI had been advocating that a law be passed imposing a ceiling on government borrowings as enabled by the constitution, but more recently, a bill is under contemplation for fiscal responsibility at the central government and several states (and has since been passed for the central government).

Financial intermediaries, especially banks, take exposures with a great degree of comfort when there is a sovereign guarantee. Such guarantees are often formally extended and notified as such to the legislative bodies and financial markets. RBI has encouraged governments to pass a legislation prescribing a ceiling on such guarantees and also charge a fee without exception to ensure credibility to guarantees and comfort to subscribers. Several state governments have passed such legislations, though some are less stringent than others. In view of the magnitudes of such guarantees by many states, banks have been advised to exercise due diligence in subscribing to them. Apart from explicit guarantees, recourse is occasionally made by governments to letters of comfort that have a similar effect, and the RBI has been dissuading such relatively nontransparent practices.

There are, in addition, what may be termed "implicit-guarantees" that have maximum linkage between fiscal and financial sectors. A predominant point of financial intermediation through banks, mutual funds, and insurance, in spite of significant reform, is undertaken by publicly owned or government-backed financial institutions. Hence, the public tends to repose confidence with a corresponding implicit direct obligation on the part of the government to protect the interests of depositors or investors. Such a reasonable expectation is not only justified on the basis of considerations of reputational risk and the concept of "holding out" or backing, but also by the obligations discharged in the past by the government of India, in several cases—some of them at the instance of the relevant regulator.

In some cases, banks and financial institutions seek and obtain instructions for direct debit of dues to them from government accounts to ensure the timely recovery of dues to them and thus bring about comfort through credit enhancement. Since large-scale recourse to such mechanisms, especially when state governments are under fiscal strain, has the potential to erode both the integrity of budget process and the de facto comfort to financial intermediaries, the RBI has been vigorously advocating the avoidance of recourse to such direct debit mechanisms.

A government has, in its asset portfolio, equity holding and some debts of financial intermediaries that it owns, and financial returns on these do impact the fiscal situation. More important, whenever pockets of vulnerability arise in financial sector, the headroom available in the fiscal situation to provide succor to financial entities needs to be assessed. Fortunately, on present reckoning, the magnitudes of the few pockets of vulnerability appear to be manageable without undue fiscal strain.

In assessing fiscal financial linkage, the scope for money financing of budgets vis-à-vis bond financing also needs to be considered. Since there are elements of open capital account, the RBI's maneuverability in the short term to monetize the government's deficit is severely circumscribed by the direction and magnitudes of such flows. Keeping these considerations in view, the RBI and the government have agreed to give the RBI the freedom to determine the extent of government monetization consistent with macroeconomic stability.

4.4 Managing the Process of Reform

4.4.1 Financial-Sector Reform and Changes in Law

Any reform has both public and private dimensions, and ideally all participants should recognize the emerging new realities, assess costs, and benefits and make attempts to cope. Reform outcomes should thus be related not only to public action but also to several other factors. In public action itself, there can be legal, policy, and procedural aspects including subordinate legislations and institutional changes. There are possibilities of significant policy and procedural changes within a given legal framework, and these need to be explored since changes in law are often difficult to get through in any democratic process.

The RBI has been articulating the need for appropriate changes in law, assisting the government in the process and has also been bringing about changes in the financial sector without necessarily waiting for changes in law. Thus, several legislative measures affecting ownership of banks, IDBI, debt recovery, regulation of nonbanking financial companies, foreign exchange transactions, and money market have been completed. Those on the anvil include measures relating to fiscal and budget management, public debt, deposit insurance, securitization and foreclosure, and prevention of money laundering. The agenda for further legal reform, as identified by several Advisory Groups related to the RBI, includes banking regulations, companies, chartered accountant, income tax, bankruptcy, negotiable instruments, contracts, Unit Trust of India, and so forth.

The legislative process is complex in a democratic setup, and it will be inadvisable to rush into legislation through a "big bang" approach. Furthermore, many elements of economic reform and the underlying legislative framework need to be harmonized. At the same time, it may not be necessary to wait for a legislative framework to change to bring about some of the reforms or initiate processes to demonstrate the usefulness of reform orientation. In fact, there are several examples of managing reform within constraints of law that need to be recalled. For example, there are some enabling but not mandated provisions that may or may not be used. Thus, the RBI has shed its direct developmental role of money financing by ceasing to operate on relevant provisions and by and large leaving money creation to the government of India. Supplemental agreement in the form of Ways and Means Advances to terminate automatic monetization of the government's deficit has been used, by way of a signed agreement between the RBI and the government of India, though a legislative compulsion is necessitated as part of the Fiscal Responsibility and Budget Management Bill.

In several cases, contracts with stipulated conditions have been framed in the absence of a specific law governing such transactions. Examples relate to regulation of clearing houses, operating current payment systems, and the functioning of electronic trading even before instructions under the Information Technology Act came into force. Similarly, it has been possible to invoke prudential regulations over RBI-regulated financial institutions to effectuate best practices in financial markets, though the legal compulsion as a regulation on all market participants may not be possible; the example of successes achieved are dematerialization of commercial paper and demateralization of debt instruments, brought about in the requirements on banks and financial institutions. There could also be use of incentives to conform, though legal or formal regulation may be difficult. Examples relate to valuation and accounting norms performed by a self-regulatory organization and adopted by banks, as well as proposals relating to information sharing with the Credit Information Bureau pending legislative initiatives. A deliberate decision may be taken not to use regulatory powers, thus enabling development of markets. For example, current account convertibility in the external sector was implemented even before a new law was introduced by recourse to large-scale relaxations. Similarly, credit guarantee was virtually given up, though a new law is yet to be enacted relinquishing the credit guarantee function of the Deposit Insurance Guarantee Corporation. In all these cases, however, a positive approach to law to enable reform was possible because of clarity about what was to be done and the ability to find legal ways to do it even if it were second best.

4.4.2 Managing Uncertainties during Reform

Reforms in the financial sector had to be implemented while keeping in view not only the desirable directions and appropriate measures carefully sequenced, but also the emerging uncertainties, in both domestic and global arenas. By all accounts, India has managed the uncertainties reasonably well. Recognizing that such uncertainties have a tendency to impact the exchange rate, it is instructive to briefly review the processes of management and draw some tentative lessons. The Gulf crisis, which triggered the reform process, was managed without any rescheduling of any contractual obligation, but with a recourse to stabilization measures and initiation of structural reforms. The current account convertibility in 1994 led to liberalization of gold imports and large capital inflows up until 1996. In 1997, the timely efforts to depreciate the currency warded off a possible crisis due to the persistence of a relatively overvalued rupee in the forex markets. This also enabled the implementation of a package of monetary and other prompt actions in resisting the contagion effects of the Asian crisis in late 1997 and early 1998. The imposition of sanctions by the U.S. government and others after the nuclear tests in India required the replacement of normal debt flows with a type of extraordinary financing.

There was also an occasion, in May–August 2000, where inexplicable changes in expectations put pressure on the currency, warranting yet another package to counter the market sentiment. In contrast the events of September 11, 2001, needed measures to reassure the markets with timely liquidity and stability in monetary conditions. The reasonable success in managing these uncertainties, while adding to forex reserves with the marginal addition to total external debt but maintaining both reasonable overall macroeconomic stability and pace of reform in the financial sector, has some tentative lessons to offer.

First, stable and appropriate policies governing overall management of the external sector are important. As part of the reform process, a policy framework was developed to gradually liberalize the external sector, move toward total convertibility on current account, encourage nondebt credit inflows while containing all external debt especially short-term debt in capital account, and make the exchange rate largely market-determined. The policy reform in the external sector, accompanied by other changes, was guided by the Report of High-Level Committee on Balance of Payments (Chairman Dr. C. Rangarajan) in April 1993 (Reserve Bank of India 1993).

Second, the impression that a closed economy is less vulnerable to crisis is not borne out by the facts. India was a closed economy on the eve of the Gulf crisis, but the impact was severe. Though it is now a relatively more open economy, it could without serious disruptions withstand several uncertainties. Third, as evident from experience, if the fundamentals are weak, the economy is more vulnerable in the face of uncertainties.

Fourth, in all instances of serious uncertainties, the existence and manifestation of harmonious relations between the government and the central bank become critical and appropriate coordination is extremely useful. Fifth, while it is difficult to anticipate or assess the uncertainties, there may be advantages in taking the risk of early action rather than late action. Sixth, while in a rapidly changing world of uncertainties, commitment to ideology can prove to be a drag on policy, especially in emerging countries that are attempting structural transformation. It has been demonstrated by events the world over, as well as by the Indian experience, that when the going is good, the government is perceived to be a problem but when the going gets tough, effective public policy may be the only solution. As such, the state has a pivotal role in stabilizing the economy when there is a spell of stormy weather.

Seventh, there may be need for several short-term actions to meet challenges, but this should not distort the medium-term vision to proceed with economic reform to improve standards of living. In other words, it is necessary for the policymakers to be conscious and more important, essential for the policymaker to convince market participants that some measures to meet the crisis are short term, while some others may get embedded into public policy in the medium term. Related to this approach and to reinforce this is the advantage to designing measures that are easily reversible, preferably with an explicit indication that the measures are reversible even as they are being announced, though a specific time frame may not be prescribed.

Eighth, with regard to the techniques and instruments of managing uncertainties, they have to evolve while keeping in view the reform process itself, especially developments in financial markets; monetary policy; the nature, composition, and evolution of market participants; and above all public opinion.

Ninth, it is necessary to have an appropriate mix of surprise elements and anticipated elements in policy actions for meeting any uncertainties. For example, when the markets are in need of comfort or assurances, when the convergence in the objectives of policymakers and the markets are matched, and such convergence is observable with regard to instruments, there is merit in taking the market into one's confidence and proceeding accordingly. Where there is a perception that the market expectations and their possible actions in that direction are not considered to be desirable by policymakers, it is always advantageous to bring an element of surprise, preferably with firmness and credibility, so that all possible anticipatory actions as well as resistances are avoided. There may be occasions when the wavelengths of markets or segments thereof and policymaker differ significantly and in such circumstances, the conduct of policy would presumably be more complex and difficult.

Finally, the issue of transparency is extremely important. There are many occasions where transparency is desirable, but there are also occasions where instant transparency is not entirely essential and could even be counterproductive. An acceptable approach seem to be one that practices transparency as a rule, but the timing of transparency could vary depending on the circumstances.

4.4.3   The RBI and Government

During the early 1960s, RBI Governor Iyengar identified four areas of potential conflict between the bank and the central government. These were interest-rate policy, deficit financing, cooperative credit policies, and management of substandard banks (Balachandran 1998). It may be of interest to note that these four areas are still some of the RBI's concerns.

During the postreform period, the relationship between the central bank and the government took a new turn through a welcome development in the supplemental agreement that took place between the government and the RBI in September 1994 on the abolition of the ad hoc treasury bills, from April 1997 on. The measure eliminated the automatic monetization of government deficits and resulted in considerable moderation of the monetized deficit in the latter half of the 1990s.

At the same time, with the gradual opening up of the economy and development of domestic financial markets, the operational framework of the RBI also changed considerably with a clearer articulation of policy goals and more and more public dissemination of a vast amount of data relating to its operations.

In fact, during the recent period, the RBI enjoyed considerable instrument independence for attaining monetary policy objectives. Significant achievements in financial reforms, including the strengthening of the RBI's banking supervision capabilities, have enhanced its credibility and instrument independence. It has been pointed out by some experts that the RBI, though not formally independent, has enjoyed a high degree of operational autonomy during the postreform period.

In terms of redefining the functions of the RBI, enabling a movement toward meaningful autonomy, Governor Jalan's statement on monetary and credit policy on April 19, 2001 (Reserve Bank of India 2001) is a landmark event. First, it was decided to divest the RBI of all the ownership functions in commercial banking, development finance, and securities trading entities. Second, a beginning was made in recommending the divestiture of RBI's supervisory functions in regard to cooperative banks, which would presumably be extended to nonbanking financial companies and later to all commercial banks. Third, the RBI signaled initiation of steps for separation of the government debt management function from monetary policy. These measures would enable the RBI to primarily focus on its role as monetary authority and enhance the possibility of a move toward greater autonomy.

The emerging issues relating to autonomy of the RBI can be addressed at different levels. First, at the level of legislative framework, several suggestions have been made to ensure appropriate autonomy, and many of them are under consideration. In particular, the Fiscal Responsibility and Budget Management Bill and other amendments to the Reserve Bank of India Act would cover significant ground. Several other suggestions relating to the legal framework, as recommended by the Advisory Groups, are yet to be taken up.

Second, at the policy level, there are three important constraints on the operational autonomy even within the existing legal framework. One, the continued fiscal dominance includes large temporary mismatches between receipts and expenditures of government warranting large involuntary financing of credit needs of government by the RBI. Two, the predominance of publicly owned financial intermediaries and nonfinancial public enterprises has created a blurring of the demarcation between funding of and by government vis-à-vis the public sector as a whole. Three, the relatively underdeveloped state of financial markets partly due to legal and institutional constraints blunts the effectiveness of instruments of monetary policy. These issues need to be resolved to enhance genuine autonomy.

Third, at the operational and procedural level, there is a problem of "old habits dying hard." In a deregulated environment, there is considerable scope to reduce micromanagement issues in the relationship between the government and the RBI. At this degree of transparency, there is a temptation to continue what has been termed the "joint-family approach"; this ignores the basic tenets of accounting principles with respect to the transactions between the RBI and government.

4.5   Some Critical Elements for Progress in Reform

In spite of difficulties in prioritizing the elements relevant for reform, an attempt is made to mention some elements that present themselves as critical in the light of experience gained so far. First, as elaborated in recent statements on monetary and credit policy by the RBI, several legislative measures are needed to enable further progress. These relate in particular, to ownership, regulatory focus, and the development of financial markets and bankruptcy procedures. Some of the serious shortcomings in the anticipated benefits of reform such as in credit delivery do need changes in the legal and incentive systems. In particular, there is a need to focus on the reduction of transaction costs in economic activity and enhancing economic incentives. Severe penalties in law, including criminal proceedings, may not be substitutes for increasing enforceability (i.e., probability of being caught, prosecuted, and punished adequately and in a timely fashion). With regard to institutions, there is a need to clearly differentiate the functions of the owner, regulator, financial intermediary, and market participant to replace the joint-family approach that is a legacy of the prereform framework.

Second, fiscal empowerment appears to be essential for obvious reasons. While the existing level of fiscal deficit may be manageable, the headroom available for meeting unforeseen circumstances appears rather limited. The problem is somewhat acute with regard to the finances of states that have serious structural problems, and their resolution is possible only through accelerated fiscal support from central government consistent with the latter's fiscal soundness. Some of the legal reforms may also be necessary for this purpose, and the imperative for further progress in the financial sector is obvious. In particular, the nature of fiscal dominance does constrain the effectiveness of monetary policy to meet unforeseen contingencies as well as maintain price stability and contain inflationary expectations.

Third, the reforms in the real sector are needed to bring about structural changes in the economy. Liberalization of the financial sector and external sector can provide the impetus for further growth and in turn help generate more rapid progress only when accompanied by reforms in the real sector, particularly in domestic trade.

Fourth, there are what may be termed "overhang" problems in the financial sector, such as nonperforming assets of banks and financial institutions. There are similar overhang problems in other areas as well, and it is necessary to make a distinction between what may be termed "flow" issues and "overhang" issues. There is merit in insulating the overhang problem from flow issues and demonstrably solving the flow problem up front. For example, with regard to the food stocks, an addition to buffer stocks occurs virtually on a continuous basis, and a policy needs to be created to tackle this flow. Any attempt to sort out the overhang accumulated excess stocks on an ad hoc basis would obviously have limited success. Any solution to the overhang problem of large magnitude is bound to be operational over the medium term and may involve admission of the magnitude of possible losses to be incurred. Yet another example relates to the power sector, where addition to capacities to generate without ensuring cost recovery adds to the problem of accumulated losses. Prima facie, the major areas with considerable overhang problems apart from the financial sector are public enterprises, pension and provident fund liabilities, and the co-operative sector. The importance of the issue is in terms of their cumulative impact on financial sector as a whole.

Fifth, it will be useful to distinguish between what the financial sector can contribute and what fiscal action can contribute to matters relating to poverty alleviation. In the interest of efficiency and stability of the financial sector, intermediation may have to be progressively multi-institutional rather than wholly bank-centered. Social obligations may have to be distributed equitably among banks and other intermediaries, but that would be difficult to achieve in the context of emerging capital markets and a relatively open economy. In such a situation, banks that are special and that are the backbone of payment systems may face problems if they are subject to disproportionate burdens. Hence, mechanisms have to be found to reconcile these dilemmas.

Furthermore, monetary policy is increasingly focused on an efficient discharge of its objective including price stability, and this no doubt would help poverty alleviation, albeit indirectly, while the more direct attack on poverty alleviation would rightfully be the preserve of fiscal policy. Monetary and financial-sector policies in India should perhaps be focusing increasingly on what Dreze and Sen (1995) call "growth-mediated security" while "support-led security," mainly consisting of direct anti-poverty interventions, are addressed mainly by fiscal and other governmental activities.

Notes

This chapter is based on a presentation by Dr. Y. V. Reddy, Deputy Governor, Reserve Bank of India, at The Indian Economy Conference, Program on Comparative Economic Development (PCED) at Cornell University, Ithaca, NY, on April 19–20, 2002. Dr. Reddy is thankful to Dr. A. Prasad and Mr. Saibal Ghosh for their valuable assistance.

1. The RBI has enunciated that in processing specific proposals for the movement toward universal banking from concerned institutions, the overwhelming consideration would be to meet the strategic objectives of the concerned financial institution for meeting the varied needs of different categories of customers, while at the same time ensuring healthy competition in the financial system through transparent and equitable regulatory framework applicable to all participants in the banking business. In such a situation, particular attention would be paid to the primary need to ensure the safety of public deposits, especially those of small depositors, and to promote the continued stability of the financial system as a whole and the banking system in particular.

2. As at the end of March 2001, as many as 95 out of the 100 scheduled commercial banks (except Regional Rural Banks) had CRAR of 9 percent and more. The corresponding figures for 1995–1996 were 54 out of a total of 92 banks.

3. The evolution of monetary policy during the 1990s has been detailed in Reddy (2001).

References

Balachandran, G. 1998. *The Reserve Bank of India: 1951–1967*. Delhi: Oxford University Press.

Dreze, J., and A. Sen, eds. 1995. *India: Economic Development and Social Opportunity*. Delhi: Oxford University Press.

Reddy, Y. V. 2000a. *Monetary and Financial Sector Reforms in India: A Central Banker's Perspective*. New Delhi: UBS Publishers.

Reddy, Y. V. 2000b. "Fiscal and Monetary Policy Interface: Recent Developments in India." *RBI Bulletin* (November):1257–1272.

Reddy, Y. V. 2001. "Developments in Monetary Policy and Financial Markets in India." *RBI Bulletin* (May):595–615.

Reserve Bank of India. 1993. "Report of High-Level Committee on Balance of Payments." (Chairman: Dr. C. Rangarajan). Mumbai: Reserve Bank of India.

Reserve Bank of India. Various years. *Annual Report*. Mumbai: Reserve Bank of India.

Reserve Bank of India. 2001. *Annual Statement on Monetary and Credit Policy*. Mumbai: Reserve Bank of India.

5

Some Macroeconomics of India's Reform Experience

Mihir Rakshit

Though some tentative steps toward liberalization were taken in the mid-1980s, it was only from 1991 on that the government of India has started implementing in earnest a fairly comprehensive economic reform program. The first section of this chapter gives a summary of the program's contents, highlighting those that seem to have had a decisive impact on the overall behavior of the economy. Section 5.2 delineates the trends of major macroeconomic indicators in the 1990s, compared with those in earlier decades. For a deeper understanding of the strength and weaknesses of the reform process, section 5.3 distinguishes among three phases in the economy's development during the 1990s: (i) payments crisis leading to adoption of reforms and a contractionary phase lasting about a year; (ii) quick recovery followed by a spell of expansion; and (iii) deceleration of growth with mounting evidence of fiscal fragility since the mid-1990s. The main factors driving the economy in the first two phases are discussed in this section. Sections 5.4 and 5.5 constitute perhaps the most controversial part of the chapter. They examine the major factors behind the disquieting developments during the third phase and seek to identify the nature and sources of policy failures. Section 5.6 concludes with a summary of my main observations and results.

5.1 Economic Reforms in the 1990s

The reform program was undertaken in the face of a severe balance-of-payments crisis that forced the government to seek financial assistance from the IMF and other sources.[1] Though India adopted a more cautious and step-by-step approach to reforms and liberalization compared with most other similarly placed emerging economies, the program bore the unmistakable stamp of the Washington consensus, characterized by emphasis on macroeconomic stabilization on the one hand and structural adjustment on the other.

The proximate cause of the payments crisis, à la the mainstream perception, was faulty macroeconomic policies, especially large fiscal deficits of the government during 1984–1991—deficits that spilled over in the country's current account of the balance of payments.[2] More fundamentally, the malady was traced to growing inefficiency of the system of production and noncompetitiveness of the country's exportables due to import substitution strategy, to subversion of market forces through a plethora of controls and quantitative restrictions, and to the public sector's dominance over the "commanding heights" of the economy. The problems faced by the country were accordingly attempted to be solved through two sets of policies, the first macroeconomic, the second efficiency enhancing, though for a number of measures the distinction was far from clear-cut.

The macrostabilization program designed to tackle the balance-of-payments problem and ensure longer-term budgetary viability consisted of (a) an 18 percent devaluation of the rupee, in two successive steps in July 1991; (b) reduction in fiscal deficit through expenditure compression, tax reforms, privatization (though mostly partial), and signals to public-sector undertakings (PSUs) to operate on commercial principles (rather than try to secure "social" goals); and (c) granting a large measure of autonomy to the Reserve Bank of India (RBI) for maintaining the country's internal-cum-external balance. These measures were supplemented by (i) transition to a system of market-driven exchange-rate system with current account convertibility of the rupee; (ii) permitting select Indian corporates to raise funds from the international capital market; and (iii) encouragement of capital inflows by way of foreign institutional investment (FII), foreign direct investment (FDI), and nonresident Indian (NRI) deposits.

The other major reforms measures relating to trade, financial markets, and industries were intended to raise allocative efficiency of investment, production, and domestic absorption, and thus to promote long-term viability of the balance of payments, sustained growth, and resilience of the economy to internal or external shocks. Abandonment of the import substitution strategy, reflected in phased liberalization of exports and imports, was complemented by policies aimed at raising productivity in domestic industries. The most important step in this direction was dereservation,[3] permitting private[4] investors to set up production units in any sector except in a few defense and strategic industries.

It was perhaps the financial sector that underwent the most thorough overhaul during the 1990s. The major features of the reform measures in this sector were (i) partial privatization of a number of public-sector banks and financial institutions; (ii) entry of private (including foreign) banks, mutual funds, and other financial intermediaries; (iii) a cutback in the statutory liquidity ratio[5] (SLR) and the cash reserve ratio (CRR) from 38.5 and 15.0 percent to 25 and 5 percent respectively;[6] (iv) adoption of international (Basel) norms for financial institutions relating to capital adequacy, income recognition, asset classification, and provisioning; (v) empowering banks (and other financial institutions) to fix their lending and deposit (borrowing) rates, except for the rate on short-term savings deposits; and (vi) abolition of control of capital issues, dematerialization of shares, institution of screen-based trading in the securities market, and setting up of the Securities and Exchange Board of India (SEBI) for making private equity and bond issues easier and rule based, and functioning of stock exchanges transparent. Adoption of Basel norms and the strengthening of regulatory-cum-supervisory role of the RBI and SEBI were intended to promote stability and shock absorptive capacity of the financial sector and hence of the macroeconomic system. Other reforms in this sector were aimed at reducing transactions costs and raising efficiency through competition and flow of resources to relatively productive lines of economic activity. The expectation was that, freed from the straitjacket of bureaucratic controls, the economy would enjoy a much faster growth of output and employment without suffering from serious external payments or fiscal imbalances.

5.2   A Balance Sheet of the Indian Economy

While all important developments of the Indian economy since 1991 cannot be attributed to the reforms program, it is useful to see how the macroeconomy fared during the 1990s compared with that in the earlier period.

From a number of viewpoints the economy's performance in the postreform era has been quite impressive. Unlike most other emerging economies that had adopted IMF-sponsored structural adjustment programs, India did not have to go through a prolonged downturn in its production and capital accumulation. Indeed, growth rates of GDP, per capita income,[7] and capital accumulation were all higher and their coefficients of variations lower during 1992–2001 than in the 1970s or 1980s (table 5.1). Much more spectacular was performance of the economy in the spheres of poverty alleviation and taming of inflation. The poverty ratio, à la official estimates, decreased from 36.0 percent in 1993–1994 to 26.1 percent in 1999–2000—a fall that was much steeper than that in the 1970s or 1980s (Government of India 2002).[8] Indeed, while from the mid-1980s to early 1990s the *absolute number* of the poor continued to hover around 320 million, the number registered a significant fall at 260 billion by 1999–2000. The economy's performance on this front was closely related to a substantial decline in consumer price inflation from double-digit levels in 1990–1993 to less than 4 percent by the end of the millennium.

The most remarkable improvement in the economy's performance was, however, in the external sphere. The trade-GDP ratio crawled from 13.6 to 14.2 percent between 1980–1981 and 1989–1990, but jumped to 22.1 percent by 2000–2001 (Reserve Bank of India 2001).[9] Other positive developments during 1990–2001 included (i) a reduction, as percentage of GDP, in external indebtedness and current account deficit from 28.7 and 3.1 percent to 22.3 and 0.5 percent, respectively; (ii) an increase in foreign exchange reserves from USD 5.8 billion (amounting to 2.5 months' import bill) to USD 42.2 billion (providing an import cover for 8.6 months); (iii) a decline in short-term debt as percentage of forex reserves from an unsustainable 146.5 to a healthy 8.2 percent; and (iv) a fall in debt service payments as a proportion of current receipts from 35.3 to 17.1 percent (Reserve Bank of India 2002).

Despite the apparent signs of strengthening of the external balance and labeling of India by the IMF and the World Bank (2002) as a less indebted nation, in 2001–2002 not only did two international agencies downgrade the credit rating of the country, but one of them put the sovereign rating below that of an Indian financial company, not renowned for its performance in recent years. Though credit rating agencies, after the East Asian and Enron debacle, have become notorious for their failure to assess the economic health of companies or countries, in the present instance the rating agencies, on which I elaborate in sections 5.4 and 5.5, was on the whole right, but for the wrong reason.[10] Before I discuss the factors driving the behavior of the economy during the 1990s, I summarize the manifestations of the economic malady, especially over the last six or seven years.

Table 5.1
Performance of Indian Economy, 1970–2001[1]

		1970–1971 to 1979–1980	1980–1981 to 1989–1990	1990–1991 to 2000–2001	1992–1993 to 2000–2001	1992–1993 to 1996–1997	1997–1998 to 2000–2001
GDP	Growth rate	2.95 (141.9)	5.81 (38.9)	5.61 (32.7)	6.1 (20.9)	6.68 (16.9)	5.35 (21.6)
Per capita GDP	Growth rate	0.73	3.67	3.68	4.17	4.75	3.42
Investment[2,3]	Growth rate	4.65 (238.4)	6.38 (88.2)	6.93 (136.3)	8.31 (91.08)	9.63 (90.89)	6.68 (99.8)
Fixed capital formation	Growth rate	3.62 (181.2)	6.72 (33.8)	6.68 (85.9)	7.39 (75.7)	8.47 (84.62)	6.03 (53.32)
Public investment	Growth rate	na	6.89 (151.3)	3.14 (238.39)	4.12 (180.7)	2.28 (343.53)	6.43 (113.75)
Private investment	Growth rate	na	7.60 (251.2)	8.75 (136.32)	10.21 (92.2)	13.01 (81.03)	6.71 (114.12)
Public consumption	Growth rate	4.42 (120.1)	6.92 (37.2)	6.23 (71.38)	7.31 (55.5)	4.66 (57.44)	10.61 (26.8)
Investment as % of GDP		18.27	22.04	22.87	22.85	23.34	22.22
Savings as % of GDP		18.38	19.51	23.20	23.15	23.50	22.80
ICOR		5.98	3.65	4.35	4.00	3.72	4.47
WPI inflation		9.4 (100.6)	7.97 (48.8)	8.04 (42.1)	7.16 (54.6)	8.74 (42.9)	5.18 (70.5)
Services	Share in GDP	34.40	38.60	44.30	44.92	43.04	47.28
	Growth rate	4.5 (36.2)	6.6 (29.9)	7.6 (24.9)	8.1 (19.6)	7.55 (24.4)	8.82 (11.4)
	Contribution to GDP growth	52.70	43.60	57.60	59.65	48.66	77.94
Industry	Share in GDP	22.80	25.00	27.10	27.12	27.11	27.13
	Growth rate	3.7 (95.8)	6.8 (31.3)	5.9 (56.7)	6.39 (44.3)	7.61 (42.6)	4.86 (26.7)
	Contribution to GDP growth	28.70	28.90	27.60	28.42	30.91	24.67
Agriculture	Share in GDP	42.80	36.40	31.15	30.40	32.42	27.88
	Growth rate	1.3 (585.7)	4.67 (125.6)	2.87 (131.2)	3.12 (125.1)	4.64 (80.8)	1.23 (297.8)
	Contribution to GDP growth	18.60	27.50	14.80	15.55	22.54	6.38

Sources: Reserve Bank of India (2001, 2002); Government of India (2002).
Notes:

[1] Figures in brackets indicate coefficient of variation (%).

[2] Growth rates of investment may not lie between private and public investment growth rates for some of the periods because they are simple averages of individual annual growth rates.

[3] Investment growth rate for the period 1980–1981 to 1989–1990 is the average from 1981–1982 to 1989–1990 since data for public investment for 1980–1981 are not available.

Not only were the average GDP and per capita income growth rates during 1997–2001 significantly lower than in 1992–1997, but they also fell short of the corresponding averages in the 1980s (table 5.1). The disconcerting developments since the mid-1990s include prolonged deceleration in agricultural and industrial growth rates along with increased volatility of the former; decline in per capita production of food grains; sharp fall in capacity utilization in industries;[11] and rise in the unemployment ratio, with yearly labor absorption coming down from 2.04 to 0.98 percent between 1983–1994 and 1994–2000 (Government of India 2002).[12]

Again, in a significant departure from the rising trend of saving and investment ratios in the earlier decades, during the 1990s the former stayed flat, while the latter declined by about 2 percentage points. This dismal performance on the saving-investment front was accompanied with palpable signs of the growing inefficiency of resource use. At the macroeconomic level this inefficiency was attested to by an increase in incremental capital-output ratio (ICOR) from 3.65 to 4.35 between 1980–1990 and 1990–2001 (table 5.1). The trend is confirmed by microeconomic studies relating to the temporal behavior of (a) the minimum capital-coefficients in industries over different periods; (b) productivity growth rates in manufacturing (from firm-level panel evidence); and (c) growth rates in labor and capital productivity in small-scale industries.[13]

However, it is the fiscal scenario, which, by common consent, constitutes the weakest link in India's macroeconomic chain and has drawn repeated flack in recent years from practically all think tanks and commentators, both domestic and international. Contrary to its behavior in the 1980s, the tax-GDP ratio in the postreform period has been characterized by a negative trend, even though per capita income has risen and agricultural to total GDP has declined.[14] Indeed, as proportions of GDP, revenue, and fiscal and primary deficits showed perceptible declines during the initial phase of the reform era, but the trend has been completely reversed since the mid-1990s. The jump in revenue deficit to more than 6 percent of GDP has made public-sector savings negative[15] since 1998–1999 and cast a long shadow over the longer-term macroeconomic prospects of the country. The most important objective of the government, reiterated in successive budgets, has been a reduction of these deficits; but the objective has proved elusive and the actual figures for the deficits have turned out to be higher than their budget estimates by wide margins.

5.3   Developments in the 1990s: An Economic Interpretation

The catalog of positive and negative developments listed earlier is not much help in understanding or drawing policy conclusions unless one analyzes the economic factors, including the reform measures, driving the economy. For this purpose I distinguish among three phases of macroeconomic developments during the 1990s: (a) crisis and contraction; (b) recovery and growth; and (c) deceleration with fiscal distress. The first two phases were of relatively short duration, but the third phase has already lasted six to seven years and shows little sign as yet of yielding to an upturn. While unraveling of the final phase will thus be my major task, an examination of earlier phases, apart from throwing light on some crucial macrolinkages in India, also suggests important lessons for policymakers.

5.3.1   Crisis and Contraction

The reform program, I have already noted, was framed in the context of the acute payments crisis India faced in mid-1991 when foreign currency reserves (at $1.1 billion) were barely enough to meet two weeks' import bill. The orthodox view traces the origins of the crisis to large fiscal deficits spilling over into unsustainably high current account deficits during 1986–1991, and more fundamentally to the bias against exports resulting from the import substitution strategy. Empirical evidence does not however provide strong support to this hypothesis. During this period not only was the average current account deficit at about 2.5 percent not preposterously large, but what is more relevant, external borrowing was not at the expense of domestic saving: Over this period investment and savings ratios increased by 5.3 and 4.2 percentage points respectively so that unlike the typical Latin American economies (in the years preceding the crisis), India supplemented additional foreign with domestic saving.[16] Again, the second half of the 1980s saw a distinct break in the country's merchandise exports, with their average growth rate (in dollar terms) jumping from 3.7 to 15.5 percent between 1980–1986 and 1986–1990.

The 1991 crisis, it seems, may be attributed to two groups of factors, one external and the other policy related. The economic collapse of the erstwhile Soviet group of countries was not inconsequential for India's trade. Much more important was the impact of the Gulf war: merchandise and invisible trade balances[17] worsened significantly with the skyrocketing of oil prices (by far the most important factor affecting

India's import bill), sanction on Iraq, and decline in inflow of remittances (with the sharp fall in jobs and incomes of NRIs in the Middle East).

As in practically all payment crises, in the Indian case expectational factors also proved decisive, and it is here that the policies pursued played a crucial part. In the 1980s rising investment and savings no doubt went hand in hand with widening current account deficits, but the modes of financing the deficit stored up troubles for the future. The period was marked by a stagnation of concessional credit, and the rules in force were heavily loaded against foreign direct investment (FDI).[18] Instead, the system in force encouraged inflow of NRI deposits and reliance on relatively short-term commercial credit.[19] These modes of borrowing were relatively costly and raised the burden of servicing external debt. Again, debt rather than equity financing added to the volatility of *net* invisible earnings and hence riskiness on the balance-of-payments front. Finally, both NRI deposits and short-term commercial loans could be easily withdrawn[20] so that their accumulation on a large scale made the situation ripe for a self-fulfilling speculative attack.[21]

With adequate foreign exchange reserves, moderate inflation, and relatively high export as well as GDP growth, foreign (including NRI) lenders were not too worried regarding the short-term balance-of-payments prospects. Foreign currency reserves did fall in 1988–1989 and 1989–1990; but the fall was more than accounted for by repayment of IMF loans—something that investors must already have allowed for. However, by the end of March 1990, short-term debt[22] had increased to a whopping 233 percent and the country's liquid liability[23] to a staggering 494 percent, of foreign currency reserves (of USD 3.37 billion). It was in this context that the Gulf crisis and its *direct* impact on the country's net current earnings set the stage for a self-fulfilling speculative attack. From the third quarter of 1990 on sources of short-term credit dried up, and there was a torrent of outflow of net NRI deposits[24] so that by the end of March 1991, foreign currency reserves (of USD 2.2 billion) as ratios of short-term debt and liquid liability amounted to no more than 25 and 12 percent respectively, even though net IMF assistance during 1990–1991 was USD 1.2 billion. The speculative attack, culminating in major reform initiatives in the economy, was thus by no means irrational:[25] It would have been foolish for overseas investors not to expect large devaluations and significant jacking up of interest rates as conditions for financial assistance from the IMF or other international agencies. It was only when value of the rupee had fallen significantly,[26] interest rates had been set at fairly high levels, and adequate foreign currency reserves had been built up through official borrowings and other devices that investors' confidence was restored and net inflows of NRI deposits turned positive.[27]

5.3.1.1 1991–1992 Downturn The crisis year, as expected, was characterized by a substantial fall in GDP growth, with absolute declines in both industrial and agricultural output (figure 5.1). While part of the decline was due to policy changes, other (autonomous) factors also played important roles in causing the downturn. The most important of these was a steep fall in agricultural growth,[28] from 4.4 percent in 1990–1991 to −1.9 percent in 1991–1992. Apart from its direct impact on GDP, a fall in farm output produces an adverse supply side effect on agro-processing industries and sets in motion a negative multiplier process in other sectors thorough a decline in consumption and input demand for manufacturing and other nonagricultural goods.[29]

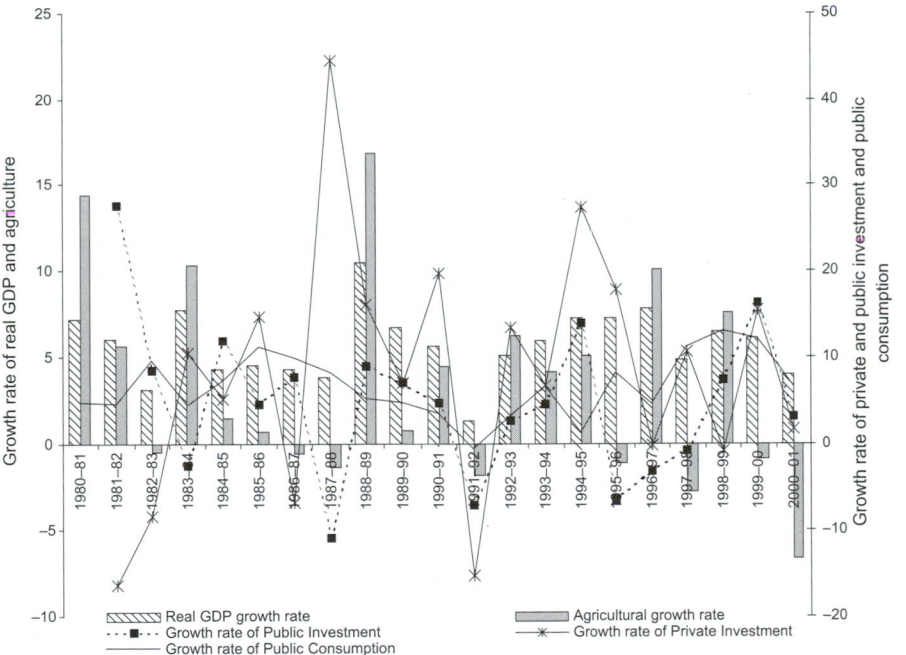

Figure 5.1
Growth of GDP and some of its components (%).

Other major factors behind the downturn were contractionary fiscal, monetary, and trade policy measures, deemed necessary for containing inflation[30] and reducing trade deficit. The fiscal squeeze was manifested in a fall in public consumption and investment expenditure, as well as in increased tax collection efforts.[31] So far as monetary policy was concerned, prime lending rates were pushed up by 3 to 4 percentage points, but in view of the double-digit inflation, real cost of borrowing actually fell. Other monetary measures proved much more potent in curbing credit, and these included a restriction of the Reserve Bank's own credit to the domestic sector;[32] the imposition of a 10 percent incremental cash reserve ratio; a directive to banks not to raise credit limits of individual borrowers (from 9 May to 8 September 1991) above that obtaining on 8 May 1991; a 45 percent ceiling on the ratio of incremental credit (other than export credit) to deposit; and stricter quantitative controls on bank loans against traders' stocks of selected agricultural goods.[33] The only factor moderating the fall in demand was large devaluation along with credit-cum-other measures to boost exports and curb imports.[34] But apart from the fact that external trade was not very important in relation to GDP, the severe compression of imports of intermediate goods (which had little domestic substitutes) tended to produce an adverse supply-side impact. No wonder expectations of domestic producers turned bleak and there was a more than 15 percent fall in private investment—a fall that reinforced the contractionary process originating in agriculture.

5.3.2   Second Phase: Turnaround and Growth, 1992–1997

With the economy experiencing a recovery and a spell of fairly rapid growth from 1992 to 1997, the contractionary phase lasted no more than a year (figure 5.1). In 1992–1997 not only was the average GDP growth (at 6.7 percent) the highest India had ever achieved over a five year period,[35] but the period was also marked by a strengthening of government finances with a downward trend in revenue, fiscal, and primary deficits as ratios of GDP (figure 5.3) and by substantial addition to the Reserve Bank of India's foreign currency reserves.[36]

As in the case of the 1991–1992 downturn, farmers' fortunes also played a major role in the second phase. Aided by a succession of good monsoons and substantial addition to productive capacity,[37] farm income registered a highly impressive 4.9 percent annual average growth during this period and produced a significantly positive demand as well as supply-side effect on the rest of the economy.

Containment of inflation[38] and a building up of foreign exchange reserves emboldened the authorities to reverse the restrictive fiscal and monetary measures adopted in 1991–1992. Increases in both public consumption and investment expenditure, significant cutbacks in income tax rates, exclusion of financial assets from the ambit of wealth tax and reduction in effective rates of capital gains tax—all these provided a direct or indirect boost to the economy and helped industries and services register significant growth after the crisis year.

Perhaps the most important route of indirect impact was the boom in private investment during 1992–1996, with an astounding average growth of 16.3 percent per annum. In order to appreciate the forces driving the boom, consider first the demand side. Agricultural growth and expansionary fiscal policies contributed to an increase in capacity utilization and return on capital employed.[39] Also important were wide-ranging reforms by way of removal or relaxation of a whole host of restrictions under which private entrepreneurs had to function. These reforms included dereservation;[40] scrapping of the approval requirement (under the Monopoly and Restrictive Trade Practices Act) for capital expansion and diversification; abolition of licensing in most industries; removal of all restrictions on imports of capital goods, raw material, and components; and rapid transition to a market-oriented exchange rate system with practically full current account convertibility. The burst of private investment during the second phase was thus partly due to a release of pent-up demand, but also reflected producers' high hopes regarding growth prospects of the Indian economy.

Stimulus to private investment demand went hand in hand with a boost to the supply of finance through an expansionary monetary policy and financial-sector liberalization. Prime lending rates were brought down from 19 percent in 1991–1992 to 17 percent the next year, and further to 14.5–15 percent by 1996–1997. CRR and SLR were reduced from 15 and 38.5 percent to 10 and 25 percent respectively.[41] At the same time under the changed regime public-sector banks could issue shares and debentures; weak nationalized banks were recapitalized; NRI deposits were made more attractive; most quantitative restrictions on bank credit were removed[42] or considerably toned down; and individual banks were left free to fix almost all their deposit and lending rates. Banks were thus in a position to raise significantly their flow of credit to private borrowers.[43]

Availability of funds for financing commercial operation was also raised through capital market reforms. Perhaps the most momentous in this regard was repeal of the Capital Issues (Control) Act under which private corporates had to seek government permission for floating shares and debentures. Capital issues became rule based under the newly constituted SEBI. Other measures of financial liberalization included opening up the mutual funds business to private entities; rules permitting easier inflows of FII and FDI; partial privatization of Development Financial Institutions so that they could raise funds through issue of bonds or shares; and facilities provided to select domestic corporates to borrow from, or issue shares in, the international capital market. The resulting widening and deepening of financial markets played an important role in the burst of investment without its growth being choked by fund constraint or steep increases in costs of borrowing.[44]

5.3.3   Deceleration with Fiscal Distress

In order to appreciate why the high growth phase came to an end and the economy entered a prolonged period of deceleration with growing fiscal fragility, it is useful to look for developments during 1992–1997 that could have had an important bearing on the country's subsequent macroeconomic travails. There were in fact palpable signs of the growth momentum losing its steam in 1996–1997, if not earlier. Growth in both industries and services fell by more than 3.5 percentage points that year, and it was the rise in household consumption, induced through an increase in agricultural output (after its slump in the preceding year), and a jump in remittances from abroad that prevented a larger slide in nonagricultural growth and enabled the economy to register some increase in overall GDP growth.[45]

While looking for sources of the slowdown during the third phase, one notes first that though the Indian economy had become much more open and 1996–1997 was a year of sharp decline in merchandise export growth in all emerging economies including India, external trade still accounted for a relatively minor fraction of India's GDP. Again, India was an important beneficiary of the IT revolution so that growth in software exports, inward remittances, and other invisibles more than made up for slowdown in merchandise exports after 1995–1996. The genesis of deceleration thus needs to be traced to operation of domestic rather than external factors.

The most important macroeconomic factors driving the overall performance of the Indian economy, my earlier analysis suggests, are agriculture and capital accumulation. From this perspective the deceleration phase of the economy can be said to have started in 1995–1996, rather than in 1997–1998. After registering three consecutive years of high growth over 1992–1995, averaging a hefty 5.1 percent, agriculture fared poorly since then, with its average growth over 1995–2001 slumping to a dismal 1.05 percent and displaying considerable ups and downs from one year to another. The behavior of investment during the two periods was similar: The first was characterized by high growth averaging 11.8 percent per annum, while in the second investment growth showed wide variations and its average amounted to only 5.8 percent.

Tracing the sources of the economy's ongoing troubles to agriculture and investment is undoubtedly helpful; but for a deeper understanding of the mechanism at work, especially for purposes of policy formulation, it is necessary to examine the reasons behind the substantial slowdown in growth in these two areas. The crucial factor constraining longer-term agricultural growth was poor progress in development of irrigation and other infrastructural facilities in rural areas. Though the trend toward slowing down of agricultural investment had started in the 1980s, the period 1992–1996 saw some revival, with an average growth of about 7.8 percent. By contrast, the average over 1996–2001 was a mere 1.2 percent. Inadequacy of agricultural investment is indicated by the fact that only about 38 percent of the area under cultivation is irrigated—something that makes adoption of new technology in the major part of arable land a highly risky venture. Limited credit facilities[46] have also created serious obstacles in the use of high yielding varieties (HYV) seeds and associated inputs by many a farmer. No wonder agricultural productivity and growth have suffered despite large year-to-year hikes in minimum support prices announced by the government. Poor growth in irrigation facilities has also left Indian agriculture highly dependent on the monsoon, raised the relative share of kharif to rabi crops,[47] and hence magnified the amplitude of fluctuations in farmers' incomes.

In industries and services also, low investment and a shortage of working capital acted as major constraints, though their nature and intensity were not exactly the same as in agriculture. Hence, it is necessary to examine (i) what held back overall investment growth (including that in agriculture); and (ii) what role financial factors played in this slowdown.

5.4   Slowdown in Investment

Perhaps the most important factor causing the declining trend in capital accumulation was a shift in public policy after 1994–1995. Over 1992–1995 public investment was progressively stepped up and recorded an average growth of more than 7 percent per annum. In each of the three following years there was an absolute decline in public investment, with the average yearly rate of fall during 1995–1998 being 3.5 percent. Since then there was some revival (figure 5.1), but the average growth for 1995–2001 was still about 2.3 percent. In order to appreciate the significance of this factor, consider the demand- and supply-side routes through which public-sector investments affect the economy's overall capital accumulation and GDP growth. Apart from the fact that such investments still account for nearly 30 percent of total capital accumulation (and more than 7 percent of GDP), they also have important indirect effects on private investment in the short as well as the medium run. In the postreform period, it is interesting to note, growth rates of both public and private investment reached their peak in 1994–1995 and showed a declining trend thereafter. Between 1992–1995 and 1995–2001, while the average increase in public-sector investment came down from 7.0 to 2.5 percent, the fall in the growth rate of private investment between the two periods was from 15.8 to 7.4 percent.[48]

There is thus a presumption that capital accumulation in the public sector tends to crowd in private investment and can have a significant impact on the economy's overall investment ratio and growth. However, the relationship between the two types of investment is not so straightforward: It may operate with some lag and depends on a number of factors, the most important of which are composition of public investment and the prevailing state of the economy. If the economy operates close to its capacity output level, additional government investment tends to raise interest rates and reduce investment by private producers.[49] But when there is an output gap (as there was in the second half of the 1990s), additional demand generated through the (government) investment multiplier raises capacity utilization and profits that in turn may induce private investment and magnify the expansionary impact. However, if this is the only mechanism for crowding-in, the effect should be larger for government consumption, remembering that such expenditure does not enhance future productive capacity of the public sector and hence poses no threat to private producers engaged in the same line of business as the government.[50] It is for this reason that crowding-in becomes significant when public capital accumulation is in areas that (a) do not attract private enterprise at the desired level; and (b) have strong supply-side linkages with the rest of the economy.

Most public investments in agriculture—for example, canal irrigation, bunding, or transport and communication linking rural and urban areas and providing easy access to information—are precisely of the kind just considered. So is provision of education and health services in rural areas, raising as it does the efficiency of entrepreneurs and workers. In quite a few of these areas externalities or public goods character of services make private investment grossly inadequate. In others investments are inhibited because of their lumpiness along with severe imperfections in the credit market. Public-sector capital accumulation in these areas induces farmers, with improvement in product as well as input markets and with an opening up of opportunities for introducing HYV technology, to invest in working capital and agricultural implements. Similar considerations suggest that private nonagricultural investment also depends crucially on a supply of infrastructural inputs as well as of trained and healthy labor. It is no wonder that the Indian experience corroborates the crowding-in impact of public-sector investment in both rural and urban areas. Between 1992–1996 and 1996–1999,[51] annual average growth of public investment in agriculture underwent a sea change, from 14.8 to −8.2 percent. The corresponding figures for private (agricultural) investment in the two periods were 5.7 and 1.3 percent, respectively. A Reserve Bank study (Reserve Bank of India 2002) also confirms the favorable impact of public-sector investment in infrastructure on private capital accumulation in manufacturing and services. Even at an aggregative level, significant crowding in is suggested by the fact that while decline in average growth of public infrastructural investment was from 5.7 percent in 1992–1995 to −0.2 percent in 1995–1999, average growth of private-sector investment fell from 15.8 to 6.8 percent between these two periods.

5.4.1 Financial Constraints

Before considering what might have led to the policy shift with respect to public investment, one also needs to appreciate the role of financial factors during the third phase of the postreform era. Belying the expectations of the first Narasimhan Committee (Reserve Bank of India

1991), cutbacks in SLR requirement and a move toward deregulation of interest rates did not raise the share of commercial bank credit to business units, especially since 1994–1995. Although by the end of 1993–1994 banks were holding SLR securities way above what they needed to, yearly additions to these securities regularly exceeded the required minimum and made the actual ratio rise from 21.9 to 44.0 percent between 1994–1995 and 1999–2000. Indeed, despite (or perhaps because of) financial liberalization, the decelerating phase of the economy was characterized by an increasing share of flow of bank credit going to the government at the expense of nonfood commercial credit:[52] the latter's share nose-dived from 80.6 percent in 1995–1996 to 48.3 percent in 2000–2001 (with more or less corresponding increases in the government's share). Particularly hard hit were small and medium farmers and other business units, many of whom found it difficult to meet their working capital requirement (Reserve Bank of India 2002).

No less glaring was capital market failure. Reforms in this market, as I have recorded, were followed by a burst of primary issues over 1992–1995, and this source of finance was as high as 40 percent of corporate investment during this period. However, since then there has been a sharp fall in the private sector's primary issues:[53] By 1999–2000 not only did they decline to only 4.1 percent of corporate investment, but their absolute sum (in real terms) was less than 16 percent of the amount issued in 1994–1995 (figure 5.2).

Remembering that a fall in business activity, whatever its origins, tends to reduce bank lending and primary capital issues, I observe that behavior of flow of funds noted earlier may be regarded as a symptom, not a separate source, of downturn. However, supply of finance was affected by policy commissions and omissions as well. Some of these were closely related to the reform program and will be taken up in section 5.5. For the moment I indicate how movement of interest rates, reflecting by and large the Reserve Bank's monetary policy stance, was not much help in countering recessionary tendencies in the economy. Of particular significance in this context was the hike in banks' prime lending rates (PLRs) by 1.5 percentage points in 1995–1996, even though both investment growth and inflation rate were falling. It is no coincidence that the long-drawn deceleration in industrial and investment growth the country has been passing through started in 1995–1996: With real PLR jumping from 4.1 to 8.8 percent and nonfood bank credit registering a 6 percent fall in real terms, monetary factors rein-

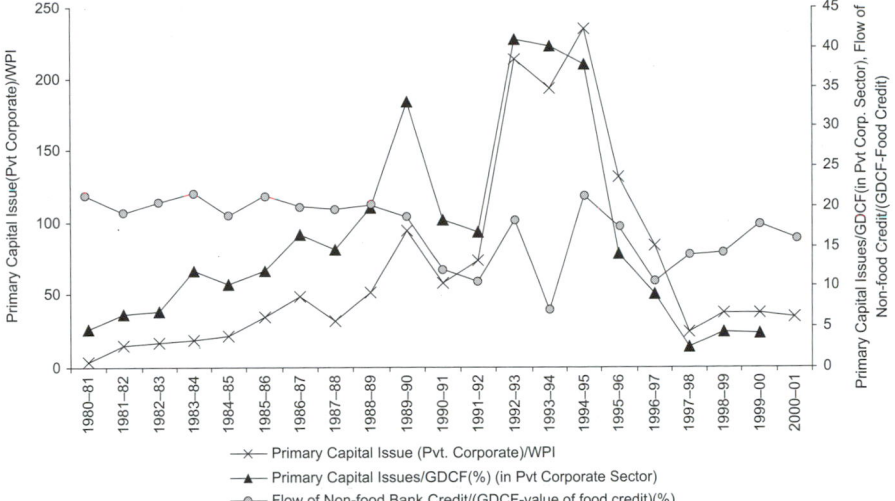

Figure 5.2
Bank credit and capital issues.

forced the impact of fiscal tightening initiated in that very year. Since then the Reserve Bank has tried to follow an easy money policy[54] and nominal interest rates have softened. However, with inflation of non-food and manufacturing prices falling at a fairly fast pace, the real cost of borrowing (even of producers who are considered creditworthy) has shown a rising trend since 1994–1995. This, along with the difficulty a number of small and medium enterprises face in accessing the formal credit and capital market, has contributed in no small measure to deceleration over the last six to seven years.

5.5 Sources of Policy Failure

My analysis so far has focused on three sets of macroeconomic policy failures behind the economic woes during the third phase of the post-reform period. The first consists of neglect of the government's role in agricultural investment, supply of infrastructural services, and human resource development—failures that make the economy recession-prone and constrain its medium- and long-term growth potential. Nor has the government adopted countercyclical fiscal measures for closing the persistent output gap. Finally, financial-sector policies have proved less than conducive to the promotion of investment, productivity, or employment. These deficiencies in their turn may be traced to two main reasons. Some of the reforms measures, while eminently sensible on their own, have, in the absence of complementary policies, turned counterproductive for the economy as whole. However, the more fundamental flaw seems to lie in the government's lack of appreciation of short- and long-run linkages between policy instruments and macrovariables, including the intermediate targets. Readers can see whether my diagnosis is supported by the nature of fiscal and financial policies adopted over the 1990s.

5.5.1 Financial Measures

Of the three macroeconomic objectives of financial policies—containing inflation, avoiding payment problems, and maintaining an adequate supply of funds for productive purposes—the record for the first two, as already noted, has been quite good, but far from satisfactory for the third. Interestingly enough, reform measures like the adoption of prudential norms are partly responsible for the diversion of bank credit away from the commercial sector. Switching from commercial loans to government securities reduces the value of risk-weighted assets and helps banks meet their capital adequacy norms. Asset classification and provisioning requirements also militate against extension of bank credit to private producers: Apart from assessment and monitoring costs entailed in such loans, banks are also put off by the risk of their turning nonperforming and thus undermining their bottom line and balance sheet under the new norms. Again, additional commercial loans require banks to raise their priority-sector credit— something that most banks find highly unattractive. It also seems that the threat, under the changed environment, of being held personally accountable in case loans become nonperforming has made officials in public-sector banks, which still account for the overwhelming part of the financial system, extremely conservative in sanctioning commercial credit. Finally, while there is a natural tendency for banks to cut back private credit and raise their holding of government securities when business conditions are not favorable, the capital adequacy norm magnifies such a procyclicity of credit (Rakshit 1998).

My analysis does not imply that imposition of prudential norms was not warranted for making banks viable and efficient. The problem lay rather in a lack of supplementary policy intervention on two fronts. The first consists of the need for more vigorous fiscal and monetary measures to neutralize the increased procyclicity of credit flows to the commercial sector. I have already drawn attention to the absence of any softening of real interest rates during the third phase, reflecting the Reserve Bank's relatively timid policies for closing the output gap. However, it is quite unlikely that a more expansionary monetary stance could have significantly raised the degree of capacity utilization. One reason for relative ineffectiveness of orthodox monetary policy lies in the fact that when banks operate with the minimum capital adequacy ratio, additional lendable resources by way of extra deposits tend to cause a shift away from commercial credit to government securities (Rakshit 1998). What is needed under these conditions is recapitalization of banks, especially when lack of cushion in capital is due to cyclical factors rather than managerial weakness.

The second and more important reason for the ineffectiveness in the Indian context is decline in the proportion of producers without any access to formal credit—a decline that is primarily structural. This highlights the need for the promotion of effective networks of credit delivery systems, linking small and medium producers in both rural and urban areas to the formal credit market. Such a network not only enhances the effectiveness of anticyclical monetary policy, but also is essential for ensuring allocative efficiency of resource use. Unfortunately, adoption of Basel norms has not been supplemented by serious attempts to build a financial structure under which credit flows to their most productive users, irrespective of their size and location. Omission of policies in this sphere was also compounded by a failure to pursue vigorous countercyclical fiscal measures—something that was essential, since an adequate credit delivery system could not be built overnight and adoption of prudential norms by itself tended to produce a contractionary impact.

There were other Reserve Bank of India policies of a structural nature that have not been conducive to the country's macroeconomic performance. Balance-of-payments vulnerability has indeed been reduced with a sharp cut in the country's short-term debt, which at the end of 2000–2001 stood at only 8 percent of the central bank's foreign exchange reserves, compared with 189 and 146 percent in 1989–1990 and 1990–1991, respectively. However, the reform period has been marked by sharp increases in both FII and NRI deposits—liabilities that are highly volatile and make the domestic currency vulnerable to speculative attacks.[55] It is for this reason that the Reserve

Bank has added significantly to its foreign currency reserves.[56] But such additions, it is important to note, have entailed considerable costs to the economy in more ways than one.

Additional foreign exchange reserves do not raise the country's productive capacity, and their marginal earnings (from abroad) fall significantly short of the return on domestic investment. This together with the fact that risk management requires a relatively high fraction of the country's liquid liability to be held in foreign currency assets implies a net loss to the economy on account of increased NRI deposits and FIIs even when these inflows *less* incremental foreign assets finance domestic capital accumulation. Since the mid-1990s in particular, incremental foreign reserves have far exceeded the country's current account deficits,[57] suggesting that the greater part of the increase in external liabilities was used to extend credit to the U.S. (or some other) government or central bank,[58] not to support domestic investment.

Again, when the economy is saddled with excess capacity, as it was during the third phase, encouraging capital inflows[59] does not make macroeconomic sense: Additional investment through domestic finance is then costless to the economy since it does not involve the (future) burden of transferring (real) resources to the rest of the world. Finally, dominance of NRI deposits and FII under the capital accounts receipts and the consequent need for building up foreign currency assets have made these the dominant factor behind variations in high power money and severely constrained the scope for anticyclical monetary policies. Thus while the degree of capacity utilization was much higher in 1988–1991 than in 1998–2001, RBI credit to the government and the commercial sector as proportions of GDP averaged 2.4 and 0.2 percent respectively during the earlier period, but slumped to 0.37 and 0.1 percent respectively during the later one.

5.5.2 Capital Market Malady

I have shown how a spate of primary issues, triggered by stock market and industrial reforms, was followed by a steep fall in the amount of funds raised through the capital market. There is little doubt that the reform measures have sharply reduced transaction costs and eliminated the risk of bad delivery, an endemic malady of the prereform capital market. Even though the stock market has, during the last seven years, proved a poor vehicle for transferring funds from savers to investors, something must have gone seriously awry. Part of the explanation lies in procyclicity of primary issues: In times of recession even far-sighted producers seeking to invest in viable projects find it difficult to raise funds from the capital market. However, two features of the reform program seem to have had an adverse impact on the working of the capital market. The first is regulatory failure, as evident from the series of scams and disappearance, with impunity, of hosts of companies that raised substantial funds from the stock market during its boom phase. This has eroded savers' confidence and posed significant obstacles to primary issues except by big companies with a proven track record. At the same time, given the relative thinness of the capital market, FII flows have significantly raised the correlation between U.S. and Indian stock prices, even though the real sector links[60] between the two economies are quite weak even now. It is no wonder that the average asset holder in India does not want to invest in shares and the most popular schemes of mutual funds are those where funds are invested in government securities.

5.5.3   Fiscal Fetishism

The most important policy failures in the postreform era have been on the fiscal front, and here the deficiencies are related to both structural adjustment and macrostabilization. In a reversal of its trend during the 1980s, the tax-GDP ratio fell by about 2 percentage points in the last decade. Over the period 1995–2000, revenue deficit, as a proportion of GDP, showed a steep rise, from 3.2 to 6.2 percent, and this in turn pulled down the overall public-sector savings ratio by nearly the same rate and constituted the most important source of decline in the country's aggregate savings ratio from 25.1 to 23.2 percent. Indeed, during the second half of the 1990s while the fiscal stance, as noted earlier, played a major role in structural impediments to growth, macroeconomic maladies, and poor performance of agriculture, all relevant criteria suggest a significant worsening of budgetary position even in the narrow sense (figure 5.3). One cannot help asking: Was there some method in the fiscal madness?

One reason for the bleak scenario was faulty design and poor administration of tax laws, reflected in low buoyancy of revenue collections, even though share of the most-difficult-to-tax component of GDP, namely, agriculture, recorded a substantial fall. More fundamentally, the malady may be traced to what may be called fiscal fetishism, manifested in a simplistic approach to reduction of fiscal deficit, considered the central concern of budgetary measures, with quite insufficient appreciation of (a) what drives the deficit in the short and

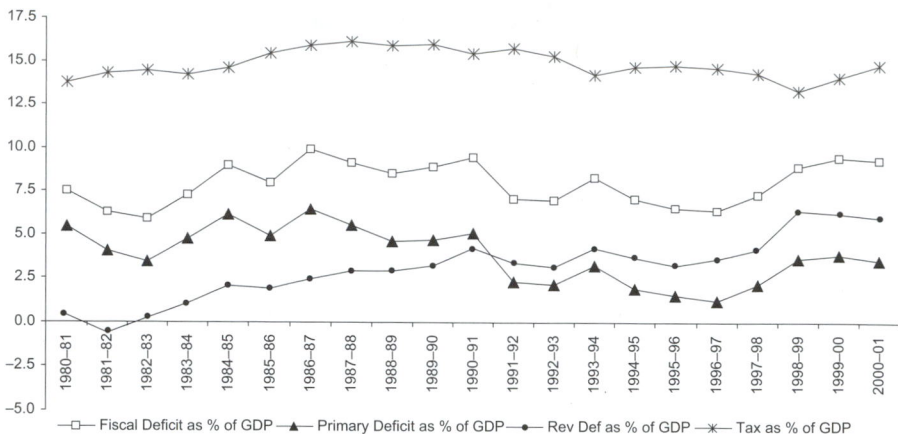

Figure 5.3
Some indicators of fiscal scenario.

medium run, or (b) how the policy instruments that the government can directly control affect, under alternative states of the economy, longer-term fiscal viability and basic objectives of budgetary policy. Our diagnosis is based on overall budgetary trends as well as on several instances of counterproductive commissions and omissions of the ministry of finance.

For a number of years the successive budgets have been characterized by overestimates of tax collections and underestimates of both revenue deficit and fiscal deficit, despite actual expenditures often falling short of their original provisions. Persistence of such estimation failure raises doubts regarding relevance of the analytical framework (if any) behind the budgetary exercise. Such doubts are strengthened by the nature of budgetary adjustments undertaken, especially since 1994–1995. With their focus on fiscal deficit, policymakers seem to think that what matters primarily is curbing government expenditure and increasing nondebt creating receipts, irrespective of the nature of changes in their composition. The period 1995–2000 was marked by 9.6 and 12.6 percent growth in government consumption and subsidies,[61] respectively; but public capital accumulation grew at a snail's pace of 1.9 percent, and its two crucial constituents, namely, investment in agriculture and infrastructure, actually *declined*, by 5.6 and 0.2 percent, respectively.[62] At the same time the government appears happy to collect disinvestment proceeds as a substitute for current receipts and has given up seignorage as a source of revenue even though interest outgoes have risen by leaps and bounds and the economy has for long been characterized by deceleration with excess capacity.

Indeed, a decisive factor behind our diagnosis is the abandonment of the government's role relating to macrostabilization. The latest manifestation of this is the Fiscal Responsibility and Budget Management Bill (Government of India 2000) lying before the parliament. Defying all economic logic and contrary to similar legislations elsewhere, the bill is intended to free the government from any responsibility(!) in trying to close an incipient or growing output gap. What is more serious, the bill's provision for an across-the-board proportionate cut in all government expenses (other than the committed ones) at the first sign of deficits exceeding their targeted levels cannot but strengthen the contractionary forces operating in the economy (Rakshit 2001a).

It is not very difficult to demonstrate how self-defeating this fiscal program is or how it erodes the country's economic fundamentals (Rakshit 2000; 2001c). Budgetary viability requires an improvement in revenue balances in the medium and the long run. Substitution of public consumption for investment reduces the government's revenue growth both directly and indirectly as nontax revenue (from public-sector capital accumulation) is reduced and a fall in GDP growth produces an adverse impact on future tax collections. Public investment in agriculture, aided by its crowding-in effect, raises agricultural productivity, acts as a stimulant to a rural economy, brings down poverty, and enables the government to reduce over time expenditure on food or fertilizer subsidies and poverty alleviation measures. On the other hand, cutbacks in infrastructural investment discourage private capital expenditure, lower economic growth, and add to the government's fiscal woes. In fact, as I have elaborated elsewhere (Rakshit 2001b), FCI's mountainous and rotting food stocks, along with the persistence of large fiscal and revenue deficits, are due in no small measure to the fiscal stance taken by the government: An increase in government investment in rural and urban infrastructural facilities will, through increased revenue receipts and decreased subsidies, strengthen the budgetary position not only in the medium and the long run, but in the short run as well (remembering that as of mid-2002 the economy was saddled with excess capacity on the one hand and more than USD 60 billion foreign exchange reserves on the other). Hence my hypothesis that the roots of policy omissions and commissions may be traced to a poor perception of the working of the Indian economy or of interlinkages among its major sectors.

5.6   Conclusions

The focus of this chapter has been on the behavior of India's macroeconomy, especially its prolonged sluggishness, in the postreform period, and on some critical policy failures. This does not mean that initiation of reforms was a major mistake or that most measures adopted since 1991 have been counterproductive. Though one might not always have approved of the precise timing of their adoption, few could doubt that policies aimed at improving the efficiency of enterprises, both private and public, through dismantling bureaucratic controls and subjecting them to market discipline and facing internal as well as external competition, were long overdue. Under this category of policies fall deregulation of industries, removal of the government's discretionary control on capital issues, adoption of best-practice accounting-cum-prudential norms, tariffication along with gradual opening up of trade, and encouragement of FDI inflows. If despite successes in the spheres of inflation control and balance-of-payments viability, the overall performance of the economy was worse in the 1990s than in the 1980s in core areas like GDP growth, unemployment, inequality or capacity utilization, it is important to identify the major weaknesses in the government's structural or macromanagement policies.

So far as structural policies were concerned, the major deficiency seemed to consist in a substantial slowdown in public investment in agriculture and infrastructural services. Given the close supply-side linkages such investment has with private capital accumulation in rural and urban areas, it is not difficult to see how the slowdown produced a negative impact on overall GDP as well as agricultural growth, raised the latter's year-to-year variability, and stood in the way of absorbing new entrants to the workforce and workers losing jobs in the process of (reform-induced) restructuring of industries or enterprises. The expectation of the government that enough private-sector investment will flow in areas it was withdrawing from proved way off the mark. The reason, apart from externalities or the public goods nature of most infrastructural services, lay in long durability, high risk, and lumpiness of investment in this sector, apart from the financing difficulty private investors had to face, especially under the new regulatory regime.

It is interesting to note in this connection that India's emergence as a major provider of IT services during the 1990s owed much to the dismantling of bureaucratic controls and external-sector liberalization; but no less important were the availability of skilled scientific and technical manpower, the congenial environment created through clustering of high-tech enterprises centering cities like Bangalore, and the massive extension of telecommunications facilities—all factors in which public investment had played a decisive role. It is also worth emphasizing that fund requirement of software and most other IT units is relatively small so that unlike capital-intensive units, their establishment was not held back by financial constraints.

This brings me to the second structural problem associated with the reform agenda. My analysis suggests that though adoption of prudential norms and capital market reforms were by and large necessary, regulatory failure and the absence of effective steps for building an adequate credit delivery system acted as serious obstacles to productive activities, especially in the unorganized sector.

Third, at a macroeconomic level the problem was aggravated by steps for attracting external funds by way of FII and NRI deposits. Stock market volatility associated with FII made households accounting for the overwhelming part of domestic saving extremely wary of investing in capital issues. As the same time considerations of balance-of-payments viability forced the Reserve Bank to hold large foreign currency reserves and reduce its supply of domestic credit—steps that impacted adversely on capital accumulation through seignorage and RBI credit to commercial sector.

Fourth, some aspects of the structural adjustment program followed by the fiscal authorities tended to weaken the country's longer-term economic fundamentals. A step-up in government consumption expenditure and a fall in revenue buoyancy under the new tax laws and their implementation caused a reversal during the 1990s from the (earlier) trend of a rising savings ratio and reduced thereby (full employment) investment and growth potential of the economy. At the same time the government failed to reform the system of user charges for electricity, irrigation, or other infrastructural products even where the beneficiaries could be easily identified and by and large did not belong to poorer sections of the community. Nor is it easy to comprehend the economic rationale behind the cutback in agricultural investment coupled with substantial year-to-year increases in procurement prices—policies that choked agricultural productivity and landed the government with mounting food subsidy bills.

Finally, the policy failures on the structural front just considered were compounded with an absence of measures for countering the prolonged slowdown and growing excess capacity. No wonder both Indian and foreign business units have found the Indian market not attractive enough to undertake investment on a significant scale.

The policy imperatives following from my analysis are fairly clear and do not require further spelling out. I have also indicated why and how, contrary to widely held beliefs, the measures suggested are in fact "prudent" and contribute to fiscal or budgetary viability. The important point to note in this regard is that the primary goal of reforms should be building up a climate for productive investment and diffusion of entrepreneurial activity across regions. It is with these objectives in view and on the basis of prevailing specifics of the Indian economy that policies need to be framed, even if they may not always tally with "common sense" or conventional wisdom: Remember the age-old adage that in macroeconomic analysis so-called common sense very often proves nonsense.

Notes

1. It seems that major changes in India's economic policy occur due not so much to domestic compulsions, but more to the loss of face of the country's leaders to the international community. The putative reason behind adoption of (what was then called) the New Agricultural Strategy (ushering in the Green Revolution) was the indignity Indira Gandhi suffered when she went to meet Lyndon Johnson for enhanced PL 480 food aid and was kept waiting in the president's antechamber for quite a while. The reform program of the 1990s also followed a similar and much more public humiliation when India's former colonial masters not only insisted on the Reserve Bank of India's gold stock as a collateral for advancing a fairly modest sum (of about USD 600 million), but also forced the government to airlift 47 tons of gold to the Bank of England in July 1991. Memory of these humiliations has perhaps played a significant role in India's huge accumulation of food stocks and foreign exchange reserves, irrespective of whether such accumulation makes any economic sense or not.

2. For an early assessment of factors behind the payment crisis, see Rakshit (1991).

3. In the earlier era a number of important industries were reserved only for the public sector, and in some others entry of private entrepreneurs was subject to government approval.

4. In many cases, entry of foreign entrepreneurs is also no longer barred.

5. The ratio refers to the minimum proportion of a bank's net demand and time liabilities (NDTL) required to be invested in government and other approved securities.

6. During the prereform era the SLR requirement together with large net RBI credit to government and a high cash reserve ratio enabled the government to appropriate at a fairly low cost a significant part of credit generated through the banking system. This meant that (a) bank profits were squeezed; and (b) private-sector borrowers were generally credit constrained or there was financial crowding-out of private investment. An important objective of financial-sector liberalization was removal of these constraints and impediments to the efficient functioning of banks.

7. The rise in per capita income growth during the 1990s was due in part to the fall in population growth rate to 1.93 percent per annum from 2.22 percent in the 1970s and 2.14 percent in the 1980s.

8. Over the six-year period 1977–1978 to 1983, the poverty ratio fell from 51.3 to 44.5 percent; the decline between 1987–1988 and 1993–1994 was from 38.9 percent to 36 percent.

9. The 1990s also saw a reversal of the declining trend in India's share of exports in world trade, with the share registering an increase from 0.5 to 0.6 percent between the beginning and the end of the decade.

10. The most important factor cited by Standard and Poor's and Moody's for downgrading India's rating (on August 7, 2001 and August 6, 2001 respectively) is persistence of large fiscal deficits, which, as explained in section 5.5, are only a symptom (and not a very important one at that) and provide few clues to the basic ills afflicting the economy.

11. A Reserve Bank study (Reserve Bank of India 2002) suggests that between 1990–1995 and 1995–2000, capacity utilization in manufacturing, with a weight of nearly 80 percent in the industrial sector, fell from 90.6 to 75.7 percent. This itself may be a gross underestimate because of reliance on the Wharton Measure of capacity output, obtained by dividing (real) fixed capital stock in a year by the *minimum* capital-output ratio registered over the reference period. Between 1990–1995 and 1995–2000, the minimum ratio was estimated to rise from 3.0 to 3.7. So in the later period either there was a fall in efficiency of resource use in manufacturing or capacity utilization was in fact lower than its estimate of 75.7 percent. The second conclusion appears more plausible in view of significant slackening in demand growth during the second half of the 1990s.

12. The rise in unemployment rate, fall in agricultural growth, and decline in per capita availability of food grains cannot be easily reconciled with the official estimate of a near 10 percentage fall in the poverty ratio between 1993–1994 and 1999–2000, remembering that (a) concentration of the poor is larger in rural than in urban areas, and (with an income-elastic demand for food grains by the poor) a substantial reduction in poverty ratio should have *raised* the economy's per capita consumption of food grains. What is more paradoxical, the decline in poverty in 1993–2000 was 7 percentage points more than in 1987–1994, even though during the earlier period employment growth was much faster and per capita consumption of food grains showed an upward trend.

13. Between 1980–1981 and 1994–1995 there was a steady fall in the (minimum) capital coefficient (over five-year periods) in manufacturing from 3.2 to 3.0; but the coefficient rose to 3.7 in the period 1995–2000 (Reserve Bank of India 2002). A panel data–based NCAER study strongly suggests a decline in mean technical efficiency of Indian firms in the 1990s compared with that in the earlier decade. SIDBI finds that between the 1980s and the period 1990–1996 the annual growth rates of labor and capital productivity in small industries declined from 6.2 and 2.6 percent to 3.7 and −1.6 percent respectively.

The results of the NCAER and SIDBI studies are reported in the Reserve Bank of India (2002).

14. A rise in per capita income implies an increase in taxable capacity. Since agriculture is taxed relatively lightly, a fall in its share in GDP should normally raise the tax-GDP ratio.

15. Public-sector savings in India consist of the government's revenue surplus and undistributed profits of public-sector undertakings.

16. Though the government continued to borrow for financing current expenditure.

17. Between 1989–1990 and 1990–1991, the trade deficit went up by nearly USD 2 billion and worsening of net invisibles amounted to about 0.5 billion.

18. The rules were so stringent that there was no FDI inflow in 1980–1986. There was some relaxation of conditions imposed during the second half of the 1980s, but the inflows, though positive from 1986 to 1987, remained insignificant during the rest of the decade.

19. Thus in 1989–1990 canalizing agencies (responsible for the major part of foreign trade) raised their recourse to short-term external credit by about USD 2 billion.

20. Long-term NRI deposits were also highly liquid, because they could be withdrawn before maturity if depositors were ready to forego some accrued interest—as they would generally be when the prospect of large devaluations or interest hikes, if not of outright default, loomed large.

21. See Rakshit (2002) on roles of self-fulfilling expectations and alternative modes of finance in causing a currency crisis.

22. Including NRI deposits of less than a one-year maturity.

23. Consisting of short-term debt and long-term NRI deposits (remembering that there were no foreign institutional investments in those days).

24. Between October 1990 and June 1991 (when foreign currency reserves, amounting to $1.1 billion, were at their smallest since the mid-1970s), net withdrawal of NRI funds totaled USD 1.3 billion.

25. Things were not helped by political instability until a new government took office in June 1991.

26. The rupee was devalued by 18 percent in two steps on 1 and 3 July 1991; but total devaluation between 1990–1991 and 1991–1992 amounted to over 31 percent.

27. Net NRI deposit flows were negative in each month from October 1990 to December 1991, with the withdrawal totaling USD 1.3 billion up to June 1991 (when foreign currency reserves were at their lowest since the mid-1970s), and USD 1.9 billion for the entire fifteen-month period. From June 1991 to 31 March 1992, financial assistance from the IMF, the World Bank, and Asian Development Bank (ADB) totaled over $3.1 billion, while India Development Bonds, Immunity Schemes (for inflow of foreign exchange by Indians), and loans against gold yielded $1.61, $0.7, and $0.6 billion respectively. These, along with austerity measures, raised currency reserves to $4.0 billion by December 1991 and to $5.63 billion at the end of March 1992.

28. This I include under autonomous factors since the most important reason for the fall was monsoon failure. The other, less important reason, namely, a hike in fertilizer prices (following the rise in those of petro products), was also external shock–induced.

29. The first-round fall in demand for these goods originates in both agricultural-sector and agro-processing industries, suffering from supply-side shocks.

30. Owing mostly to a fall in agricultural output and a rise in prices of petroleum and other imported inputs. Inflation reached its peak at 16.7 percent in August 1991, but fell to 13.6 percent by March 1992.

31. Between 1990–1991 and 1991–1992 public consumption and investment in real terms were reduced by 0.7 and 7.2 percent respectively, while there was a near 1 percentage point rise in revenue receipts as a proportion of GDP, even though industrial income and value added in government, which accounted for a sizeable part of GDP, registered a decline.

32. So that the major part of the rise in reserve money was accounted for by accretion of foreign reserves.

33. During 1991–1992 bank credit to the commercial sector registered a 4.3 percent decline, which (with an inflation rate of 10.1 percent) implied a fall of more than 14 percent in real terms. Part of the fall was due however to the operation of demand rather than supply-side factors.

34. In real terms exports rose by 19 percent and imports fell by 9.7 percent.

35. Although the base year 1991–1992 was a depressed one.

36. From their nadir at USD 1.1 billion in the last week of June 1991, foreign currency reserves rose to USD 5.6 billion at end March 1992 and reached a healthy USD 22.4 billion by the end of 1996–1997.

37. Note that capital accumulation impacts agricultural output with a lag of one year or more. During the second phase the importance of agricultural investment may be appreciated from the fact that it averaged 7.3 percent over the period 1991–1996.

38. In respect to which the role of agricultural output growth can hardly be overemphasized.

39. Tax brakes implied that for any given rate of capacity utilization, return became higher.

40. The number of areas reserved for the public sector was reduced from 17 to 6, and these included railways and some strategic areas like atomic energy and defense industries.

41. Though the reductions were initiated from 1992–1993, the major cuts in the two ratios were effected in the later part of the period.

42. The Reserve Bank removed the 45 percent ceiling on the incremental credit deposit ratio (excluding export credit) and restrictions on loans for consumer durables and on other nonpriority-sector personal loans.

43. However, as I discuss in section 5.3.3, other reforms measures like introduction of prudential norms, tended to curb such credit.

44. Note that flow of bank credit to the commercial sector actually declined in 1993–1994; but this was more than made up for by additional funds secured through primary issues (figure 5.2) and disbursement from institutions like IDBI and so forth. In 1996–1997 however additional flow of funds from nonbank financial institutions fell short of

the total decline in primary capital issues and incremental (nonfood) bank credit. This, as is to be expected, was associated with a fall in private investment.

45. The 10.1 percent increase in agricultural income and near doubling of remittances (from USD 2.22 to 4.42 billion) provided a significant boost to aggregate demand— something that is reflected in about a 10 percent increase in household consumption (in real terms) in 1996–1997. Quite clearly, neither of the two factors could be of an enduring nature.

46. Something I will discuss.

47. The reason is that while scope for further expansion of rabi output has slowed down, there is as yet scope for extension of HYV technology in kharif crops, provided the monsoon is good and adequate credit is available in time.

48. Although growth of private investment peaked in 1994–1995, its high growth phase was 1992–1996, characterized by an annual average increase of 16.3 percent. This slumped to 5.3 percent over 1996–2001.

49. Though the crowding-out is partial and aggregate investment rises. However, when public investment is expected to raise future profitability of private producers, their investment demand may rise sufficiently to bring about a crowding-in effect even under full employment conditions.

50. Despite their negative impact on private producers, additional public investments in such activities may still raise aggregate investment, given their salubrious impact on private investment in other sectors.

51. CSO data for breakup between private and public investment in agriculture are available only up to the period 1998–1999.

52. Credit extended to Food Corporation of India is guaranteed by the government and stands on a different footing from other commercial credit.

53. Since a number of public-sector banks and term lending institutions like IDBI floated shares and bonds during this period, it is not very useful to compare aggregate primary issues with total capital formation.

54. Except for a brief spell at the height of the Asian crisis in 1998.

55. I have already noted in connection with the 1991 crisis how even long-term NRI deposits can be easily withdrawn. Volatility of FII is well attested in the history of both the Latin American Crisis and the East Asian Currency Crisis (Rakshit 2002).

56. In 2000–2001 external liquid liability (including long-term NRI deposits, short-term debt, and FII) amounted to more than USD 40 billion and was in fact larger than the Reserve Bank's foreign currency assets.

57. In 1998–2001 the incremental forex reserves of the banking system averaged 2 percent of GDP, while the current account deficit 0.9 percent.

58. That is what holding foreign currency reserves amounts to.

59. Other than FDI. See Rakshit (2002).

60. Except for IT industries.

61. Subsidies are for the central government. Their total for state governments is not available.

62. Owing to nonavailability of the CSO estimate, the two rates are for the period 1995–1999.

References

Government of India. 2000. *Fiscal Responsibility and Budget Management Bill.*

Government of India. 2002. *Economic Survey 2001–2002.*

Rakshit. 1991. "The Macroeconomic Adjustment Programme: A Critique." *Economic and Political Weekly* 26, no. 34 (August):1977–1988.

Rakshit, M. 1998. "Financial Fragility: Sources and Remedies II." *Money & Finance* 7 (October–December):28–50.

Rakshit, M. 2000. "On Correcting Fiscal Imbalances in the Indian Economy: Some Perspectives." *Money & Finance* 2, no. 2 (July–September):47.

Rakshit, M. 2001a. "Restoring Fiscal Balance through Legislative Fiat: The Indian Experiment." *Economic and Political Weekly* 36, no. 23 (June):2053–2062.

Rakshit, M. 2001b. "Some Public Economics of Food Subsidy and Buffer Stock Operations in India: Part I." *Money & Finance* 2, no. 4–5 (January–June):90–124.

Rakshit, M. 2001c. "Contentious Issues in Fiscal Policy: A Suggested Resolution." *Money & Finance* 2, no. 7 (October–December):23–60.

Rakshit, M. 2002. *The East Asian Currency Crisis.* New Delhi: Oxford University Press.

Reserve Bank of India. 1991. *Report of the Committee on Financial System.* Narasimham Committee Report, Mumbai.

Reserve Bank of India. 2001. *Handbook of Statistics on Indian Economy.* Mumbai.

Reserve Bank of India. 2002. *Report on Currency and Finance 2001–02.* Mumbai.

World Bank. 2002. *Global Development Finance.* Washington, DC: World Bank.

6 State-Level Fiscal Reforms in India

M. Govinda Rao

6.1 Introduction

6.1.1 Need for Subnational Fiscal Reforms

Launching the Indian economy to a higher growth trajectory during the Tenth Plan crucially depends on state-level fiscal reforms. The constitution assigns a preeminent role to states in agricultural development, poverty alleviation and human development, and coequal position in the provision of physical infrastructure. The predominant role in allocation and cooperative role in distribution makes states' fiscal operations critical for macroeconomic stabilization as well. Although the constitution places limitations on the states' borrowing powers, in actual practice they are able to run large deficits, and that makes fiscal reforms at the state level critical for achieving overall fiscal consolidation in the country. Thus, fiscal reform at the state level is important from the viewpoint of both macroeconomic stability and microeconomic allocative efficiency.

Much of the discussion on fiscal restructuring in Indian context has remained at the central level in spite of the fact that the states incur almost 55 percent of total expenditures and raise 37 percent of total revenues. Ironically, even at the central level, after a decade of fiscal restructuring, fiscal consolidation has remained elusive. Analysis shows that on a comparable basis, there has hardly been any reduction in the central government's fiscal deficit.[1] On the contrary, there has been a steady increase in revenue deficits and a sharp reduction in the share of capital expenditures indicating significant deterioration in the quality of fiscal imbalance (Rao and Amar Nath 2000). International comparison too shows that of the seventy-four countries with more than 10 million people, only seven countries including India recorded a government deficit higher than 7 percent, with India third after Turkey

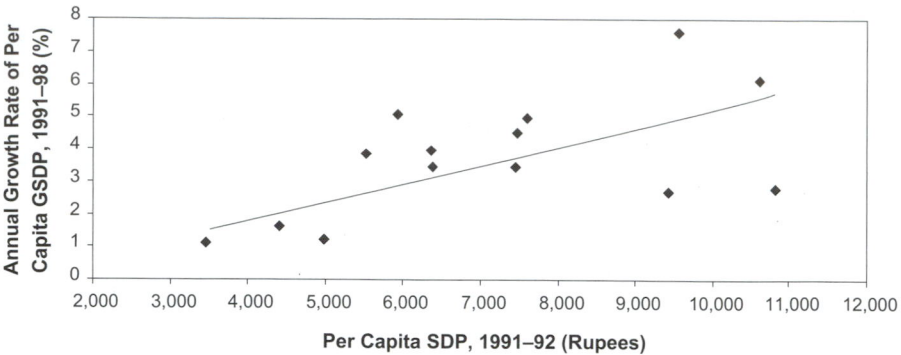

Figure 6.1
Relationship between level of income and growth rates.

and Zimbabwe (Acharya 2001). The unsatisfactory nature of finances constrains the ability of the central government to transfer adequate resources to the states.

6.1.2   Increasing Disparities

Analysis shows that the divergence in growth performances among states has increased, particularly in the 1990s, after market-based reforms were initiated (Ahluwalia 2000; Rao, Kalirajan, and Shand 1999). In the 1990s, by and large, more affluent states (except Punjab and Haryana) have shown a better growth performance than the poorer states (figure 6.1). Those with a market-friendly environment, market supporting institutions, and a better infrastructure could grow faster than those without.[2] Improvement in the quality of infrastructure is one of the key prerequisites for accelerating and sustaining growth rates. This can be achieved only by improving the fiscal health of the states. The problem is particularly relevant in less developed states where the government will have to make significant investments in augmenting physical and social infrastructure.

6.1.3   State-Level Fiscal Problems

There has been a severe deterioration in fiscal health at the state level. Both revenue and fiscal deficits have increased sharply, particularly after 1997–1998. Fiscal stress has increased the states' indebtedness including contingent liabilities and caused severe cutbacks in infrastructure spending. The states have also found a variety of ways to soften their budget constraints. Fiscal deterioration in poorer states has been more acute than in richer states. In this context, two important issues are noteworthy. First, lending by multilateral banks to states could contribute to fiscal instability. Second, as the transfer system will become performance-based in the future, it is important to clearly identify performance indicators. Therefore, reforming the transfer system is equally important.

Fiscal deterioration has occurred despite the attempts to contain expenditures by the states. Declining buoyancy of both tax and nontax revenues in the 1990s is a matter of concern. In this, the most important factor is the sharply deteriorating performance of state electricity boards (SEBs). On the expenditure side, the principal factor causing fiscal imbalances was the revision of salaries and pensions. The remedial measures will have to focus on not only phasing out fiscal imbalances, but also imparting efficiency in tax policy to enhance revenue productivity.

Achieving the growth rates envisaged in the "Approach to the Tenth Five Year Plan" (Government of India 2001) calls for immediate fiscal correction measures. This chapter analyzes the problem of state finances in India with a view to identifying the policy and institutional reforms to achieve fiscal rectitude. Section 6.2 examines trends in fiscal imbalances at the state level and its contribution to overall fiscal imbalances in the country. Section 6.3 analyzes the sources and causes of fiscal imbalances on the revenue and expenditure sides and helps identify the policy measures required to restore fiscal balance. This is followed by an analysis of revenue and expenditure policies to identify the sources of allocative inefficiency in states' fiscal operations in section 6.4. The last section brings out major challenges faced by the states in achieving fiscal consolidation.

6.2   Trends in State Finances: Macroeconomic Implications

6.2.1   Trends in Fiscal Imbalances

The trend in fiscal imbalances since the 1980s is presented in figure 6.2. It appears that the primary, revenue, and fiscal deficits of the states have deteriorated sharply, particularly since 1998–1999. Interestingly, this trend in the revenue deficit started as early as the mid-1980s. In the early 1980s, the states generated a revenue surplus of 1 percent of GDP. By 1987–1988, however, the surplus had vanished. The fiscal adjustment during the early 1990s helped reduce the deficit from about 1 percent in 1990–1991 to 0.4 percent in 1993–1994. Up until 1997–

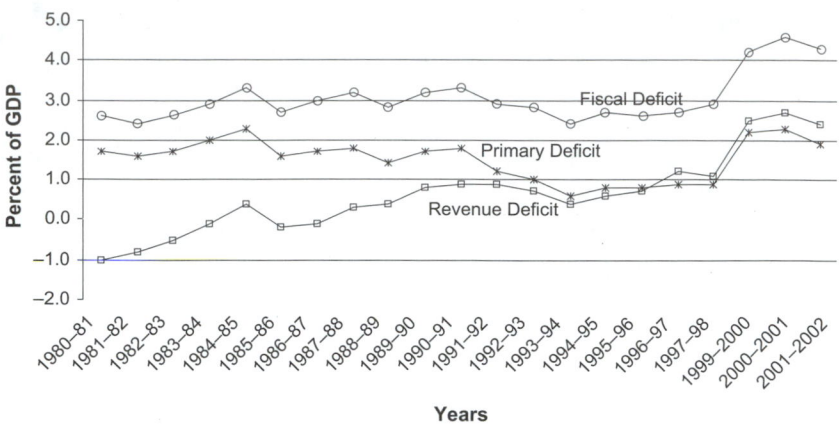

Figure 6.2
Trends in states' fiscal imbalances, 1980–1981 to 2000–2002.

1998, there was a gradual increase in the deficit, but following the impact of the pay revision the deficit jumped sharply to 2.5 percent in 1998–1999. It was expected to be close to 3 percent in 2000–2001.

The states' flexibility to control their fiscal deficit, however, is lower than their control over the revenue deficit because their overall borrowing is determined by the central government. Analysis shows that until 1995–1996, the fiscal adjustment program succeeded in reducing deficits. However, in subsequent years, the imbalance worsened coinciding with pay revisions of state government employees in 1998–1999. Thus, the proportion of fiscal deficit, which fluctuated between 2.5 and 3 percent until 1997–1998, increased sharply to 4.2 percent in 1998–1999 and further to 4.6 percent in 1999–2000. The impact of pay revision particularly on autonomous bodies assisted by the government continued into 2000–2001.

Thus, fiscal, primary, and revenue deficits have deteriorated sharply since 1997–1998, coinciding with pay revisions in the states. Further, the share of revenue deficit in fiscal deficit has also shown sharp increases over the years. Until 1986–1987, the states collectively generated revenue surpluses. By 1990–1991, a little over a quarter of borrowed funds were used to finance current expenditures. Even in 1997–1998, the proportion of revenue deficit in fiscal deficit was just about 38 percent. However, the proportion of borrowed funds used to finance current expenditures increased sharply to 60 percent in 2000–2001 reflecting the effect of pay revisions. Similarly, the proportion of primary deficit to fiscal deficit has shown a steady increase from about 30 percent in 1995–1996 to over 50 percent in 1999–2000. This shows that fiscal deficit position at the state level has become increasingly unsustainable in recent years, particularly since 1997–1998.

Increasing fiscal imbalances in the states has not merely constrained their ability to provide efficient social and physical infrastructure; they have significantly contributed to macroeconomic instability in the country. The deficits incurred by the states constitute a significant and increasing proportion of the overall fiscal imbalances in the country. States' fiscal deficit, which was just about 35 percent of total fiscal deficit in 1990–1991, increased to almost one-half of total fiscal deficit in 1999–2000 (table 6.1).

Attempts to contain fiscal deficits have caused a sharp decline in the quality of deficits as well. The share of revenue deficit in fiscal deficit increased from 38 percent in 1997–1998 to 60 percent in 1998–1999 following pay revisions. Hardening resource position has crowded out capital expenditures. Capital expenditure, as a ratio of GDP, declined from 3.6 percent in the early 1980s to 1.8 percent in 2000–2001 (figure 6.3). The share of capital expenditure in total spending declined from 26 percent to about 13 percent during the period. This has led to increasing infrastructure bottlenecks. Thus, the deterioration in the fiscal position of states has rendered their fiscal operations increasingly unsustainable, contributed to macroeconomic instability, and constrained the provision of social and physical infrastructure.

Deterioration in fiscal imbalances noted earlier is not just a general phenomenon. It is seen in the case of each of the individual states. Table 6A.1 shows that, of the fourteen nonspecial category states, six showed improvements from 1990–1991 to 1995–1996 with respect to revenue deficits and nine showed improvements with respect to fiscal deficits by varying magnitudes. Also, in the case of special category states, there was significant improvement in their revenue accounts (2.5 percent of net state domestic product, or NSDP) and fiscal deficits (4.7 percent of NSDP). However, thereafter the situation deteriorated sharply.

States' fiscal deficits are mainly financed by market borrowings and central loans. According to Article 293 of the Constitution, the states, if they are indebted to the central government, have to seek its permission to borrow. However, all the states are indebted to the central government and states' market borrowing is determined by the Ministry of Finance in consultation with the Planning Commission and the

Table 6.1
Trend in states' fiscal imbalances

Year	Percent of revenue deficit to GDP	Percent of fiscal deficit to GDP	Percent of rev. def. to fiscal def.	Percent of primary def. to fiscal def.	Percent of states' rev. def. to total rev. def.	Percent of states' fis. def. to total fis. def.	States' capital exp. as % of total state exp.	Percent of states' capital exp. to GDP
1980–1981	−1.0	2.6	−38.5	65.4	−250.0	34.7	26.0	3.6
1985–1986	−0.2	2.7	−7.4	59.3	−10.5	33.8	20.0	2.9
1990–1991	0.9	3.3	27.3	54.5	21.4	35.1	15.8	2.4
1995–1996	0.7	2.6	26.9	30.8	21.9	40.0	14.0	2.0
1996–1997	1.2	2.7	44.4	33.3	33.3	42.2	11.4	1.6
1997–1998	1.1	2.9	37.9	31.0	26.8	39.7	13.3	1.8
1998–1999	2.5	4.2	59.5	52.4	39.7	47.2	12.6	1.8
1999–2000	2.7	4.6	58.7	50.0	43.5	48.9	12.6	1.9
2000–2001 (RE)	2.4	4.3	55.8	44.2	40.7	47.3	13.1	1.8

Sources: Public Finance Statistics, Ministry of Finance, Government of India.

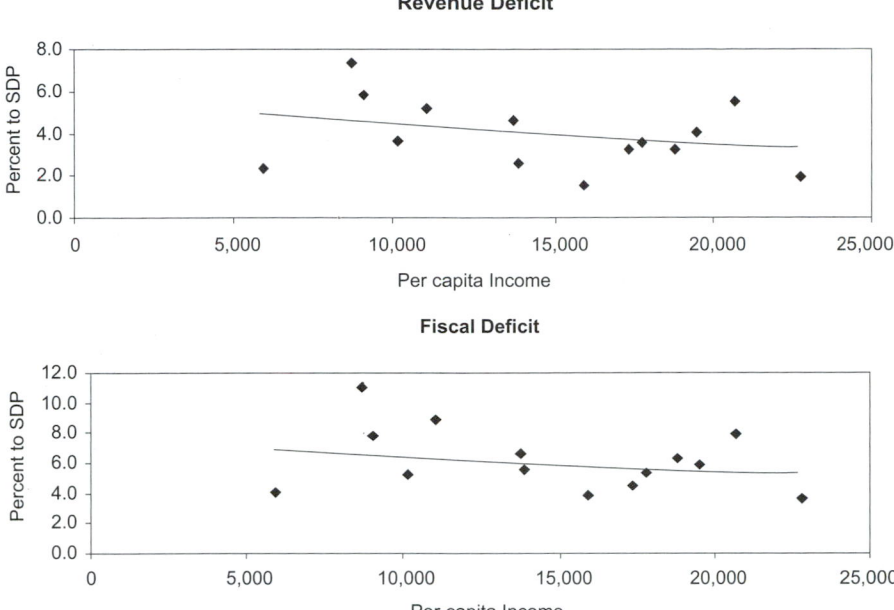

Figure 6.3
Relationship between per capita SDP and states' fiscal imbalances.

Reserve Bank of India (RBI). In addition to these, states also get 80 percent of net collections of small savings. Other liabilities of the states are in the public accounts, mainly the provident funds.

The persistence of large and growing fiscal deficits in the states over the years has led to a steady accumulation of debt. Measured by accumulated stock of debt as a ratio of GDP, states' indebtedness fell from 19.4 percent in 1990–1991 to 17.8 percent in 1996–1997 but increased thereafter to 23.1 percent in 2000–2001. In fact, since 1995–1996, the debt stock increased at the compound annual rate of 17.9 percent, whereas revenue receipts increased only at 11.2 percent. Consequently, the share of interest payments in total expenditure increased from 13 percent in 1990–1991 to 21.6 percent in 2000–2001 to crowd out productive expenditures.

6.2.2 Fiscal Imbalances in Individual States

As shown in table 6A.1, the deterioration in the fiscal situation coinciding with pay revision after 1997–1998 is seen in each of the individual states; it was particularly severe in special category states. Both

Table 6.2
Frequency table of fiscal imbalances in states

Percent of NSDP	1990–1991	1995–1996	1999–2000
Revenue deficit			
<0	1	1	—
0–1.5	6	8	—
1.5–3.0	5	4	4
3.0–4.5	2	1	4
>4.5	—	—	6
Fiscal deficit			
<2.5	2	1	—
2.5–5.0	6	11	3
5.0–7.5	5	2	6
>7.5	1	—	5

Source: Estimated from Reserve Bank of India bulletins.

revenue and fiscal deficits as percentages of NSDP in these states deteriorated by over 6 percentage points. In the case of 14 nonspecial category states revenue and fiscal deficits deteriorated by 2.8 percentage points to NSDP.

There was, however, wide variation in the deterioration in the fiscal situation in different nonspecial category states. The worst was in West Bengal, where both revenue and fiscal deficits as percentages of NSDP worsened by about 5 percentage points. The deterioration in revenue deficit was also very high in Punjab (4.4), Rajasthan (4.2), and Maharashtra (3.7). In the case of fiscal deficits, marked deterioration was seen in Bihar (5.3), Punjab (3.9), Orissa (3.4), Gujarat (3.3), and Maharashtra (3.1). Thus, the severe deterioration in fiscal imbalances is seen also in some of the high-income states and those that are traditionally known for their fiscal austerity such as Gujarat and Maharashtra.

The spread of the states with different ranges of revenue and fiscal deficits presented in table 6.2 highlights the sharp deterioration. Of the fourteen major states in 1995–1996, thirteen had revenue deficits of less than 3 percent of NSDP in 1995–1996. In contrast, in 1999–2000, revenue deficits in ten states was more than 3 percent, and in six states it was more than 4.5 percent. Similarly, fiscal deficits in thirteen of the fourteen major states was less than 5 percent of NSDP in 1995–1996. In contrast to 1999–2000, it was more than 5 percent in eleven states and more than 7.5 percent in five states.

By and large, the problem of fiscal imbalances is more acute in poorer than in richer states. A notable exception to this is Punjab, while although having the highest per capita SDP, has had very high revenue and fiscal deficits. The correlation coefficient of per capita SDP with revenue deficit is −0.319 for fourteen nonspecial category states and −0.438 when Punjab is excluded from the sample. The correlation coefficient of per capita SDP with fiscal deficit is −0.331 for nonspecial category states and −0.446 when Punjab is excluded. Thus, in general the severity of fiscal crunch is felt more by the poorer than by the richer states.

6.2.3 Hidden Imbalances and Softening Budget Constraints

An important implementation rule of fiscal decentralization is the need to have a hard budget constraint for subnational governments (Bahl 2002). Although in principle, the states have hard budgets, in practice, they can soften the constraint in a variety of ways (Lahiri 2000; Anand, Bagchi, and Sen 2002). The practice of collecting taxes in advance and keeping contractors' bills pending is well known. The states can also increase their liabilities in Public Accounts, particularly small savings loans. Another method used is by creating special purpose vehicles for investments in activities such as irrigation. States also resort to borrowing from public enterprises. In recent years, the states have been borrowing heavily from financial institutions such as NABARD, LIC, HUDCO, and IDFC to finance infrastructure. I have already referred to borrowing from multilateral lending agencies. All these are in addition to the ways and means advances and overdrafts from the RBI.

Thus, the fiscal position discussed earlier does not reveal fiscal imbalances of the states in their entirety. Significant contingent liabilities are caused by the state government guarantees and indemnities given to urban local bodies, public enterprises, and autonomous institutions. Available information shows that recorded contingent liabilities in 1999–2000 was Rs. 1,24,813 crore or almost 6.4 percent of GDP.

Until the mid-1990s, the interest payments were kept artificially low due to financial repression. With the alignment of interest rates to market rates, interest outlay increased significantly. In addition, small savings is an expensive source of borrowing. Thus, both the volume of borrowing and the average interest rate have increased. Yet, small savings borrowing is an important method of overcoming budget constraints. In fact, some states (Karnataka) mandate that a proportion of salary arrears have to be invested in small savings.

Another major source of fiscal imbalance not reflected in the budgets is losses incurred by public enterprises, notably, SEBs. In 2000–2001, estimated losses of SEBs was over Rs. 26,000 crore of which only Rs. 6,000 crore is taken into account in the state budgets (by way of explicit subsidy given to SEBs). The loss of SEBs account for 1.2 percent of GDP of which only 0.2 percent is shown as explicit subsidies in state budgets. The performance of SEBs has had adverse repercussions on central finances as well. As of 28 February 2001, dues payable by SEBs to central enterprises were Rs. 41,473 crore (2 percent of GDP) comprised of Rs. 25,727 crore principal and the remaining in interest payments. Of this total, Delhi Vidyut Board alone owed Rs. 5,380 crore (13 percent) and state utilities owed Rs. 36,000 crore.

Many states have tried to overcome their immediate fiscal problems by taking structural adjustment loans from multilateral lending institutions. Notable among the states availing such facilities are Andhra Pradesh, Karnataka, and Uttar Pradesh who borrowed from the World Bank as well as Gujarat and Madhya Pradesh who borrowed from the Asian Development Bank (ADB). Other states are also in the fray seeking loans from these institutions. Although the central government guarantees repayments of these loans, the states are required to initiate an action plan to improve their repayment capacity. However, while the loans have added to the states' indebtedness, fiscal reforms undertaken by them thus far have failed to address satisfactorily the fundamental issues of tax reforms, public expenditure restructuring, and reform of SEBs. Unless the issue is addressed immediately, this could cause further deterioration in the states' finances.

6.3   Sources of Fiscal Imbalances in States

6.3.1   Trends in Revenues and Expenditures

Fiscal imbalances in the states are structural; expenditures have grown faster than revenues during the last decade by 2.2 percentage points and the difference has been increasing (table 6.3). Given the difference between levels of expenditures and revenues' growth rate, differences translate into substantial revenue deficit. The slowest growing item was the transfers from the central government (10 percent) and given the precariousness of central finances, it is unlikely that transfers will register a much faster growth than in the past. Nevertheless, it is important to rationalize the central transfers both from the viewpoint of

Table 6.3
Average annual growth rates of states' revenues and expenditures

	14 nonspecial category states		25 states	
	1980–1981 to 1989–1990	1990–1991 to 1998–1999	1980–1981 to 1989–1990	1990–1991 to 1999–2000
Own tax revenue	15.82	14.09	15.92	14.08
Own nontax revenue	13.13	11.51	12.54	12.38
Total transfers	14.58	10.99	15.84	11.50
Total revenues	14.91	12.62	15.30	12.83
Revenue expenditure	16.69	14.82	17.07	14.94
Capital expenditure	8.80	11.39	9.69	11.13
Total expenditure	15.07	14.38	15.53	14.43

Sources: Public Finance Statistics, Ministry of Finance, Government of India.

designing them to offset states' fiscal disabilities as well as ensuring minimum standards of services and incentivizing them.

Restoring fiscal balance, however, will have to be achieved mainly by the states' own efforts. Therefore, slower growth is cause for concern. Growth of states' own tax revenues lagged behind that of revenue expenditures by about 1 percentage point. The nontax revenues lagged behind revenue expenditures by 4 percentage points. This is mainly due to the states' inability to make proper cost recoveries from public services provided and generate adequate returns from public investments.

The declining growth of revenues also point to structural factors exacerbating fiscal imbalances. Notably, growth of each source of revenue decelerated in the 1990s from what it had been in the 1980s. The growth rate of states' own tax revenue decelerated by 1.8 percentage points and nontax revenue by 1.6 percentage points. Interestingly, in the 1990s, efforts to contain expenditures by the states reduced the growth rate of expenditures from 16.7 percent in the 1980s to 14.8 percent in the 1990s.

Thus, for over two decades, states' revenues have grown at significantly lower rates than revenue expenditures. This has created increasing public dissavings year after year. The deceleration in the growth of revenues has put increasing pressure on revenue and fiscal deficits. What is more, lower and decelerating growth in revenues has crowded out capital expenditures. Thus, the impact of fiscal constraints at the state level has been not only to create severe fiscal imbalance, but also to crowd out productive capital expenditures.

Declining revenue-GDP ratio is a major source of fiscal imbalances (table 6.4). The revenue-GDP ratio in the states increased in the early part of the 1980s, but declined from 12 percent in 1985–1986 to 9.8 percent in 1998–1999. Of this, an approximately 1.5 percentage point decline occurred after the mid-1990s, with the revenue-GDP ratio falling from 11.3 percent in 1995–1996 to 9.8 percent in 1998–1999. Since the mid-1990s, a decline of about 0.6 points was in central transfers, 0.5 points in states' nontax revenues, and 0.4 points in states' tax revenues. Thus, states' revenue-GDP ratio from each of the major sources has shown a declining trend during the 1990s, which has accelerated since the mid-1990s. This is really cause for concern.

Declining revenues have contained the expenditure-GDP ratio as well. While the ratio increased by 1 percentage point until 1990, it declined by about the same magnitude until 1998–1999, although it is expected to increase again taking the full effect of the pay revision to 15.5 percent. Hardening resources and increasing pressure on revenue expenditures have also been responsible for crowded out capital expenditures. The latter declined from 2.4 percent in 1990–1991 to 1.8 percent in 1999–2000. Further, within revenue expenditures, economic services declined from 3.7 percent to 2.9 percent during the period. Expenditure on social services declined from 4.9 percent in 1990–1991 to 4.6 percent in 1998–1999 until the effect of pay revision increased it to 5 percent. Expenditure on administrative services increased steadily throughout the two decades. Of particular concern has been the sharp increase in the interest payments from 1.5 percent in 1990–1991 to 2.3 percent in 1999–2000.

The trends show that in each of the states except Kerala there has been deceleration in the growth of revenues (table 6A.2). This has constrained increases in expenditures, particularly capital expenditures in every state. The trends also show that during the period 1990–2000, in general, the poorer states performed worse than better-off states. The lowest growth in own revenues was seen in Bihar (10.2), followed by West Bengal (11.2 percent) and Uttar Pradesh (11.6 percent). In other poorer states such as Madhya Pradesh and Orissa too, revenues also recorded low growth rates. This constrained the growth of expenditures, particularly capital expenditures states. Thus, capital expenditure in real terms declined in Madhya Pradesh (3.2 percent) and was virtually stagnant in Bihar (6.8 percent), Uttar Pradesh (7.2 percent), and Orissa (7.3 percent), even in absolute terms as the growth rates

Table 6.4
Percent of states' revenues and expenditures to GDP

	1980–1981	1985–1986	1990–1991	1995–1996	1998–1999	1999–2000 RE
States' revenues						
Own tax revenue	4.60	5.23	5.34	5.20	4.89	5.21
Own nontax revenue	2.27	1.90	1.62	1.92	1.36	1.49
Own revenues	6.87	7.14	6.96	7.12	6.25	6.70
Total transfers	4.46	4.89	4.73	4.20	3.58	4.04
Total revenues	11.33	12.02	11.69	11.32	9.83	10.74
States' expenditures						
Revenue expenditure	10.30	11.79	12.62	12.05	12.36	13.68
General services	*	3.49	4.03	4.63	4.97	5.68
Interest payments	0.85	1.06	1.52	1.84	2.02	2.30
Social services	*	4.81	4.92	4.43	4.56	5.09
Economic services	*	3.49	3.67	2.99	2.82	2.91
Capital expenditure	3.62	2.94	2.37	1.87	1.67	1.81
Total expenditure	13.92	14.73	14.99	13.92	14.02	15.50

Source: Public Finance Statistics (relevant years), Ministry of Finance, Government of India.
Note: Due to differences in budgetary classification, the figures are not estimated. RE = revised estimates.

recorded in them were barely equal to increase in wholesale price index. Punjab (3.2 percent) recorded the lowest growth in capital expenditures even though revenue receipts in the 1990s increased at 14.7 percent because at the same time revenue expenditure grew 15.8 percent.

6.3.2   Reasons for the Slow Growth of Tax Revenues

Analysis shows that each of the major state taxes has shown a deceleration in growth in the 1990s as opposed to the 1980s (table 6.5). Deceleration has been particularly marked in the case of taxes on land and agriculture, stamps and registration, state excises, and sales taxes. The taxes on land and agriculture generate a negligible amount of revenue, and even this grew only at 8.7 percent per year during the 1990s. Revenue from sales taxes constitutes two-thirds of states' own tax revenues, and during the 1990s deceleration in the growth of sales taxes by about 1.7 percentage points was a major factor responsible for the decline in states' tax revenue-GDP ratio, particularly after 1995–1996.

Low revenue productivity of taxes on land and agricultural incomes has been a much-debated issue. From the viewpoint of horizontal equity and revenue productivity, levying a tax on agricultural incomes is necessary. Yet the architecture of the tax has not been implemented on paper for want of political willingness. In fact, states have not been able to levy the tax on agricultural income declared in the tax returns submitted to the central income tax department. Even the proposal to assign the tax to the rural local governments (Rajaraman and Bhende 1998) has not found favor with the states. The fragmented nature of income tax has provided an easy avenue for evasion and avoidance of personal income tax.

The principal reason for the deceleration in the growth rate of sales taxes has to be found in the inability to extend the base to the services sector. During the last decade, the services sector has grown at 7.8 percent per year, much higher than both the primary (2.8 percent) and secondary (5.7 percent) sectors, and since the mid-1990s, over 70 percent of the growth of the economy was attributed to this sector (Acharya 2001). Since the states are allowed to levy taxes only on goods, the production and consumption of services remains outside the tax net. In the medium term, buoyancies in states' taxes can be improved only when the states are enabled to extend sales taxes to services (Rao 2001). This would also help to evolve a comprehensive,

Table 6.5
Growth rates and buoyancies of revenues and expenditures

	Revenue-GDP percentage		Growth rates (percent per annum)		Buoyancy	
	1990–1991	1999–2000	1980–1990	1990–2000	1980–1990	1990–2000
1. *States' own tax revenue*						
Tax on agricultural income	0.14	0.08	14.52	7.18	1.08	0.60
Stamps and registration	0.37	0.43	16.68	15.88	1.22	1.13
Sales tax	3.14	2.96	15.27	13.39	1.11	0.94
State excise	0.84	0.71	16.44	12.14	1.20	0.82
Taxes on transport	0.31	0.26	9.56	12.06	0.69	0.82
Total—Own tax revenue	5.34	5.21	15.04	13.44	1.12	0.94
2. *Own nontax revenue*	1.62	1.49	12.30	12.51	0.89	0.84
3. *Transfers*	4.73	4.04	15.52	11.68	1.11	0.77
Total revenue receipts	11.69	10.74	14.63	12.70	1.08	0.86

Source: Public Finance Statistics, Ministry of Finance, Government of India.

destination-based value-added tax (VAT) at the state level. This, however, requires an amendment to the Constitution to put consumption of services in the concurrent list.

The bases of state taxes are also rendered narrow because of large-scale exemptions, evasion, and avoidance of taxes. In the case of sales tax, for example, besides wide-ranging exemptions, there are generous schemes of incentives in terms of tax exemption and deferment. While the efficacy of such fiscal incentives in promoting industrialization is limited, foregone revenue is significant. These incentives do not enhance the availability of capital in the country but merely redistribute the existing capital in distortionary ways.

The efficiency implications of sales taxation are discussed in section 6.4. Here, it is necessary to state that the prevailing tax system has caused severe distortions due to complexity in its structure, cascading of the tax due to input and capital goods taxation, and wide-ranging incentives and exemptions. In addition, Union Territories have been subnational tax havens. Similarly, exemption given to sales in canteen stores meant for the armed forces has been subject to widespread misuse of both sales tax and state excise duty. Finally, providing sales exemptions on the basis of end use of the commodity not only provides an easy means to evade taxes but also leads to severe allocative distortions. It is necessary to put an end to such discretionary exemption practices.

The problem is similar with other taxes as well. Levying a registration fee on transfer of immovable property at high and differentiated rates has led to widespread tax evasion by undervaluing the value of the property transacted. Absence of a mechanism to objectively determine the benchmark values by stratifying properties according to the factors influencing the value of land and building costs has led to widespread tax evasion as an acceptable practice in the society.

Lack of proper information systems and administrative machinery to implement taxes is a general shortcoming in all states. Much remains to be done to simplify the tax system and strengthen tax administration and enforcement. Hardly any cooperation exists between one tax department of a state and another, much less between central and state tax departments. Complications in the tax system add to complexity in administration and most states are ill-equipped to administer the taxes designed to fulfill multiple objectives, thus adding to compliance cost and reducing revenue productivity.

6.3.3 Declining Nontax Revenues

Inability to recover reasonable returns from large investments has been a major reason for the low and declining growth in nontax revenues. By 31 March 1999, states' outstanding investments in statutory corporations were Rs. 75,000 crore, and about Rs. 42,000 crore were invested in the government companies. Together, they yielded hardly any return. In most cases, public enterprises do not recover even a fraction of the capital cost and depreciation, let alone generate any return on investments (Government of India 2000).

Almost 85 percent of the investment in state-level public enterprises is on electricity utilities. Poor financial performance of SEBs has been a major cause of drain on states' exchequers. The Electricity (Supply) Act of 1948 stipulates that SEBs should yield 3 percent return on their net fixed assets. With the value of fixed assets at Rs. 68,000, they should have contributed Rs. 2,040 crore to revenues. In actual practice, however, they have generated a commercial loss of Rs. 23,000 crore or 33.8 percent of the value of fixed assets in 1999–2000 (Government of India 2001). The losses excluding the state government subsidy amounted to Rs. 18,200 crore.

While the average cost of power by the SEBs was Rs. 2.83 per unit, the average revenue realized was only Rs. 1.99 per unit. The difference was due to poor efficiency in the supply of power and irrational pricing policies. The transmission and distribution losses were high (23.7 percent), mainly due to theft of power. The subsidy to agricultural sector was estimated at Rs. 24,541 crore, and Rs. 8,103 crore was due to domestic consumption. Industrial and commercial sectors had to pay more than the average cost, and the excess payment amounted to Rs. 8,407 crore. After accounting for a Rs. 4,800 crore explicit subsidy given by the states, uncovered losses were Rs. 20,032 crore. Further, the financial position of the SEBs has been steadily deteriorating over the years. Unless immediate steps are taken to improve efficiency, ensure universal metering, and rationalize the tariff structure, the SEBs will continue to strain state finances.

The previous picture of financial drain due to poor functioning of SEBs hides the enormous interstate differences (table 6A.3). In Andhra Pradesh, in 1999–2000 commercial losses were more than the value of capital stock! The losses were more than 50 percent of the value of capital in West Bengal (66 percent), Jammu Kashmir (57 percent), Madhya Pradesh (56 percent), Rajasthan (52 percent), and Gujarat

(52 percent). The efficiency parameters and volume of subsidies also varied widely among states. Even more problematic is the fact that the commercial losses as a ratio of net fixed assets have shown steady decline in all the states all the way through the 1990s, and the policy measures implemented thus far have been ineffective in reversing the trend.

Restoring fiscal balance is inextricably linked to the improvement in the SEBs and State Road Transport Corporations (SRTCs). In fact, SEB losses add to the deficit by an additional Rs. 26,000 crore or about 1.3 percent of GDP. With this, revenue deficit is estimated at close to 3 percent of GDP. Similarly, losses of SRTCs in 1997–1998 amounted to Rs. 1,282 crore, and their finances have shown a steady deterioration over the years. The situation is similar with other state enterprises as well. The Accountant Generals' reports in many of the states point out that there are a number of state-level public enterprises with accumulated losses amounting to several times the value of their fixed assets.

Poor fiscal condition of the states should also be attributed to poor cost recovery from public services. The NIPFP study for 1996–1997 showed that cost recovery in social services was as low as 8.4 percent of the cost of providing services, and in the case of economic services it was 16.6 percent. Analysis of various social and economic services in Karnataka shows that cost recoveries not only are low but also have shown a decline over the years (Rao and Amar Nath 2001). Detailed sectorwise studies in Karnataka demonstrate considerable scope for raising revenues from targeting subsidies in agriculture (Deshpande and Bhende 2001), irrigation (Raju and Amar Nath 2001), power (Vivekananda 2001), industry (Gayithri 2001), higher education (Narayana 2001), and water supply sectors (Saleth and Sastry 2001). The studies show that the malice of poor cost recovery does not lie merely in noneconomic pricing of these services. Often, the problem is one of poor efficiency in their provision, and increasing prices will simply pass on the burden of production/distribution inefficiency to the consumers.

6.3.4 Expanding Expenditures

Disaggregated analysis of state expenditures (table 6.6) brings out some important stylized facts with implications for macroeconomic stability and allocative and technical efficiency in states' public expenditure policy. These are summarized in what follows:

Table 6.6
Trends in state expenditure

	Percentages of states' expenditure to GDP		Growth rate (percent per annum)	
	1990–1991	1999–2000	1985–1995	1990–2000
Total revenue expenditure	12.62	13.68	15.16	13.92
1. *General services*	4.03	5.68	17.85	16.84
Of which—Interest payment	1.52	2.30	19.99	17.39
2. *Social services*	4.92	5.09	13.30	13.82
Education	2.73	2.91	14.44	14.09
Health and family welfare	0.81	0.75	12.58	12.71
3. *Economic services*	3.67	2.91	14.41	9.75
Agriculture and allied activities	1.10	0.88	13.33	9.83
Rural development	0.88	0.69	13.20	9.35
Irrigation	0.60	0.48	11.99	11.53
Power	0.17	0.29	29.33	14.59
Industry and minerals	0.21	0.12	11.40	8.12
Transport and communications	0.41	0.29	13.95	9.77
Capital expenditure	2.37	1.81	9.48	10.55
Total expenditure	14.62	15.50	14.24	13.48

• Despite attempts to contain the growth of expenditures during the decade 1991–2000, the states' revenue expenditure-GDP ratio increased by 0.9 point. This contributed to the severity of fiscal imbalance at the state level broadly by the same magnitude as the reduction in the revenue-GDP ratio. The share of revenue expenditures in GDP increased from 12.6 percent to 13.7 percent during the period.

• A substantial proportion of the increase in revenue expenditures is due to interest payments. Both the volume of liabilities and average rate of interest have increased significantly. An increasing share of states' loans are used for revenue expenditures, the vicious cycle of higher interest payments and increasing expenditures feeding back into larger borrowings. The problem is exacerbated by low productivity of even capital expenditures. The proliferation of projects spreads the resources thinly, and inadequate financial allocation causes severe cost and time overruns.

• The principal reason for an increase in expenditures, however, is the pay and pension revision. The impact of pay revision has been much more severe on the states than the central government because the share of salary expenditure in states is higher; revisions had to be extended to aided institutions and local bodies other than the government administration. Thus, general service expenditures excluding interest payment increased by almost 1 percentage point during the decade, reflecting the increases in pay scales and pension payments. An nearly 0.7 percentage point increase occurred in just the last two years. Overall, much of the 1.3 percentage point increase in noninterest revenue expenditures seen in the last two years could be attributed to the implementation of pay revision. In absolute terms, compensation to employees (pay and pensions) in states increased from Rs. 73,432 crore in 1996–1997 to Rs. 89,748 crore in 1997–1998 and further to Rs. 111,891 crore in 1998–1999. Thus the increase of Rs. 16,000 crore in 1997–1998 was followed by an additional increase of Rs. 22,000 crore in 1998–1999 (Acharya 2001).

• Despite a significant increase in the salary component of social services expenditures, the expenditure-GDP ratio remained more or less constant at about 5 percent of GDP. Constancy in the social services expenditure-GDP ratio in the wake of increasing salary costs implies a reduction in nonsalary inputs with an adverse impact on their quality.

• The impact of declining revenue-GDP ratio and the inevitability of meeting increasing commitments on pay and pension revisions and interest payments have caused the capital expenditure-GDP ratio to fall from 2.4 percent in 1990–1991 to 1.8 percent in 1999–2000. Within revenue expenditures, a sharp decline in the expenditure-GDP ratio with respect to economic services signifies the inability of the states to make adequate provision for maintenance of physical infrastructure. The effect has been to put pressure on both the availability and quality of physical infrastructure.

• A major structural cause of expenditure proliferation is the artificial and often meaningless distinction made between plan and nonplan expenditures. Implicit in this is the assumption that plan expenditures are productive and nonplan expenditures are not. This is incorrect, because a number of projects classified as "plan" in the revenue account are merely salary payments that are not productive. Similarly, completed plan schemes are classified as "nonplan." Maintenance expenditures on roads, irrigation works, and buildings are certainly productive, and inadequate provision for containing nonplan expenditures has been a major shortcoming in expenditure management. Often, for convenience and strategic reasons, various developmental projects are initiated on the nonplan side. The classification itself is unscientific, and this has led to inadequate expenditure allocation to maintenance of assets. Emphasis on increasing the plan size of every successive plan, irrespective of resources available, has caused a proliferation of plan schemes even when they cannot be justified economically. As I mentioned earlier, emphasis on increasing the plan size has also had the effect of allocating expenditures to a large number of projects, resulting in thinly spread resources and causing time and cost overruns.

· Increasing the emphasis on plan expenditures by containing nonplan expenditures has had another undesirable effect on state finances. One way to increase the plan size is to classify some of the expenditures considered to be nonplan in earlier years as plan. Besides, the emphasis has shifted to revenue expenditures under the plan category. During earlier plans, the revenue component of plan expenditures in nonspecial category states was only about 30 percent, and therefore the grant-loan component of plan assistance was 30:70. At present, the revenue component of plan expenditures is almost 55 percent, and the consequence of this has been to finance increasing proportions of revenue expenditures from borrowed funds year after year.

6.3.5 Inequity and Disincentives from Central Transfers

Reform in the transfer system is outside the purview of individual states. Yet it is important to address the issue to make the transfer system adequate, efficient, and equitable. The fiscal adjustment at the central government has decelerated the growth of transfers to states from 14.6 percent in the 1980s to 11 percent in the 1990s. It is also necessary to note that that the transfer system has not been able to offset fiscal disabilities satisfactorily (Rao 1997; Rao and Singh 2002). The income elasticity of transfers for fourteen major states declined from -0.35 in 1990–1991 to -0.20 in 1998–1999.

The problems associated with central transfers are well known and have been analyzed by several studies. Multiple agencies dispensing transfers have constrained the targeting of general-purpose transfers to offset fiscal disabilities. It would be appropriate to make all current transfers through the instrumentality of the Finance Commission and all loan assistance through the Planning Commission. The Planning Commission should be confined to infrastructure projects, and the distinction between plans and nonplans in the revenue budget should be done away with.[3] The Finance Commission grants have serious design problems, and the "fiscal dentistry" is alleged to have had the consequence of widening "budgetary cavities."

The specific-purpose transfers comprise central-sector and centrally sponsored schemes. There has been a proliferation of these schemes, and at present they number more than 175. Besides spreading the resources thinly, these programs distort states' choices in expenditure allocation, multiply bureaucracy, and cause a thin spread of resources across several schemes. Because centrally sponsored schemes also require matching contributions from the states, the extent of distortion in resource allocation is higher and expenditure centralization is much larger than what is indicated by the expenditure shares of the states.

Based on the recommendation of the eleventh Finance Commission, attempts are being made to incentivize the revenue deficit grants. In particular, 15 percent of the deficit grants has been recommended by the Finance Commission to be earmarked with an equal contribution from the central government to be distributed to the states according to their fiscal performance. Each state will be given a share in excess or short of its initial eligibility (population share), depending on its fiscal performance. The states will be required to put out their Medium Term Fiscal Reforms Programme (MTFRP), and performance will be measured on the basis of a single monitorable fiscal objective, namely, the improvement in the revenue deficit by at least 5 percent of its revenues. If a state fails to fulfil the condition, the fund will be rolled over to the next year. If the withheld portion is not claimed by 2005–2006, the fund will lapse. Twelve of the twenty-eight states have already signed the Memorandum of Understanding (MOU) with the central government to operationalize the scheme, and the remaining are expected to follow. The problem with the scheme is that the amount of funds available for incentive payments may not be enough to incentivize the transfers. Further, the scheme is designed to incentivize only incremental changes in revenue deficit irrespective of the size of the deficit. Moreover, the central government, which is a bigger source of fiscal imbalance, has not put in any scheme to rein in its own deficits, and even the Fiscal Responsibility Act proposed to bring in a measure of discipline has been a nonstarter.

6.4   Efficiency Implications of Subnational Fiscal Operations

6.4.1   Need for Efficiency in Subnational Fiscal Policy
Efficiency in terms of both minimizing distortions in tax policy and cost-effective provision of services has not received much attention. This can partly be explained by the fact that in a closed economy, inef-

ficiencies of tax and expenditure systems are neither transparent nor important. It is therefore not surprising that the emphasis has been to raise revenues to finance large public-sector plans without concern for allocative distortions. Indeed, policymakers pursued multiple objectives from tax policy besides raising revenues to complicate the tax systems such as equity, regulating consumption, and attracting investment and regional allocation of resources. Competition among the states to attract trade and investment has added to the complexity. On the expenditure side, the emphasis has been to increase the size of every plan, with no emphasis on efficiency in resource use. Thus, even performance measurement, if done at all, has been in terms of inputs or meeting financial targets and not outputs or outcomes. Thus, allocative and technical efficiency in the design and implementation of public spending policy has not received any attention.

In open economies, it is imperative to minimize distortions in tax policy, ensure proper pricing of quasi-public goods and services provided by the state governments, and improve efficiency in public service delivery. Achieving competitiveness in the economy calls for minimizing relative price distortions arising from subnational tax and pricing policies, providing high-quality physical infrastructure, and ensuring human development.

6.4.2 Efficiency Implications of Subnational Tax Policy

Subnational tax policy causes inefficiencies in resource allocation by distorting relative prices and violating common market principles in a federation. The tax policy can cause excessive and unintended distortions of the pursuit of multiple objectives, from year-to-year and ad hoc policy changes guided by exigencies of revenue or responding to special interest groups. Similarly, violation of the principles of common market arises from the impediments placed on free movement of factors and products throughout the federation. Such impediments segment the markets and create inefficiencies in resource allocation.

The sales tax—the most important source of states' own tax revenue —is also the most important source of distortion. Administrative considerations have led to the levy of the tax predominantly at the first point of sale. All preretail sales taxes cause cascading. The tax is levied also on inputs and capital goods, which exacerbates the problem. Pursuit of multiple objectives has caused minute differences in tax rates. Interstate competition in sales tax to attract trade and investments has complicated the tax structure further. In this "race to the bottom," the Union Territories have played a destabilizing role. The competition has led the states to adopt the self-defeating schemes of fiscal incentives in terms of sales tax holidays and deferment. In addition, to meet exigencies of revenue, the states have levied turnover taxes, additional sales taxes, and entry taxes. All these have contributed to complicated, cascading, and opaque tax systems. The tax on tax and markup on tax have altered relative prices in unintended ways. The complicated tax systems and wide discretions to officials have resulted in negotiated tax payments and high compliance costs. In addition, the central sales tax levied by the exporting state has distorted relative prices and segmented the market. This has also been a major source of inequitable interstate tax exportation.

Despite widespread awareness of the distortions caused by Octroi,[4] the states of Gujarat, Maharashtra, Orissa, and Punjab have assigned their urban local bodies to levy this tax on the entry of goods into local areas for consumption, use, or sale. In these states, this levy is a major source of market segmentation, impedes internal trade, and causes allocative distortions and rent seeking. In addition, as this is a checkpost-based levy, it enlarges scope for rent seeking. In spite of an awareness of the ills of the levy, it has continued to be levied by urban local bodies in some states.

The taxes on the transfer of property, as they are levied at present, have hindered the development of the organized market for immovable properties in the country. The levy of high and differentiated rates of stamp duty and registration fees has led to widespread undervaluation of immovable properties and tax evasion. There is no incentive for honest reporting of the value of transactions, and this prevents the development of a transparent market for immovable properties. The levy has hindered the very development of a transparent organized market for immovable properties.

It is often said that "tax administration is tax reform." A major source of distortion in the subnational tax policy in India is weak administration and an ineffective enforcement mechanism. Complicated tax structures, weak governance, and poor information contribute to poor tax compliance. Enforcing a complicated tax system requires sophisticated administrative machinery. The prevailing administrative machinery is unable to effectively enforce the tax. The ineffective enforcement mechanism not only reduces revenue productivity of the tax system, but also causes serious distortions and inequity.

6.4.3 Efficiency Implications of Subnational Expenditures

Productivity of subnational expenditures depends upon the efficiency public service provision and the creation of a positive business environment. While efficiency in the provision of public services has important implications for the volume of resources/savings that should be drawn from private investment, the volume and spread of physical and social infrastructure provided by public expenditures determine the private business environment. If it is assumed that central public finance operation is neutral in its impact across regions, resource distortion can be caused by the spread of interstate differences in the provision of physical and social infrastructure. The causes of allocative and technical inefficiency in the public expenditure policies of the states have been pointed out in the previous sections. One of the important reasons for the inefficiency is that proliferation of expenditure on salaries, pensions, interest payments, and subsidies has crowded out outlay on the creation and maintenance of physical infrastructure. Even in the case of social services, increasing salary expenditures have reduced technical efficiency, as the required complement of nonsalary inputs for the provision of education (books, blackboards, laboratory equipment) and health (equipment, medicine) has been crowded out. The artificial distinction between plan and nonplan expenditures has caused expenditure profligacy on the one hand, and low productivity of public expenditures on the other. Besides these, distortions in states' choices are created also by the proliferation of central-sector and centrally sponsored schemes.

For providing required standards of public services and effecting their even spread across the country, all the states should be allowed to provide a given normative bundle of public services. This does not mean that all the states should provide an identical bundle of public services. Of course, it is important to ensure that all states provide certain minimum normative standards for such high "merit good" services as basic education and healthcare. With respect to other services, the emphasis has to be on the provision of infrastructure at standards necessary to harness their resource potential.

Analysis shows a significant positive relationship of infrastructure availability with per capita NSDP (figure 6.4). This indicates that the Indian federation has failed to offset the fiscal disabilities of the states. Because the infrastructure standards in states with low per capita NSDP are lower, even when these states are resource rich, they are unable to exploit their growth potential. This does not necessarily

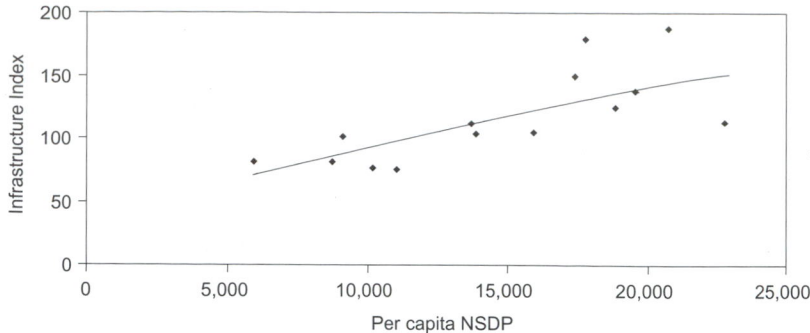

Figure 6.4
Relationship between per capital NSDP and infrastructure index. *Sources*: Infrastructure
index: Government of India (2000). Per capita NSDP: Central Statistical Organisation,
Ministry of Planning, Government of India.

mean that the low level of per capita incomes or their low growth rates
have necessarily been caused by infrastructure constraints. In fact, both
the low level of incomes and the poor state of infrastructure facilities
are consequences of shortcomings in policies, their implementation
mechanisms, and institutions.

6.5   Ten Years of Subnational Fiscal Reform and the Challenges Ahead

The last decade has seen a steady deterioration in state finances. To a
considerable extent, this deterioration has been caused by deceleration
in central transfers and spillovers of central policy on pay revision. Nor
have the states been fiscally prudent. There has been a steady deterioration in states' own tax revenues, a significant drain on states'
resources due to losses from public enterprises, and a proliferation of
implicit and explicit subsidies and transfers. Thus, despite a decade of
reforms, fiscal consolidation at the state level has remained elusive.

An additional dimension to states' finances in recent years has been
the lending by multilateral lending institutions (World Bank and ADB)
to states. Although the loans are made conditional on the states undertaking effective fiscal reforms, there will be a tendency to dilute the
conditions since the repayment liability for loans eventually lies with
the central government. Loan pushing by these lending institutions can
result in excessive borrowing by the states. Aside from the usual problems associated with loans, these loans also carry the additional foreign exchange risk. It is extremely important that an effective fiscal

reform program be put in place in order to avoid serious problems arising from excessive borrowing.

The record of fiscal conditionality at the state level has not been very encouraging. A number of states with poor fiscal performance have had to seek repeated refuge with the Ministry of Finance for bailouts from overdraft regulations after signing MOUs, the contents of which were not made public. Despite this, it was found necessary to issue a directive to the Finance Commission to link transfers with a monitorable program of reducing revenue deficits, thereby lessening the importance of those MOUs. In terms of both the size of the transfers linked to fiscal performance and its design, it is doubtful whether the new MOUs will inculcate greater fiscal discipline among the states.

Of course, there has been an increased awareness of the need to undertake fiscal reforms. To get a comprehensive picture of the state of their finances, most nonspecial category states have decided to publish their contingent liabilities. Some of the states (notably, Andhra Pradesh, Karnataka, Kerala, Maharashtra, Tamil Nadu, and Uttar Pradesh) have, in recent years, brought out White Papers to increase public awareness of their problems. Some of the states have also prepared a medium-term fiscal plan for policy institutional reforms to restore fiscal balance in the medium term of five years. Initiatives to undertake in-depth analysis and make detailed recommendations on tax reforms and administrative restructuring have been implemented in states such as Karnataka, where a Tax Reforms Commission and Administrative Reforms Commission were appointed. Some of the states are also in the process of initiating measures to legislate on the fiscal responsibility to provide legislative control over fiscal imbalances.

However, these measures have been merely cosmetic and have not been able to arrest the declining revenues and increasing revenue expenditures. The states have contained expenditures until 1997–1998 by compressing spending on the creation and maintenance of infrastructure. After the pay revision, even the pretense of containing expenditures had to be given up as the pay revision increased the expenditure-GDP ratio by 2 percentage points to destabilize state finances. The sharp increase in salary outlay has also reduced technical efficiency in social services expenditures.

Even though the new market-friendly open environment is marked by the reduced role of government, state governments will have to face the challenge of providing quality social and physical infrastructures. Providing a quality infrastructure would require a much larger expenditure allocation. In particular, increasing allocation to human development in the wake of dwindling revenues and competing demands from other services will be the most difficult challenge the states will have to face in the short and medium term. Restructuring the administrative machinery, downsizing bureaucracy and prioritizing expenditure allocation to provide quality infrastructure, and creating a business-friendly environment are the critical challenges the states face in achieving fiscal consolidation. Equally important is the need to contain expenditures on interest payments. It is important not to resort to high cost sources of borrowing through small savings schemes.

Increased provision to social sectors and physical infrastructure can be made only when the slide in the revenue-GDP ratio is reversed. The declining trend in the states' own revenue ratios since 1990–1991 has to be reversed. The states have no means to tax either the production or consumption of services, and thus increasing the tax ratio is likely to present a serious challenge to the states. The challenge is even more serious in improving the productivity of nontax revenues. In an era of fragmented polity and coalition politics, the states have found it difficult to increase user charges and fees. Measures to effect significant cost recoveries on quasi-public and private services as well as phasing out loss-making commercial public enterprises are necessary to ensure revenue productivity and reduce distortions.

Fiscal fortunes of the states are inextricably intertwined with power-sector reform. As mentioned earlier, commercial losses of the SEBs alone amounted to 1.2 percent of GDP in 2000–2001. The SEBs owed Rs. 41,473 Crore or 1.9 percent of GDP to central public-sector undertakings at the end of February 2001, consisting of 1.2 percent as principal and 0.7 percent as interest payment. Thus, improvement in SEBs would have a favorable impact on central finances as well. However, this requires significant policy and institutional changes. These include measures to improve physical productivity, reduce transmission and distribution losses, and rationalize tariffs. Despite discussions on the unbundling of electricity supply industry, privatization of generation and distribution, and measures to improve productivity, much remains to be done in terms of both designing the policy reforms and implementing them. Many states have appointed regulatory commissions, but they do not have the power and functional autonomy to determine tariffs according to long-run marginal cost (LRMC). Most regulatory commissions filled with retired bureaucrats do not have the expertise to undertake scientific studies in order to determine tariffs based on LRMC. The most important impediment to power-sector reform is political will.

Other areas of reform pertain to restructuring various state-level public enterprises. Some states have taken initiatives in this regard, but much remains to be done. Most public enterprises, even when they are of commercial nature, have accumulated losses more than their asset values. Voluntary retirement schemes (VRS) have been initiated in some states, but invariably the more productive employees take advantage of this opportunity. Moreover, the social consequences of such measures have not always been desirable, because the emphasis has been to reduce employment and not to rehabilitate the retired employees.

Micro-level reforms of the tax systems are equally important to ensure that the resources for investment in infrastructure are generated in the least distortionary manner. The states had taken initiatives to substitute the prevailing cascading type sales tax with the VAT by April 2002. Transition to VAT is necessary not only to impart efficiency to the tax system but also to enhance revenue productivity. There is, however, a real danger of this reform being implemented in a half-baked manner.

A number of conceptual and operational issues have to be resolved before making a transition to VAT. These relate to the treatment of declared goods, additional excise duty items, and, even more important, interstate sales and purchases. Besides, a destination-based comprehensive VAT is a tax on goods and services, so it is necessary to enable the states to levy taxes on services. Therefore, the Constitution should be amended to provide concurrent power of taxing services to states. The proposal to give selected services to states will create complications and distortions in the tax system and cause only a distorted VAT.

There is much to be said for sequencing sales tax reforms. Although the State Finance Ministers' Committee listed the steps in 1995, neither the states nor the central government has followed them. The first step involved in the exercise is to set the floor rates, and it was hoped that interstate competition would result in the convergence of the actual rates around the floor rates. Such a transition would have helped to achieve both simplification and harmonization of the sales tax system. Unfortunately, noncooperative games played by the states' Union Territories have imparted greater complexity and disharmony to the tax system. From this position, transition to the VAT with two rates would not be easy. Simplification of the tax system, strengthening of the administrative and enforcement machinery, introduction of a self-assessment scheme, creating a robust information system, and computerization of tax administration are important steps that would improve voluntary compliance to the tax.

Thus, the states have to traverse far in restructuring their finances. These require reforms in expenditure and tax systems, power-sector reform and restructuring state enterprises, administrative reengineering, building of a proper information system, and computerization of tax administration. What has been achieved so far has been negligible. The fiscal reform journey toward achieving fiscal balance, consolidation, generation of quality infrastructure, and a competitive environment will be long and arduous, and opposition to reforms from vested interests will be strong. Political will and administrative competence, creating an awareness of the need for reform in the general public, are the most important ingredients that will be needed in abundance to achieve the desired goals.

Appendix

Table 6A.1
Statewise fiscal imbalances: Percent of NSDP

	1990–1991		1995–1996		1999–2000	
	Revenue deficit	Fiscal deficit	Revenue deficit	Fiscal deficit	Revenue deficit	Fiscal deficit
Andhra Pradesh	0.46	2.79	1.03	3.36	2.34	5.16
Bihar	2.17	6.11	2.81	4.09	5.45	9.37
Gujarat	2.51	6.42	0.34	2.71	2.75	6.01
Haryana	0.16	3.04	1.35	3.84	3.02	5.76
Karnataka	0.33	2.30	−0.12	2.76	1.71	3.29
Kerala	2.67	5.06	1.15	3.71	3.88	5.49
Madhya Pradesh	0.62	3.17	0.83	2.85	2.93	4.45
Maharashtra	0.09	2.65	0.43	2.93	4.11	6.03
Orissa	0.19	5.98	3.38	5.85	6.24	9.35
Punjab	3.36	7.67	1.31	3.98	5.74	7.93
Rajasthan	−0.76	2.45	1.67	6.13	5.92	8.85
Tamil Nadu	1.74	3.55	0.44	1.79	3.09	4.16
Uttar Pradesh	2.16	5.39	2.29	4.28	4.68	7.24
West Bengal	3.03	4.85	1.86	4.02	6.71	9.06
Major states	1.33	4.18	1.17	3.50	4.06	6.34
Special category states	−0.40	8.04	−2.53	4.65	3.70	10.69
All states	0.93	3.30	0.73	2.60	2.94	4.75

Notes: "All states" is the aggregate of 25 states. For "Major states" and "Special category states," the estimates are ratios to NSDP new series. For "All states," it is ratio to GDP new series (1993).

Table 6A.2
Average annual growth rates of states' revenues and expenditures

	1980–1981 to 1989–1990					1990–1991 to 1999–2000				
	Own tax revenue	Own revenues	Revenue expenditure	Interest payments	Capital expenditure	Own tax revenue	Own revenues	Revenue expenditure	Interest payments	Capital expenditure
Andhra Pradesh	17.15	16.57	17.13	22.28	11.15	14.30	13.76	15.54	20.99	7.84
Bihar	14.28	19.57	16.36	21.31	10.63	11.78	10.18	10.89	11.29	6.78
Gujarat	16.05	16.34	17.90	24.70	8.13	14.92	15.51	16.56	18.51	14.77
Haryana	15.79	15.87	17.19	21.58	6.94	13.33	14.86	17.66	19.38	9.79
Karnataka	16.43	14.78	16.49	22.55	6.78	14.61	14.20	15.09	18.43	10.99
Kerala	15.97	13.33	15.68	23.77	8.92	16.98	16.61	16.62	18.53	14.44
Madhya Pradesh	16.20	14.40	16.89	23.62	6.48	14.03	12.95	14.65	17.44	4.30
Maharashtra	15.77	15.44	16.67	24.31	9.13	14.16	13.13	15.45	18.87	13.66
Orissa	16.60	12.93	14.73	22.66	12.67	12.47	12.36	15.20	18.52	7.30
Punjab	14.22	13.42	16.47	16.21	15.86	12.44	14.68	15.78	27.54	3.15
Rajasthan	17.05	14.39	17.71	20.53	7.62	15.72	13.35	15.63	20.92	12.87
Tamil Nadu	14.61	13.54	16.27	17.53	2.90	15.24	14.38	13.28	20.78	22.48
Uttar Pradesh	15.43	14.87	17.84	24.20	7.53	13.14	11.64	13.54	19.53	7.18
West Bengal	16.26	14.24	14.78	19.77	9.90	11.23	11.25	15.44	21.45	21.18
Major states	15.82	15.10	16.69	22.00	8.80	14.09	13.50	14.82	19.26	11.39
Special category states	19.36	12.99	21.14	28.06	17.00	13.79	17.30	16.12	16.03	9.42
All states	15.92	14.95	17.07	22.50	9.69	14.08	13.68	14.94	18.99	11.13

Note: Growth rates have been estimated by fitting semi-log trend equations.

Table 6A.3

Performance of state electricity boards and electricity departments: Selected indicators

State electricity board	Plant load factor (percent)	Forced outages (percent)	T & D losses (percent)	Share of agri. con-sumption (percent)	Cost of supply (paise/kwh)	Average price per unit (paise/kwh)	Commercial losses (Rs. crore).	Rate of return on capital (percent)
State electricity boards								
Andhra Pradesh	83.2	5.9	31.0	40.5	295.5	177.0	2755.2	−130.7
Assam	18.2	52.0	35.0	3.1	511.4	312.1	357.5	−31.5
Bihar	19.7	40.6	22.0	20.2	318.5	200.1	679.8	−47.9
Durgapur Projects Ltd.	24.8	49.5						
Delhi (DVB)	49.9	22.6	45.0	1.2	490.1	283.8	1209.3	−34.0
Gujarat	63.4	12.9	19.4	43.2	307.7	206.0	2577.0	−52.0
Haryana	53.0	26.3	25.0	44.7	343.1	214.7	944.3	−41.9
Karnataka	82.3	2.8	30.0	46.3	255.5	204.9	781.8	−30.9
Kerala			20.8	4.4	244.3	187.5	266.7	−9.3
Madhya Pradesh	69.4	10.6	20.5	44.9	260.8	159.9	2173.5	−55.6
Maharashtra	71.7	9.2	16.7	32.5	261.2	229.7	961.0	−10.7
Meghalaya			20.3	0.1	229.9	131.4	52.6	−24.7
Orissa	85.6	1.6	6.0		184.2	138.7	332.8	−29.5
Punjab	74.7	9.5	16.9	32.5	247.2	171.6	1304.1	−37.6
Rajasthan	82.3	3.7	22.0	36.9	334.6	194.4	1512.3	−52.6
Tamil Nadu	72.3	10.9	16.5	27.2	253.1	209.1	1227.2	−18.2
Uttar Pradesh	49.8	25.6	25.0	34.2	288.1	182.0	4154.9	−25.1
West Bengal Power Development Corporation	56.2	19.3			143.9			

West Bengal (SEB)	39.8	31.6	28.0	12.2	318.4	223.4	859.1	−66.9
All SEBs	**63.7**	**15.6**	**23.7**	**31.9**	**283.7**	**199.9**	**23027.9**	**−33.8**
Electricity departments								
Arunachal Pradesh			20.5		608.0	150.0	52.4	
Goa			24.3	1.1	283.7	280.0	4.0	
Manipur			40.0	6.0	431.5	163.0	69.0	
Mizoram			42.5		516.1	96.0	49.2	
Nagaland			28.5		393.3	189.9	28.8	
Pondicherry			13.3	9.1	177.5	167.0	12.1	
Sikkim			20.0		209.0	100.0	12.8	
Tripura			28.0	21.9	294.0	96.3	83.3	
All electricity departments			**23.5**	**6.7**	**277.6**	**186.5**	**311.5**	
All India	**67.3**	**13.1**		**31.6**	**283.6**	**199.0**	**18537.6**	

Sources: Annual Report on the Working of State Electricity Boards and Electricity Departments, Planning Commission, Government of India, June 2001.

Notes

1. Fiscal deficit is the total borrowing requirements and is defined as total expenditure minus total revenues and capital receipts. Revenue deficit is the excess of revenue expenditures over revenue receipts. Primary deficit is fiscal deficit excluding the interest payments.

2. The correlation coefficient of per capita income and growth rates for fourteen major States was 0.57. If Punjab and Haryana, the two states with a predominantly agricultural sector are excluded, the correlation coefficient is 0.87.

3. For a detailed analysis of these issues, see Rao and Singh (2002).

4. Octroi is a tax on the entry of goods into a local area for consumption, use, or sale. This is a checkpost-based levy collected at entry points into urban local bodies.

References

Acharya, Shankar. 2001. *India's Macroeconomic Management in the Nineties*. New Delhi: Indian Council of Research in International Economic Relations.

Ahluwalia, Montek. 2000. "Economic Performance of States in Post-Reforms Period." *Economic and Political Weekly* (May 6):1637–1648.

Anand, Mukesh, Amaresh Bagchi, and Tapas K. Sen. 2002. "Fiscal Discipline at the State Level: Perverse Incentives and Paths to Reform." Working Paper no. 1, January.

Bahl, Roy, W. 2002. "Implementation Rules for Fiscal Decentralization." In *Poverty, Development and Fiscal Policy, Essays in Honour of Raja Chelliah*, ed. Govinda Rao, 253–277. New Delhi: Oxford University Press.

Deshpande, R. S., and M. J. Bhende. 2001. "Volume and Composition of Subsidies in Food and Agriculture Sector." Mimeo., Institute for Social and Economic Change, Bangalore.

Gayithri, K. 2001. "Housing Subsidies in Karnataka." Mimeo., Institute for Social and Economic Change, Bangalore.

Government of India. 2000. "Report of the Finance Commission." Ministry of Finance, Government of India.

Government of India. 2001. "Approach to Tenth Five Year Plan." Planning Commission, New Delhi.

Kurian, N. J. 1999. "State Government Finances." *Economic and Political Weekly* (May 8):1115–1125.

Lahiri, Ashok. 2000. "Subnational Public Finance in India." *Economic and Political Weekly* (April 29):1539–1549.

Narayana, M. R. 2001. "Volume and Composition of Budgetary Subsidies to Higher Education in Karnataka State." Mimeo., Institute for Social and Economic Change, Bangalore.

Rajaraman, Indira, and M. J. Bhende. 1998. "A Land-Based Agricultural Presumptive Tax Designed for Levy by Panchayat." *Economic and Political Weekly* (April 4):765–778.

Raju, K. V., and H. K. Amar Nath. 2001. "Irrigation Subsidies in Karnataka: A Growing Constraint for Reforms." Mimeo., Institute for Social and Economic Change, Bangalore.

Rao, Hemlata, and H. K. Amar Nath. 2001. "A Macro View of Government Subsidies in Karnataka." Mimeo., Institute for Social and Economic Change, Bangalore.

Rao, M. Govinda. 1997. "Intergovernmental Transfers in India." In *Financing Decentralized Expenditures*, ed. Ehtisham Ahmad, 234–266. Cheltenham, UK: Edward Elgar.

Rao, M. Govinda. 2001. "Taxing Services: Issues and Strategy." *Economic and Political Weekly* (October 20):3999–4006.

Rao, M. Govinda. 2002. "Fiscal Decentralisation in Indian Federalism." In *Fiscal Decentralization in Developing Countries*, ed. Ehtisham Ahmad and Vito Tanzi, 78–114. Cheltenham, UK: Edward Elgar.

Rao, M. Govinda, and H. K. Amar Nath. 2000. "Fiscal Correction in India—Illusion and Reality." *Economic and Political Weekly* (August 5):2806–2809.

Rao, M. Govinda, and Nirvikar Singh. 2002. "Fiscal Transfers in a Developing Country— The Case of India." Paper presented at the Seminar in Comparative Federalism, University of Birmingham, January 18–19.

Rao, M. Govinda, K. P. Kalirajan, and Ric Shand. 1999. "Convergence of Incomes in Indian States—A Divergent View." *Economic and Political Weekly* (March 27–April 2):769–778.

Saleth, M. R., and G. S. Sastry. 2001. "Subsidy in Water Supply and Sanitation Sector in Karnataka: Magnitude, Effects and Policy Issues." Mimeo., Institute for Social and Economic Change, Bangalore.

Vivekananda, M. 2001. "Subsidies in Power Sector." Mimeo., Institute for Social and Economic Change, Bangalore.

IV

Poverty and Public Goods

7 Policies for Pro-Poor Growth in India

Manuela Ferro, David
Rosenblatt, and Nicholas Stern

7.1 Introduction

Economic reforms in India in recent decades have spurred economic growth and contributed to a decline in poverty. Annual per capita growth accelerated from less than 1 percent per year over the 1960s and 1970s to around 3 percent per year in the 1990s.[1] This implied about a one-third increase in consumption per capita over the last decade and a 5 to 10 percentage point reduction in national poverty rates, depending on the methodology followed.[2] The acceleration of economic growth represents an important achievement, and given that one-third of the world's poor live in India, it is an achievement of real significance for world poverty.[3] Policy reforms have played a key role in this progress.

Despite this progress, millions of India's citizens still live in poverty; India cannot relax efforts to provide more opportunities for its poor. There are lessons from the recent experience in India and elsewhere that can guide policies and actions to accelerate growth and poverty reduction in India. There is great potential that could be released by stronger reforms.

The main contribution of this chapter is a strategic policy framework for identifying and organizing those policies that can accelerate poverty reduction in India in the next decade. This framework rests on two pillars: policies for improving the *investment climate* to accelerate growth, and policies for *empowering* poor people to participate in and benefit from this growth. The investment climate embodies the "policy, institutional and behavioral environment, both present and expected, that influences the returns and risks associated with investment."[4] In speaking of empowerment, we are referring to the ability of people to shape their own lives. Thus, it is a process that enables people to participate in and benefit from economic growth. This pillar embodies traditional notions of human capital development but also includes individuals' ability to influence the public policies that affect them, their ability to build and protect their assets, and their ability to gain access to public and private resources and services. The second pillar embodies policies that not only enable growth in incomes (i.e., means), but also contribute directly to the end goal of expansion of individual choice. Before turning to the specific policies grouped under each of these pillars, we present a survey of recent performance. This survey establishes some empirical regularities to guide the policy priorities within the investment climate and empowerment framework.

Empirical studies (Ravallion and Datt 1998a, 2002; Sundaram and Tendulkar 2002; Deaton 2002) presented at a January 2002 workshop on Poverty Measurement, Monitoring and Evaluation in India highlight five key statistical regularities that provide an initial basis for evaluating the policy priorities for future pro-poor growth.

First, economic growth has been a leading determinant of poverty reduction. Figure 7.1 provides the decade-by-decade progress in economic growth and poverty reduction.[5] Most of the reduction in poverty in the recent period has been a result of the increase in average consumption driven by economic growth (Deaton and Dreze 2002). Econometric analysis (Ravallion and Datt 1998a, 2002) using twenty-three surveys in the 1958–1991 period and private consumption per capita data from the national accounts reveal an elasticity of -1.2 (regressing the log of the headcount poverty index against the log of private consumption per capita). Cross-country studies on the relationship between growth and poverty reduction provide additional evidence on the key role of growth (Ravallion 2001). Clearly, policies that enhance overall economic growth will be key levers to improving the incomes of poor people in India. However, there are important disaggregations for state, rural-urban, and sources of growth (see figure 7.1).

Second, there has been a divergence in poverty reduction across Indian states (figure 7.2). Poorer northern states (Bihar, Madhya Pradesh, Rajasthan, Uttar Pradesh, and Orissa) have lagged behind the other major states in lowering poverty incidence over the last two decades. As noted by Deaton and Dreze (2002), the states with the poorest initial conditions grew more slowly than the rest, resulting in an increase in inequality across regions. One part of the explanation is that regional

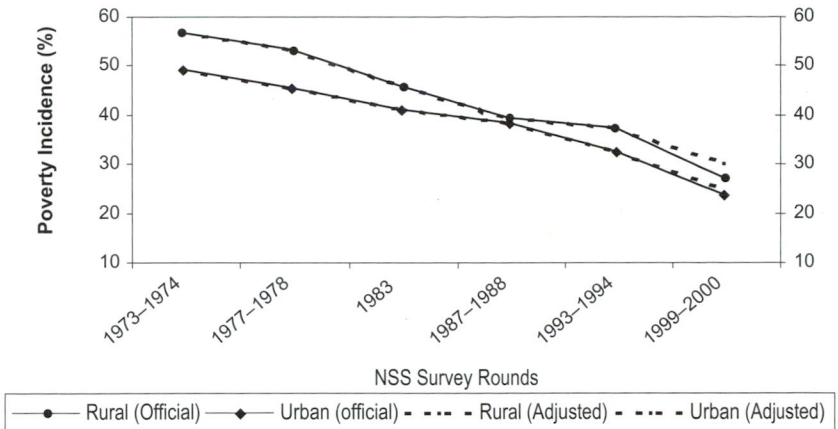

Figure 7.1
Aggregate poverty reduction in India. All-India trends in poverty, 1970s through 2000.
Sources: Official estimates: Government of India. Adjusted estimates: Deaton (2002).

Poverty Incidence

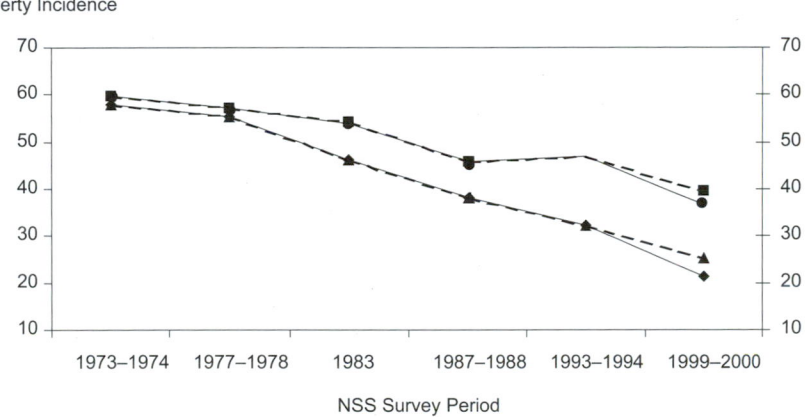

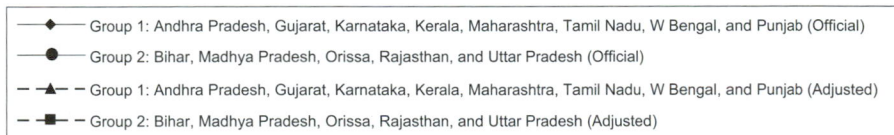

Figure 7.2
Regional variation in poverty reduction. Progress at reducing poverty: North/central states versus other major states. *Sources:* See figure 7.1.

economic growth has been slower in the poorer northern states, leading to an increased concentration of poverty in the north. Recent research by the World Bank and the Confederation of Indian Industry reveals that a weaker investment climate in lagging states may be behind this slower growth, as will be discussed in more detail.

Third, the sectoral and urban-rural composition of growth has had an impact on the poverty-reducing power of economic growth (Ravallion and Datt 1998a, 2002). Growth in average consumption in rural areas has had a greater impact than growth in urban areas in terms of reducing aggregate poverty incidence.

Fourth, agricultural productivity is a primary determinant of poverty reduction in rural areas. Ravallion and Datt (1998b) have shown that in the 1958–1994 period, agricultural productivity growth has played a significant role in reducing poverty, directly via higher farm yields to small producers and higher real wages to agricultural laborers. However, as noted in Deaton and Dreze (2002), the growth of real agricultural wages decelerated during the mid- and late 1990s.[6]

Fifth, nonfarm growth has been complementary to agricultural productivity's contribution to poverty reduction. In addition, the impact of nonfarm growth on poverty reduction has varied strongly across states in India, depending upon the initial human resource levels of the states, the degree of rural-urban disparities, and the extent of landlessness in rural areas (Ravallion and Datt 2001).

These empirical regularities provide us with valuable insights on how current and future policies should be designed to enhance pro-poor growth in India. Policies that foster overall economic growth have the greatest potential for reducing poverty further. In particular, policies that can accelerate economic growth in the poorer northern states, where poverty is increasingly concentrated, will be key to reducing poverty in India. Increases in agricultural productivity and nonfarm growth, brought about by a more conducive investment climate for small- and medium-scale firms, can continue to be the engine of growth and poverty reduction. In the sections that follow, policy priorities for India are established by devising a strategic policy framework, informed by the microlevel evidence discussed earlier.

The challenge is to build on past achievements and lessons learned and to accelerate the progress of recent decades. It can be done. Other countries, like China, have managed to set in place market-oriented reforms that have accelerated dramatically both growth and poverty reduction.

7.2   Policies for Pro-Poor Growth: The Twin Pillars of Investment Climate and Empowerment

We have seen the importance of growth for poverty reduction. How can we promote growth in which poor people are able to participate—in other words, pro-poor growth? A strategic policy framework for pro-poor growth can be built upon the twin pillars of improving the investment climate to accelerate growth and empowering poor people to contribute to and benefit from this growth. The investment climate is concerned with the factors that determine the level of current investment, as well as the productivity of existing investments and the stability of those returns over the medium term. In other words, it is the climate for entrepreneurship. As such, the investment climate necessarily involves institutions, rules, and governance as well as traditional questions of fiscal policy, public expenditure management, and taxation. In this way, it is an analytical framework that draws on concepts from both the traditional public finance literature and modern institutional economics. The "climate" implies this generality, but it also implies the externalities or economies of scale that can occur as the conditions for investment improve. In this sense, the framework also draws on concepts from contemporary growth theory and the earlier work of Hirschman and Schumpeter. It should be noted that the role of small and medium-sized enterprises is critical. If the investment climate is improved for small and medium companies, it is likely that larger firms will benefit as well.

Within the realm of the investment climate, one can organize the policies and institutional arrangements around three broad categories: (1) macroeconomic stability and openness; (2) economic governance and institutions, including both the implementation of efficiency-enhancing regulation and the elimination of regulations that lead to waste and rent-seeking behavior; and (3) infrastructure.

This analytical framework has inspired empirical research that begins with firm-level surveys. The surveys collect information on the regulatory requirements facing firms and the costs and productivity of those firms. One such survey was completed for a number of Indian states in 2001, and we draw here on the results to distinguish some of the priority areas for policy reforms to enhance pro-poor growth.

By "empowerment," we mean the ability of people to shape their own lives. Empowerment is the process that enables people to contribute to, and participate in, economic growth. Traditional notions of human capital development—notably education and health—are included in this process, as is individuals' ability to influence the public policies that affect them, to build and protect their assets, and to gain access to public and private resources and services.

7.3 Policy Priorities for Improving the Investment Climate

Macroeconomic conditions, economic governance, and infrastructure interact to determine the investment climate. A review of recent Indian economic history can contribute to our understanding of how these factors determine growth and poverty reduction. In addition, new evidence has been compiled, at the microlevel, on the relative importance of the various elements of the investment climate in determining both growth and the growth elasticity of poverty reduction. The evidence that follows establishes that an improvement in India's investment climate has been a key cause of stronger economic growth over the past decade. However, the investment climate remains weak, and further improvements are necessary if the growth process is to be sustained.

7.3.1 Macroeconomic Conditions
To invest and to secure adequate returns on their investments, firms need to have some confidence in the dimension and scope of the domestic and foreign markets to which they plan to sell their goods. They need to have continued and stable access to inputs—whether imported or produced domestically. Unstable macroeconomic conditions—often resulting from unsustainable fiscal positions which in turn often have structural roots—undermine firms' ability to make production decisions and engage in production. Equally important to these processes is maintaining open trade both across domestic regions and overseas.

7.3.2 Macrostability
India has made great progress in establishing more stable and positive macroeconomic performance during the 1990s. There is a well-known theoretical and empirical literature that links growth and macroeconomic stability. Fischer (1993) and others have found strong evidence that macroeconomic instability, and in particular high inflation, reduce growth. India has done relatively well in this regard, with inflation averaging about 9 percent over the past two decades, with two peak episodes of higher inflation in 1981 and 1991. It should be noted, however, that even regional differences in inflation rates within India have

been found to be positively associated with higher poverty rates (Ravallion and Datt 1998a). The current low interest rates keep the overall debt burden of the state manageable.

However, maintaining fairly low inflation and interest rates into the future may prove more difficult. India's fiscal deficits have been increasing sharply during the last several years, and so has the stock of public debt. The public-sector deficit-to-GDP ratio has averaged 10 percent per year between 1988–1989 and 2001–2002, and public-sector debt has reached 91 percent of GDP in 2001–2002.[7] Across the developing world in the post–World War II period, rarely has any country managed to incur such large deficits for so long without encountering a macroeconomic crisis, in the form of either a balance-of-payments problem, a debt crisis, or bouts of high inflation.[8] India, with its relatively closed capital account, large and increasing private savings rate, high economic growth rate, significant use of quasi-fiscal activities such as seigniorage and financial repression, and due to careful management of and a favorable position in its external sector, has so far managed to avoid the macroeconomic pitfalls that are known to follow periods of persistently high fiscal deficits.

Macrostability depends on monetary and exchange-rate policies as well as fiscal policies. The greatest threat to India's hard-earned macrostability is clearly on the fiscal front, which we discuss in some detail. The focus of our discussion is on four areas: (1) revenue performance; (2) state-level fiscal imbalances; (3) subsidies and off-budget deficits in the power sector; and (4) off-budget deficits associated with the banking system.

India's tax system performs poorly in mobilizing revenue on a scale that meets expenditure. India's ratio of combined center-states tax to GDP is around 14–15 percent—a relatively low level by international standards. India's public sector will both need to generate more revenues and combat waste in expenditures if it is to face the challenge of effective expansion in the delivery of social-sector services. The important challenge of mobilizing resources by eliminating waste and misdirected subsidies on the expenditure side is discussed in more detail later. India's high fiscal deficits have been sustained in recent years without an exploding debt-to-GDP ratio by a favorable interest-rate/growth-rate differential. It would be dangerous to take the continuation of this differential for granted.

The main features of India's current tax system that negatively impact the investment climate are (i) bureaucratic harassment; (ii) limited revenue mobilization leading to fiscal deficits that crowd out private investment; (iii) inadequate revenues for financing human development, social protection, and infrastructure; and (iv) basic distortions from overtaxing a narrow base. Over the medium term, improvements in both tax policy and administration will be critical for improving the investment climate.

It should be noted that the primary role of taxation should be to finance government expenditures, not redistribution. Efforts to redistribute via the tax system often prove to be unproductive. Meanwhile, properly administered expenditure programs—including social safety nets—can be highly effective means of redistribution. Lakin (2001) provides evidence of the distributive impacts of taxation and expenditure in the United Kingdom. The evidence clearly shows the minimal impact of the tax code, and the dramatic impact of government expenditures in reducing income inequality.

In the short run, improving tax collection will have to rely on improved administration. The microeconomic structure of taxation in India is burdensome, distortionary and inefficient. In fact, the fundamentals of India's tax structure have changed little since the Government of India Act of 1935. This act established the basic assignments of revenues and responsibilities of the center and the states, which were subsequently embodied in the Indian constitution of 1947.

In terms of the relative importance of sources of revenue, there have been important changes. Revenue from taxes that are not shared between states and central government have grown faster than those that are shared. Services, now the fastest growing sector of the economy, are virtually left out of the tax base. Much of the tax burden currently falls on industrial firms. In the medium term, therefore, reforms to modernize both tax policy and administration will need to be implemented. In many ways, many of the recommendations in Chelliah (1992) remain valid and are being implemented today.

The planned introduction of the value-added tax (VAT), a robust and efficient tax instrument, has the potential to boost revenue. In particular, it is the most potent instrument for taxing services. Unless it is implemented in an effective way, the structural shift to services in the economy, a natural and desirable feature of growth, will undermine revenue growth over the foreseeable future. We note that the introduction of VAT in a federal context, such as India, however, poses additional problems; it thus requires careful preparation for its introduction to be successful and well received by the public (Chelliah 1992; Burgess and Stern 1993). There are very valuable analysis and policy recommendations in the recent report of the committee chaired by Govinda Rao.

Roughly 45 percent of the consolidated public-sector deficit in recent years has been attributable to state governments. Over the 1990s, the fiscal deficit of state governments increased from around 3 percent of GDP in 1990–1991 to over 4 percent in 2000–2001. There has been a secular deterioration in the revenue deficit, which had started already in the 1980s. What has changed over the 1990s? First, higher interest rates in the early 1990s, and the accumulation of domestic debt in the late 1990s, led to an increase in the interest burden. Second, the salary burden increased dramatically, going from 5.4 to 6.8 percent of GDP between 1996–1997 and 1999–2000. At least part of this increase can be attributed to state governments' adoption of the recommendations of the Fifth Pay Commission. Continued increases in the Dearness Allowance have compounded the problem. If left unchecked, this continued expansion of the wage bill will translate into an expanding pension liability. Third, the efficiency of the current taxation system, of both policy and administration, has been declining. There is a real fiscal crisis in the making at the state level.

Those state governments that are spending more than their entire revenue on salaries, pensions, and interest payments, will certainly be severely limited in addressing poverty reduction. As N. C. Saxena stated at the November 2000 States' Forum in Delhi: "There are doctors, but there are no medicines; there are engineers, but there are no funds for construction and maintenance; there are teachers, but there are not enough school buildings." Indeed, governments in such situations may start to resemble employment agencies rather than institutions for the promotion of development or poverty reduction.

India's fiscal situation is actually worse if one includes the full impact of off-budget power deficits and off-budget borrowing at the state level. Poor performance of large public enterprises, in particular power utilities and public financial institutions, is likely to continue to translate into increased fiscal pressures in the near future. Today, combined state utility financial losses are estimated at approximately Rs. 260 billion, somewhat more than US$5 billion a year. Central to this problem is the power sector. To put these losses into perspective, Rs. 260 billion is half of what all the state governments in India combined are spending on all levels of education every year, and three times what they are spending on water supply. If current trends continue, in another three years state utility financial losses will reach Rs. 450 billion per year.

Power-sector losses are funded by various government agencies. State governments pay part of the bill, through budgetary subsidies. Utilities borrow some of the rest, but often do not pay their bills. The latest estimate of state power utility arrears to central government power utilities is Rs. 420 billion. Power-sector losses are placing massive stress on virtually all state governments. They also threaten the financial health of central utilities and of the financial institutions that fund the sector.

Another source of pressure on India's public finances is the banking system. Over the past decade, for instance, the Indian government—as the largest shareholder in the banking system—has allocated significant resources, an estimated Rs. 180 billion, to recapitalize ailing public-sector banks and fend off insolvency. This effort notwithstanding, the capital position of many public-sector banks remains weak.

So far, India's increasing fiscal deficits have not led to large external imbalances and pressures on its international reserves, as they did in the 1980s and early 1990s, when both the fiscal situation and the current account of the balance of payments deteriorated sharply. The fiscal imbalances have had, however, damaging effects on private investment and on growth. In fact, a substantial portion of the increase in private savings—which grew from 20 to 23.5 percent of GDP between 1992–1993 and 1999–2000—has been absorbed to finance the fiscal deficit. Public investment, on the other hand, is being crowded out by mounting recurrent expenditures on wages and operating losses of public enterprises. The fiscal deterioration we are witnessing today most likely has had and will have a negative impact on growth.

In response to this fragility, some positive steps have been taken toward reversing the current fiscal threats. Fiscal Responsibility legislation at the central level of government has been tabled in the Parliament (although the 2002–2003 budget has not made a reference to it). Enactment and observance of this legislation could help bring the central government deficit down. Simple and clear rules, like expenditure freezes, can be a transparent and effective way to achieve fiscal adjustment. Multiyear fiscal targets and multiyear budgeting could serve not only to assist aggregate fiscal outcomes, but also to improve the quality of expenditures. Another tool that has been effectively employed in other countries has been automatic adjustment mechanisms requiring policy changes midyear when partial year results deviate from fiscal targets. When coupled with similar efforts at the state level, especially for the larger states, this legislation could help reduce the risks of macroeconomic instability and lower pressure on interest rates. The fiscal targets could be reinforced, if loopholes to hard budget constraints via inappropriate or ad hoc transfers or intergovernmental lending are closed as well. Establishing fiscal institutions based on medium-term rules and targets would enhance fiscal stability and thus help improve the investment climate in India.

There are initiatives and active discussions of measures for hardening the budget constraint of public utilities—namely, state power utilities—by restricting their ability to accumulate arrears to central utilities and suppliers. Other recent initiatives of the government, such as the "incentivization" of state-level reforms through the Fiscal Reform Facility or the Accelerated Power Development and Reform Program, may encourage improved fiscal performance at the state level. Even though the amounts involved are relatively small compared to the size of state budgets, these initiatives could go a long way in encouraging more sustainable fiscal policies at the state level. The process begins by first improving the quality of fiscal reporting to include public enterprises in the consolidated fiscal deficit. Then one can establish fiscal rules for the broader deficit concept. Karnataka is one state that is advancing along these lines.

In addition, there appears to be renewed impetus toward divestment of state ownership in large enterprises, which will create space for more efficient, improved service delivery—namely, in transportation—and lower pressures on public finances. There also appears to be increased awareness and support for the need to reform the power sector, an issue that we return to in the discussion of infrastructure.

7.3.3 Trade

Increased trade integration into the world economy has created great opportunities for India. A lesson of development experience is that rapid overall economic growth depends on rapid export growth. The strategy of inward-oriented development, in which exports are not encouraged because imports are kept to a minimum, proved to be ineffective everywhere, even in the most populous countries such as Brazil, China, India, and the former Soviet Union (Bajpai and Sachs 1998). Indeed, much of the rapid growth of the past decade in India was due to economy-wide macrolevel reforms, reforms that accelerated the transformation from a state-led, inward-oriented economy into a more market-oriented and open one. But further increases in the productivity of Indian firms will require other changes at the institutional and microlevel, as well as further opening of the economy. A number of studies—most recently, Frankel and Romer (1999), Dollar

Table 7.1
Foreign direct investment: India and selected countries

	1995	1996	1997	1998	1999	2000
India	2,144	2,426	3,577	2,635	2,169	2,315
China	35,849	40,180	44,237	43,751	38,753	38,399
Malaysia	4,178	5,078	5,137	2,163	3,895	3,788
Philippines	1,478	1,517	1,222	2,287	573	2,029
Thailand	2,068	2,336	3,895	7,315	6,213	3,366
Brazil	4,859	11,200	19,650	31,913	28,576	32,779

Source: IMF International Finance Statistics.
Note: US$ million.

and Kraay (2001), and World Bank (2002a)—find that openness to trade and direct foreign investment accelerate growth, because such openness encourages innovation and productivity gains. India's overall high tariff rates, especially on intermediate products that are used by exporters, impose a heavy indirect tax on export competitiveness (Bajpai and Sachs 1998). The proposed reductions in maximum import duties from 35 to 30 percent and the establishment of a plan to simplify the existing four custom slabs to two by 2004—with a minimum of 10 percent for raw materials and intermediate goods and a maximum of 20 percent for final products—represent a step in the right direction for India's trade regime. Continuing the process of opening the economy to the world is one of the challenges and opportunities for public policy in India.

7.3.4   Foreign Investment
While China's export-led growth strategy was based on core policy and economic management decisions that invited foreign investors to provide the capital and expertise to achieve export competitiveness in a wide range of sectors, India's policies toward foreign direct investment (FDI) have been more ambivalent. On the one hand, the government promotes FDI; on the other, it maintains significant regulations against full foreign ownership, or insists on lengthy approval processes (table 7.1).

7.3.5   Economic Governance
Governments need to regulate firms in all market economies. Regulating pollution emissions, curbing monopolistic practices, ensuring worker safety—these are all legitimate and important roles of the government. But in India the more critical issues are the extent and nature

of regulation, its effectiveness and transparency, and the opportunities for corruption it provides. A business environment survey carried out by the World Bank in a large number of countries revealed that managers reported spending 5 percent of their time dealing with government officials in Latin American countries, and about twice that in the transition economies of Eastern Europe. In India, the average share of managers' time spent dealing with bureaucracy was 16 percent (World Bank 2000).

Despite this sobering assessment, if one recalls the situation of the early 1980s, there have been improvements. A study on the role of law and legal institutions in economic development in India (Anant and Mitra 1998) attributes part of the productivity increases of the 1990s to the delicensing of thirty-two groups of industries in 1985, followed by the elimination of licensing in all but twenty-six industries. But the regulatory and administrative burdens on businesses remain high, restricting both the growth of existing businesses and the start of new businesses, in several areas of potential comparative advantage for India. Excessive regulation of industrial relations is often singled out as an important reason why India is not doing as well as it should in terms of export growth (Sachs, Varshney, and Bajpai 1999). These areas of regulation are important, because much of the productivity growth that comes from a more open and competitive economy comes from the movement of capital and labor from less productive to more productive activities, and in particular to new firms. For instance, garments, toys, shoes, and leather products continue to be reserved, to a varying extent, for small-scale producers. Such restrictions virtually assure China's dominance in these sectors, compared with India. Entry and exit regulations impose high costs on firms in India and may also help explain the high level of productivity dispersion observed across firms in India. Dispersion levels are comparable to Indonesia's, more than double Malaysia's, and triple the Republic of Korea's. Well-known examples of barriers to exit include India's bankruptcy and liquidation procedures, with recent estimates showing that over 60 percent of liquidation cases before the High Courts have been in process for more than ten years (Mathur 1993).

Two other examples are key. One is the restrictive nature of labor regulations in India, which imposes high costs on firms, especially small- and medium-scale firms. The result is that formal-sector firms (those that are registered and pay taxes) are reluctant to create additional jobs. India's restrictive labor regulations thus result in a large pool of laborers in the informal sector, employed in small, tax-evading enterprises. The 2002–2003 budget announced reforms to the labor legislation, which would reduce the regulatory and administrative burden on small and medium enterprises. Progress in this area is important, since it would eliminate the need for small and medium firms to obtain government approval before exit or retrenchment is announced. A more flexible labor market could have an important positive effect on employment creation, including off-farm jobs in rural areas.

The other example has to do with the delays in having goods cleared by customs, which act as another "tax" on firms. In India, it takes 50 percent longer to clear goods from customs than it does in the Republic of Korea and Thailand. There is also a large variance in the time spent in clearing goods, adding to uncertainty. Numerous other examples exist across India. We would like to underscore here that the issue is not whether or not to regulate, but whether such regulations serve the public interest and are implemented efficiently, without harassment and corruption.

Finally, as mentioned earlier, the tax system itself creates additional bureaucratic harassment that inhibits investment. Better tax administration also would serve to improve the investment climate.

Such barriers pose a particular problem for *small and medium-sized firms*, since they tend to have less developed political contacts for overcoming these barriers, and the fixed start-up costs are more difficult to finance, relative to larger firms. This has an important effect on employment, including off-farm employment in rural areas. There are some positive signs that deregulation in agricultural markets, fundamental for increased efficiency in agricultural production, may be forthcoming. The 2002–2003 budget, for instance, signals the government's willingness to advance with significant decontrol and deregulation of agricultural products to create a country-wide integrated market for agricultural products.

It should be noted that these regulatory issues are not just federal government responsibilities. They also involve regulations imposed by state and local governments. These are sometimes even more problematic in terms of burden and harassment than are federal regulations. At the end of section 7.3.6, we present some evidence on how state policies have resulted in differential economic outcomes across states.

7.3.6   Infrastructure
Under the rubric of infrastructure are the state of power supply, telecommunications services, transport, and water supply. Of these, power

supply is viewed by many, and with good reason, as by far the strongest and most widespread bottleneck to investment and growth of the nonfarm sector in India at the moment. The state of power supply affects agricultural activities too. Access to reliable power at reasonable cost is a prime concern for most manufacturing firms and is critical to improving productivity of businesses in India. Industry in India suffers doubly from poor power-sector policies: It receives low-quality power and is forced to pay tariffs above cost to cross-subsidize residential and agricultural consumers. First, because of the poor supply of power they receive, firms are often forced to purchase and run their own power generator, an activity that inevitably increases business costs, especially for small- and medium-scale firms. Second, they face among the highest industrial power tariffs in the world (Rs. 4 to 5 per kWh or US7–10 cents in India, versus 6–7 cents in Western Europe, 3–4 cents in China, or 6–7 cents in Brazil-Thailand-Bolivia). Third, variable voltage in the power supply can damage telephone equipment or irrigation pumps. In addition, farmers often leave the supply on at night—to get whatever energy might be available—leading to occasional flooding, waste of water and energy, and soil erosion. The main reasons behind the poor financial and technical performance of power utilities include inadequate tariffs for nonindustrial consumers and excessive losses, a large part of which is due to weaknesses in metering, billing, and collection and to outright theft. Reforms in this sector are urgent.

India's northern states, where poverty reduction and growth have been lowest, suffer from shortfalls in every infrastructure dimension. This is especially true in rural areas, where water, power, telecommunications, and roads are generally provided without cost, or at least with a heavy subsidy, and as a result are almost not provided at all. State governments are the main actors in infrastructure in India, and it would be difficult to overemphasize the urgency of infrastructure reforms, particularly in these states, if poverty reduction is to accelerate in these heavily populated states. Rural India needs clean water and basic health services, as well as reliable infrastructure supplied at prices increasingly nearer commercial prices rather than provided for free.

7.3.7 Human Capital Development

Education, health, and social protection programs cut across both pillars of investment climate and empowerment. In India, states are responsible for much of the delivery of these services, creating a natural experiment for measuring the impact of these policies in affecting pro-poor growth. Research by Ravallion and Datt (2001) has demonstrated that states with lower literacy and poorer health status in India have experienced a lower impact on poverty reduction per percentage point increase in nonfarm output. Part of the investment climate involves the ability to locate and recruit capable and healthy workers. As we discuss in more detail later in this chapter, institutions that allow more direct public participation in administering resources—for example, parent participation in school programs—can have a strong impact on the quality of human capital investment.

National social safety net programs include the Public Distribution System (PDS) (costing Indian taxpayers about 0.5 percent of GDP), Integrated Child Development Services, employment guarantee schemes, the integrated rural development program, and other social welfare programs targeted for the elderly, disabled, or other particular circumstances. Most of these programs involve state governments in their implementation. While efforts could be made to improve the effectiveness of many of these programs, I focus here on the PDS.

Problems with the PDS as a social protection instrument have been well known for some time. Mired in administrative problems, it has been costly, and its targeting—both at the national and state levels— often has been faulty.[9] A more effective basis for social protection could be constructed through targeted income transfer programs that could be comprised of either cash transfers or food vouchers, or some combination of the two. Some states are experimenting with vouchers, and it seems that some states are also now starting to improve targeting techniques for these programs. Targeted social programs can also be used to address "demand-side" problems in the social sectors—for example, how to keep children in school once the schools are built and staffed. Other countries have been successful in conditioning transfers on school attendance and other social objectives (e.g., *Bolsa Escola* in Brazil and *Progresa* in Mexico). These are cases that show how specific antipoverty programs in developing countries, if run well, can contribute to the reduction of poverty. However, one must recognize that in a country as poor as India, and with such weak tax collections, income transfers may play a smaller part in redistribution than they can in richer countries with better developed tax systems and administration for transfers. Nevertheless they can be very important for providing relief in extreme circumstances, such as natural disasters; they do have a potential in education and health incentive systems; and well-targeted systems do have a role to play in helping very poor people.

7.3.8   The Impact of the Investment Climate: Research on Indian States

Businesses and individuals engaging in economic activities in any Indian state face certain common factors in the investment climate, and more particularly the macroeconomic and national elements—for example, exchange rates, banking system regulation, external trade policy, and national infrastructure. However, as mentioned earlier, states also have an important role to play in local regulations, the administration of state-level infrastructure (including power-sector issues), policies for human capital development, and state taxes and fees. As a result, the federal structure of India allows us to study the impact of the investment climate on economic decisions and the resulting economic growth in a way that can yield specific lessons for poverty reduction.

There is a strong correlation between indicators of investment climate and productivity. A World Bank team, in conjunction with the Confederation of Indian Industry (CII), conducted a large-scale survey of about 1,400 firms from eight tradable goods sectors in ten states to assess the impact of the investment climate. The survey found that West Bengal, Kerala, and Uttar Pradesh (UP) had rather poor investment climates compared to states such as Tamil Nadu, Maharashtra, Karnataka, and Andhra Pradesh (AP). This was reflected in variables such as the reliability of the power supply, the number of times per month that factories are visited by government officials, and Internet connectivity. For example, the number of visits by government officials per month was twice as high in UP as in AP. In states such as AP and Tamil Nadu, the typical small firm was using the Internet to communicate with suppliers and customers.

This study reveals the importance of the investment climate. The firms in the good climate states have been investing more and growing faster, and the aggregate performance of these states has been better than in the poor climate states. For example, firms in poor investment climate states produced, on average, 44 percent less value added per worker than firms in good investment climate states. In the 1990s the good climate states grew at 5 percent per capita while the poor climate states grew at 3 percent, and there was faster poverty reduction in the good climate states as well.

A research team at the World Bank has just finished a similar survey in China, and preliminary data indicate that the investment climate in China's flagship locations—Shanghai, Guangzhou—is quite good at the microlevel. The results show that, in both Indian states and Chinese provinces, the investment climate has a strong impact on productivity growth and on both domestic and foreign investment. A number of Indian states have been fairly successful at attracting foreign investment. Even the better performing states, however, could grow faster if their state governments and the central government were to enact the reforms to improve their investment climate.

There is little doubt that India's weak investment climate has prevented it from fulfilling its vast potential. Its growth rate, while increasing in recent years, remains way below that of China. As the joint World Bank-CII study has established, India's low-cost advantage relative to other countries is whittled away by higher effective costs of power, interest rates, bureaucratic harassment, and regulatory hurdles. The low level of FDI into India is a signal of the importance of tackling problems in the investment climate.

7.3.9 Microevidence and Policy Priorities

Returning to the empirical regularities discussed in the first section, one can draw some tentative conclusions based on the earlier discussion of the investment climate. The empirical surveys and econometric evidence on investment climate variables add one policy dimension to the more aggregate regressions discussed in section 7.1.

Clearly, growth itself will be a necessary condition for poverty reduction. On a macrolevel, fiscal imbalances must be addressed to avoid an inflationary bias and potential future economic crises. So far, the impact of these imbalances primarily has been via depressed investment levels. In addition, evidence from states across India reveals that growth has varied widely, and an important part of this variation is determined by differences in the investment climate across states.

Second, there is a broad agenda for improving the general rural economy—both in terms of agricultural productivity and nonfarm business development. Here again, investment climate variables play a key role: They remove the bureaucratic barriers to small business creation and agricultural innovation, establish the infrastructure links at the "border" between the rural and urban economies, and provide the basic human skills and basic health conditions for the workforce.

7.4 Policy Priorities to Empower Poor People

The fight against poverty in India cannot be waged through an improved investment climate alone. Growth will be more pro-poor if poor people have a higher level of human capital and an opportunity to shape the decisions that affect their lives.

Some of the human capital issues discussed here also form a vital link between the "investment climate" and "empowerment." Basic education and health standards form a key part of the investment climate, as firms require workers with basic skills and physical health. These skill requirements tend to increase as countries advance. So both poor groups' participation in growth and the changing demands emerging from the private sector require a dynamic response from the government in promoting the development of human capital. Both improving governance and changing the role of the state to refocus its activities on core services can serve the dual purposes of improving the investment climate and empowering the poorer segments of society.

The people themselves can be more active and effective in fostering reform of the state, if the government provides them with the information—qualitative and quantitative data—with which to form opinions and enforce accountability. Better information both makes the government more accountable to the people and assists in the design and implementation of social programs.

7.4.1 Education

India has made substantial progress in basic education over the past decade. One key result has been an increase in literacy from 52 percent to 65 percent over the 1991–2001 period. And the gender composition of these gains is of great importance: Men's literacy rose from 64 to 76 percent, while women's literacy rose from 39 to 54 percent (Census of India 2001). The first step in this process has been to keep children in school. Enrollment rates at the primary level have increased substantially during the 1990s, especially for girls. Programs like the District Primary Education Programme (DPEP) probably have played an important role by targeting districts with low female literacy rates. In UP, for instance, with the backing of a supportive state policy, efforts have been simultaneously directed at the community and the school system to create a favorable environment for girls' education, with community participation in governance playing an important role.

India, however, has much ground to cover to catch up with other Asian countries in education indicators. China, Indonesia, and Sri Lanka all have higher literacy rates. Furthermore, literacy is an aggregate indicator, and behind the aggregates is great inequality in access to and quality of public education. It is well known that India's elite groups are among the most educated people in the world. The challenge for the Indian public sector is to raise standards for other groups and substantially reduce the education gap between rich and poor and between urban and rural populations and to eliminate the gender gap. Enrollment for children of the poorest families (per capita income less than Rs. 3,000) is 25 percentage points below the richest households (per capita income greater than Rs. 10,000). Education is of increasing importance, given the growth of nonfarm employment, which now provides 40 percent or more of rural incomes.

7.4.2   Health

Health outcomes have improved over the last twenty years. This is reflected in the fact that life expectancy increased from 50 to 61 years over the 1970–1993 period. Infant mortality declined from 137 to 74 per 1,000 live births over the same period, and to 65 per 1,000 by 1996. However, the latter figure is about twice the level recorded in China.[10] Maternal mortality, although declining, remains stubbornly high, particularly in the poorer northern states of India. Another somber statistic is the fact that approximately half of all children below four years of age continue to suffer from severe or moderate malnutrition.[11] In addition, even though India has been fighting the spread of HIV/AIDS for over a decade now, the country already has the largest number of infected people of any country in the world with recent estimates of approximately 4 million cases—more than any country in the world except South Africa.

Both health and education shares of total government expenditures are somewhat low by international standards. This may be partly, but directly, attributed to some of the spending on power and other economic subsidies that (1) create open-ended fiscal demands; (2) lack transparency in the budgetary process; (3) lack adequate targeting to poor people; and (4) generate large economic distortions. Once again, we see a reemerging theme of the changing role of the state and the need to improve governance and focus government activities. In addition, regulatory issues overlap our previous investment climate discussion. For example, there have been problems in recent years with a lack of regulation of the quality of private-sector providers of health services. This is a particular concern since the majority of poor people often seek medical care from private-sector providers to supplement or complement weak or absent public-sector health care.

Research by Ravallion and Datt (2001) has demonstrated that states with lower literacy and poorer health status in India have experienced a lower impact on poverty reduction per percentage point increase in nonfarm output. Both growth and inclusion matter for poverty reduction.

7.4.3   Data for Empowerment and Improved Social Programs

Data constitute a key input for two reasons. One reason is the practical issue of monitoring the performance of social programs with an eye to improving their administration and design. A second is that knowledge empowers—power that comes from the general public's improved understanding of how social programs function and in what areas are the greatest social needs.

As the role of the state in India has changed, so has the demand for the type of statistical information required for policy analysis and design. With programs that involve less central planning, the new emphasis is on monitoring and evaluating economic and social performance and the effectiveness of overall policies and specific programs during and after implementation. This allows assessment of both the general direction of economic policies and the specifics of program design and administration. This implies improvements to the overall statistical system from data collection to processing and final dissemination, including both the timeliness and accuracy of information and the public's access to that information.

In particular, to have adequate knowledge of living conditions, household surveys should be strengthened, to improve both the data on basic poverty measures as well as measures of access to basic services, vulnerability, wages, food prices, and so forth. In addition, basic national accounts statistics are in great need of improvement, in particular at the state level. Finally, more developed firm surveys—with systematic collection of information on the investment climate—would provide policymakers and the general public with a clearer understanding of the barriers faced by small firms and farms.

7.4.4   Government Structure and Accountability

India has a number of traditional strengths in its government structure: a long-standing democratic tradition is a special asset that sets India apart from many other developing countries. Other functional traditions, like relatively strong auditing standards, also serve the country well. Two areas deserve attention for improving accountability of India's public sector. One is the quality, dissemination, timeliness, and accuracy of fiscal and socioeconomic data; the other is the federal structure of India's public sector. In section 7.3.8, the emerging state fiscal crisis was mentioned in the context of federalism. Federalism also creates opportunities in terms of improved accountability and the empowerment of local groups to participate in government decisions.

As discussed earlier, publicly disclosed data are critical to improving general policies and targeted poverty programs, but it is also key to general government accountability. The first step toward accountability is to provide the public with timely, accurate, and comprehensive information on the activities, expenses, and financing of the public sector.

In the fiscal and macro area, India has made substantial progress, especially in terms of the reporting of central government data. India's subscription to the IMF's Special Data Dissemination Standard (SDDS) is an important step in the right direction. Internal auditing, at least at the central government level, is generally considered to be effective. On the other hand, general government data—including the states—are often published with some delay. But the critical problems lie in the off-budget accounts, as well as subsidies (e.g., as we have emphasized in the power sector) or "tax expenditures." Such measures and processes inhibit the public's ability to understand government's expenditures, thus limiting the public's power to hold government accountable for its actions.

One important example of progress in disclosing information to the public is Karnataka's Right to Information Act. This act establishes citizen's charters for key government departments. The charters, which establish citizens' rights with regard to public services, were prepared with citizens' inputs and were widely disseminated to the public. In addition, the charters establish a grievance mechanism (*voice*) for citizens to report on service failures. In Rajasthan, strong pressure from civil society has contributed to greater government openness and thus accountability.

Decentralization is one means to improve government accountability, particularly in geographically or demographically large nations, such as India. It may be easier for poor people to voice their opinions at the local level, and greater responsibility at the local level can allow local governments to design public policies according to the particular preferences and needs of the local population. Empirically, it is difficult to draw a precise conclusion on the impact of decentralization in India. Most observers probably would agree that the increasing role of the states in India has had a beneficial impact along these lines, and it seems to be an inevitable part of the process of reducing central government controls on economic and political life more generally.

Decentralization does, however, pose certain risks. There are many ways to get it wrong—one risk, discussed earlier, is that it can complicate fiscal management. Another risk is that subnational governments could be captured by elite groups within their jurisdiction. Under these circumstances, lack of accountability and other governance problems can be replicated at the subnational level. Important elements include the role of democratic institutions at the subnational level and the establishment of information flows and transparency discussed earlier.

The 73rd and 74th Constitutional Amendments have provided the framework for an enhanced role of local governments—below the state level. This next phase of decentralization itself has largely been entrusted to the state governments in that it is up to each individual state to determine the final shape of fiscal federalism with respect to local governments within its jurisdiction. This state discretion is eminently sensible, given the wide diversity of demographic, geographic, and socioeconomic conditions across states. In fact, it would be curious to devise a central plan for decentralization to the local level. Note that this more flexible approach contrasts with some historical antecedents, like the 1935 Government of India Act that provided excessively detailed planning of the structure of taxation in the federal system. On the other hand, some general guidelines are provided by the 73rd and 74th Constitutional Amendments, and it may be necessary for the central government, with perhaps the support of multilateral organizations, to provide advice and technical assistance to states and local governments during this process.

7.4.5   Political Dimension

An important political dimension to empowerment is the enhancement of the ability of particular groups to become more involved in democratic political processes. Constitutional rules, an independent press, division of power among branches and levels of government, anticorruption rules, and freedom of information all have an important role to play in promoting good governance[12] and empowering citizens. Reforms of the political regime can also play a role. One example from India is the constitutional amendments that require a minimum level of women's leadership of local village and district councils.

In 1998, West Bengal held elections for the first time, applying the 1992 constitutional commitment (73rd and 74th Amendments) that one-third of elected leadership positions be held for women. One-third of village councils were randomly selected, and in those jurisdictions, the position of chairperson was restricted to women candidates. (In village councils where the restrictions did not apply, only 6.5 percent of chairpersons were women.) A recent study (Chattopadhyay and Duflo 2001) examined the expenditure decisions of village councils in West Bengal following the new system of elections. The study found that placing women in leadership positions in village councils changed the types of public good investments that the village councils made. The effects were noticeable. There was more investment in drinking water infrastructure and road construction, and less in informal schools. The change in the allocation of investments corresponded to the preferences expressed by women.

In brief, political and governmental structures influence the decision-making process for social policies critical for empowerment. Information flows, including concrete quantitative data, inform the public and the intellectual community, so that they can hold government accountable for its actions. The data also inform technical staff of government agencies in charge of developing the design of social programs. These processes are all essential to determining the quantity and quality of investment in people—in particular, poor people—and this investment allows individuals to participate in, and contribute to, the growth process.

7.5 Conclusion: Policy Options

During the last decade, India has been successful in continuing its progress in reducing poverty. To this extent, the growth pattern was broadly pro-poor.

To a large extent, the success in poverty reduction can be attributed to a shift in the role of the state and a decision to gradually open India's economy to the rest of the world. Compared to the past, India's government today is less active in directing the economic activities of individuals in society, and more active in supporting human capital development, as well as the development of domestic and external markets for goods and services. This has translated into faster growth, income poverty reduction, and notable improvements in the education status of a significant share of the Indian population.

Yet there is considerable scope for accelerating growth and poverty reduction in India. Production costs are high, especially for small- and

medium-scale firms, and productivity gains are held back by an un-
friendly investment climate. This is particularly true in the poorer,
slower growing states of northern India, those where it is particularly
critical to accelerate private-sector growth and job creation.

Improving the investment climate will require decisive action from
both the central and state governments. This includes enacting legislation to facilitate entry into and exit from business and make the labor
market more flexible; it also involves reducing bureaucratic harassment (which increases both costs and risk) and further opening the
Indian economy through reduced trade restrictions and increased
openness to foreign investment. Also key to reducing costs and risk is
improved delivery of infrastructure services, particularly power supply. India's northern states suffer from shortfalls in every infrastructure
dimension. This is especially true in rural areas, where water, power,
telecommunications, and roads are generally provided without cost or
at least with a heavy subsidy, and as a result are of very low quality
and reliability—if they are provided at all. These measures will go a
long way to improving the competitiveness of Indian firms and farms,
supporting their expansion in number and scale, and thus fostering
economic opportunities and job creation.

Improvements in the quality and quantity of infrastructure, however, will require higher levels of public and private expenditures, on
both investment and maintenance. In recent years, public investment
in infrastructure has been crowded out by a bloated civil service wage
bill and mounting interest payments. Bringing the cost of the civil service to an affordable level will greatly contribute to both an improved
composition of public expenditure, with greater fiscal space created for
infrastructure, and will help reduce the fiscal imbalances responsible
for the mounting interest burden. Improving infrastructure delivery by
the public sector will also require more effective resource mobilization,
through more effective taxation—namely, through a more effective
administration, the introduction of VAT, and inclusion of services in
the tax base—and greatly increased cost recovery on publicly provided
services, such as irrigation and energy.

Reduction of India's large fiscal imbalances in the near future will be
critical to ensuring macroeconomic stability, without which sustained
growth and poverty reduction cannot take place. In the short run, the
crowding out of private investment hampers growth; however, in
the medium term, macroeconomic stability is increasingly threatened
by rising fiscal deficits at the state and central levels, and by large

liabilities arising from the financial and power sectors. Indebtedness levels cannot rise indefinitely without leading to weaknesses in the financial system. In addition to increased revenue mobilization, improving intergovernmental fiscal relations—clear rules for transfers within the public sector, adequate state-level tax instruments, and institutions that encourage greater discipline at both the state and federal levels—will be a necessary condition for establishing fiscal responsibility of states.

Growth will be more pro-poor if poor people have a higher level of human capital and an opportunity to shape the decisions that affect their lives. Some of the human capital issues discussed in this chapter also form a vital link between the "investment climate" and "empowerment." Basic education and health standards form a key part of the investment climate, as firms increasingly require workers with basic skills and physical health. These skill requirements tend to rise as countries advance. Although considerable progress in improving education levels occurred in the 1990s, India's citizens remain handicapped by low average levels of education and a poor health status. Overcoming this handicap is a critical challenge for India. It will require combined action by and finance from public and private actors, and a determined effort to include the previously excluded segments of society, women, religious and ethnic minorities, and those in the less favored castes categories. In addition, improving education levels, health status, and participation in political processes enhance poor people's opportunities to control their destiny. This increased opportunity is an end in itself, while the human capital development described here also improves income-generating potential (a means).

Improved mechanisms for public accountability will empower the poor to demand the quality and mix of public services that they need. For this to occur, the government must open its activities to public scrutiny, provide the public with the information it needs to express its opinions to the government, and establish mechanisms to take into account citizens' feedback. Accountability is at the root of the reform process.

The twin-pillar approach of investment climate and empowerment allowed us to identify key policies that address the empirical regularities at the beginning of this chapter. For example, macroeconomic stability and tax reform can lead to improved growth rates in the short run, while at the same time empowering the poor by increasing the fiscal resources available for investment in human capital. Energy-sector reforms can have a similar impact, and a differential impact, as some states progress more rapidly than others. The reform agenda outlined in this chapter is challenging, but feasible, and the rewards from stronger pro-poor growth could be enormous.

Notes

Ferro and Rosenblatt are Senior Economists at the World Bank. Stern is the Senior Vice President and Chief Economist of the World Bank. The views presented here are the authors' and do not necessarily represent the views of the World Bank Group. The authors would like to thank, without implications, comments and inputs from Shahrokh Fardoust, Coralie Gevers, Amy Heyman, Stephen Howes Abhas Kumar Jha, Valerie Kozel, and Priya Mathur, as well from participants to the Indian Economy Conference at Cornell University, April 2002. Portions of this chapter draw on a speech made by Stern at the 25th Anniversary of the National Institute for Public Finance and Policy, 10 January 2002 in New Delhi.

1. There are conceptual and measurement differences that lead to a discrepancy between per capita income growth rates implied by national accounts statistics and household level statistics from the National Sample Survey Organization.

2. Changes in the survey methodology in the 55th Round of the National Sample Survey (1999–2000) rendered the latest official poverty estimates not strictly comparable to previous rounds. Recent empirical work has attempted to correct for the changes in the survey methodology. Most estimates point to a reduction in poverty incidence of 5 to 10 percentage points during the 1990s.

3. Using internationally comparable poverty estimate for the mid-1990s, based on an international poverty line of US$1 per day, with adjustments for purchasing power across countries (Datt and Ravallion 2002).

4. Stern (2001).

5. Bhalla (2002) emphasizes that these poverty measures may exaggerate the degree of poverty in India.

6. Other scholars have linked agricultural investment and productivity with colonial land tenure systems. In regions where property rights were given to landlords, as opposed to cultivators, lower productivity has prevailed into the modern period. See Banerjee and Iyer (2002).

7. Public sector refers to nonfinancial public sector only.

8. Among countries with populations of over 20 million, the Indian central government's average fiscal deficit during the 1987–1997 decade was exceeded by the deficits of only three countries: Nigeria, Pakistan, and Brazil (see Srinivasan 2001).

9. Radhakrishna and Subbarao (1997).

10. World Bank (2000). See also appendix table 4.1.

11. World Bank (2000, 23).

12. See the World Bank (2002b) chapter 5, for a more thorough discussion of these issues.

References

Anant, T. C. A., and N. Mitra. 1998. "The Role of Law and Legal Institutions in Asian Economic Development: The Case of India." Harvard Institute for International Development Discussion Paper Number 662, November.

Bajpai, Nirupam, and Jeffrey Sachs. 1998. "Strengthening India's Strategy for Economic Growth." *Economic and Political Weekly* (July):1935–1942.

Banerjee, Abhijit, and Lakshmi Iyer. 2002. "History, Institutions and Economic Performance: The Legacy of Colonial Land Tenure Systems in India." Paper delivered at World Bank research seminar, March.

Bhalla, Surjit S. 2002. "Imagine There's No Country—Poverty, Inequality and Growth in the Era of Globalization." Washington, DC: Institute for International Economics.

Burgess, Robin, and Nicholas Stern. 1993. "VAT in India: Problems and Options." IPR Working Paper Series Number IPR37, July.

Census of India. 2001. "Census of India." New Delhi, India: Office of the Registrar General.

Chattopadhyay, Raghabendra, and Esther Duflo. 2001. "Women's Leadership and Policy Decisions: Evidence from a Nationwide Randomized Experiment in India." NBER Working Paper Series Number 8615.

Chelliah, Raja. 1992. "Issues before Tenth Finance Commission." *Economic and Political Weekly*, no. 27.

Datt, Gaurav, and Martin Ravallion. 2002. "Is India's Economic Growth Leaving the Poor Behind?" *Journal of Economic Perspectives* 16, no. 3:89–108.

Deaton, Angus. 2002. "Adjusted Indian Poverty Estimates for 1999–2000." Paper delivered at the India Workshop on Poverty Measurement, Monitoring and Evaluation, January 11–12.

Deaton, Angus, and Jean Dreze. 2002. "Poverty and Inequality in India: A Re-Examination." *Economic and Political Weekly* (September 7).

Dollar, David, and Aart Kraay. 2001. "Growth is Good for the Poor." World Bank Policy Research Working Paper 2587, April.

Fischer, Stanley. 1993. "Role of Macroeconomic Factors in Growth." NBER Working Paper Series Number 4565 and *Journal of Monetary Economics* 32:485–512.

Frankel, Jeffrey, and David Romer. 1999. "Does Trade Cause Growth?" *American Economic Review* 89, no. 3:379–399.

Kozel, Valerie. 2002. "Summary of January Poverty Workshop." World Bank.

Lakin, Caroline. 2001. "The Effects of Taxes and Benefits on Household Income, 1999–2000." *Economic Trends*, no. 569.

Mathur, Ajeet. 1993. "Industrial Restructuring and the National Renewal Fund." Mimeo., Asian Development Bank, Manila.

Radhakrishna, R., and K. Subbarao. 1997. "India's Public Distribution System: A National and International Perspective." World Bank Discussion Paper 380.

Ravallion, Martin. 2001. "Growth, Inequality and Poverty: Looking Beyond Averages." *World Development* 29, no. 11.

Ravallion, Martin, and Guarav Datt. 1998a. "Why Have Some Indian States Done Better Than Others at Reducing Rural Poverty?" *Economica*, no. 65.

Ravallion, Martin, and Guarav Datt. 1998b. "Farm Productivity and Rural Poverty in India." *Journal of Development Studies*, no. 34 (April).

Ravallion, Martin, and Guarav Datt. 2001. "Why Has Economic Growth Been More Pro-Poor in Some States of India Than Others?" *International Monetary Fund Seminar Series*, no. 2001-59 (July).

Ravallion, Martin, and Guarav Datt. 2002. "Growth and Poverty in India: What Have We Learnt from the NSS?" India Workshop on Poverty Measurement, Monitoring and Evaluation, January 11–12.

Sachs, Jeffrey, Ashutosh Varshney, and Nirupam Bajpai. 1999. *India in the Era of Economic Reforms*. New Delhi, New York: Oxford University Press.

Srinivasan, T. N. 2001. "India's Fiscal Situation: Is a Crisis Ahead?" Working Paper no. 92, Center for Research on Economic Development and Policy Reform, Stanford University.

Stern, Nicholas. 2001. "A Strategy for Development." Keynote address to the Annual Bank Conference on Economic Developments, May. Washington, DC: The World Bank.

Sundaram, K. and Suresh D. Tendulkar. 2002. "Recent Debates on Database for Measurement of Poverty in India: Some Fresh Evidence." Paper delivered at the India Workshop on Poverty Measurement, Monitoring and Evaluation, January 11–12, New Delhi.

World Bank. 2000. "India: Reducing Poverty, Accelerating Development." A World Bank Country Study, Oxford.

World Bank. 2002a. "Globalization, Growth and Poverty: Building an Inclusive World Economy." A Policy Research Report, Oxford.

World Bank. 2002b. "Building Institutions for Markets." A World Development Report, Oxford.

8

Who Is Getting the Public Goods in India? Some Evidence and Some Speculation

Abhijit V. Banerjee

The way one grows up in India, it has long been known, depends on where one grows up. The average child growing up in Orissa in the 1980s was seven times more likely to die in infancy than his or her equivalent in Kerala.[1] His or her mother is four and half times more likely to die giving birth in Assam than in Kerala.[2] And if she happened to be a girl and born in Rajasthan in the 1980s, the likelihood of her being literate by the time she was fourteen was about a quarter of what it would have been had she grown up in Kerala.[3]

This is, as Dreze and Sen (1995), among others, have argued, entirely what one might have expected: In 1991, rural Kerala had seventeen times as many hospital beds per head as Orissa and ten times as many as Assam. The fraction of people in rural Orissa with access to medical facilities in their village in 1981 was less than 11 percent compared to 96 percent in Kerala. In 1991, 93 percent of all villages in Kerala had a middle school, but the corresponding fraction in Orissa and Assam was less than 25 percent and in Uttar Pradash (UP) it was less than 15 percent.

What is less often emphasized but equally striking is the extent of variation within a single state: According to the 1991 census, less than 7 percent of the villages in the Vishakhapatnam district in Andhra Pradesh (AP) had middle schools and just over 46 percent had some educational facility, as opposed to 55 percent and 100 percent in Guntur. The district of Rangareddy had only 6 percent of villages with primary health subcenters as opposed to almost 40 percent in Anantapur. Less than 1 percent of villages in Vishakhapatnam had tapped water compared to 59 percent in West Godavari. Forty-eight percent of villages in Vishakhapatnam were using electrical power as opposed to essentially 100 percent in Krishna. Twenty percent of villages in Vishakhapatnam had a post office and 25 percent had a metalled road, as opposed to 93 percent for both in Guntur.

8.1   Potential Determinants of Public Good Access

What, if anything, marks out these places that seem to be missing out so dramatically on their fair share of these public goods? One part of the answer is surely geography.

Where it rains a lot, storing water may be less of an issue than better drainage. It may change the disease burden, making certain types of health care more important. More rain also has the potential to make the land more productive, making it easier to sustain higher population densities, which, in turn, affects the cost of making public goods more accessible.

Being coastal, as Sachs and Werner have emphasized, can change the way one lives one's life: One is naturally more exposed to international trade, and trade brings with it ideas from outside. One might imagine a coastal population being more assertive about its demands for public goods. One might also expect the coast to be a different agro-climatic zone, with corresponding differences in the demands for public goods.

Other aspects of the geography may also make a difference: It, for example, is more difficult to build roads in mountainous areas and farming rocky hillsides is obviously very different from agriculture in the river valleys.

History, one imagines, must have also left its mark: While nothing in India has entirely escaped the impact of colonial rule, one might imagine that the areas that were never formally under British rule (the so-called Princely States) provide a potentially interesting contrast. The explicit policy of the colonial state was to invest in infrastructure only where its direct economic interests could be expected to be served by such investment, at least outside the urban areas. Railways, irrigation, and roads were built only where such investment could directly contribute to the expansion of trade, and it was largely taken as given that if people in rural areas wanted to have access to modern medicine and "English" education, they should be prepared to travel to the nearest big town. While this was not necessarily what the people wanted, the colonial state was powerful enough not to need to embrace populism.

The Princely States obviously faced rather different compulsions: Some of them felt the need to do something for their people, and even those who did not could not afford too much discontent within, since their power was rather limited and there was always the risk that the British would, as they had in the case of Oudh, invoke mismanagement as a reason to swallow them up. Of course, the need to limit popular unhappiness does not necessarily produce investment in schools and roads. It could also lead to an increased reliance on "feudal" or religious structures, as a means of social control: This could lead to less investment in schools, given that schools are often, not unreasonably, seen as the fount of radical ideas. Either way, however, one might expect a different pattern of public investment in the Princely States. Moreover, it is plausible that these states fostered a rather different popular attitude towards the state and generated a quite different pattern of political alignment and wealth and income inequality among their people.

I have argued elsewhere (Banerjee and Iyer 2002) that the pattern of political alignments and the distribution of income and wealth may also be expected to vary systematically within British India: This is because there were three quite different types of land tenure systems within British India. These systems mainly defined who had the liability for paying the land tax to the British and by implication, who had "property rights" on the land. The systems were landlord-based systems (also known as *zamindari* or *malguzari*), individual cultivator-based systems (*raiyatwari*), and village-based systems (*mahalwari*). The map in figure 8.1 illustrates the geographic distribution of these areas.

In the landlord areas, a landlord was put in charge of the revenue collection, and the British administration had no direct dealings with the cultivating peasants. Landlords were in effect given property rights on the land, though some measures for protecting the rights of tenants and subproprietors were introduced in later years.

Under the raiyatwari system the revenue settlement was made directly with the raiyat or cultivator. In these areas, an extensive cadastral survey of the land was done and a detailed record-of-rights was prepared, which served as the legal title to the land for the cultivator. Revenue rates were calculated as the money value of a share of the estimated average annual output. This share typically varied from place to place, was different for different soil types, and was also adjusted in response to changes in the productivity of the land.

Under the mahalwari system, village bodies that jointly owned the village were responsible for the land revenue. The composition of the village body varied from place to place: In some areas it was a single person or family and hence very much like the landlord system, while in other areas, the village bodies were larger and each person was responsible for a fixed share of the revenue. This share was either

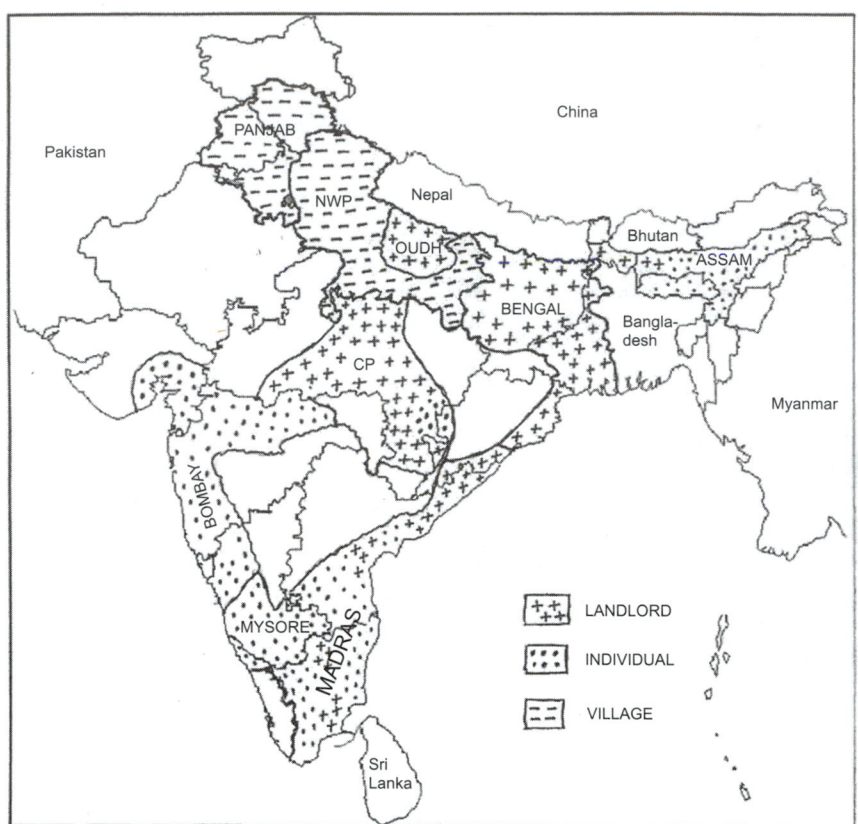

Figure 8.1
Map of India.

determined by ancestry (the *pattidari* system), or based on actual possession of the land (the *bhaiachara* system), the latter being very much like the raiyatwari system.

Why might one expect public investment to vary between areas with more or less landlord control? In particular, why would these differences persist and not be wiped out as soon as the landlord class was abolished in the early 1950s? One obvious and potentially persistent effect of being a landlord area is on the distribution of land and wealth. Bagchi (1976) suggests one possible mechanism: Since the landlords were given the authority to extract as much as they wanted from their tenants, the gains in output or productivity in these areas were more likely to be concentrated in a few hands. Landlord areas were also the only areas subject to the Permanent Settlement of 1793 (which fixed rents forever in nominal terms) and even where the settlement was not permanent, the political power of the landlord class made it less likely that their rates would be raised when their surplus grew. Therefore, we would expect a much more unequal distribution of wealth and of course, land, in landlord areas. By contrast, in individual cultivator areas, rents were typically raised frequently by the British in an attempt to extract as much as possible from the tenant. There was, as a result, comparatively little differentiation within the rural population of these areas until, in the latter years of the nineteenth century, the focus of the British moved away from extracting as much as they could from the peasants. At this point, there was indeed increasing differentiation within the peasant class, but even the smaller peasants could benefit from the increases in productivity. One would thus expect a more equal distribution of land and wealth in the non-landlord areas. This effect may have been reinforced by another factor, also pointed out by Bagchi. He argues that in the landlord areas, the British handed over a significant part of their political and judicial power to the landlord. This allowed landlords to impose terms on the peasants that they would not have been able to otherwise and contributed to the impoverishment of the peasantry.

The data we have confirms these expectations: We do find that provinces with a higher non-landlord proportion have lower Gini measures of land inequality in 1885. Even as late as 1990, the size distribution of land holdings looks quite different across these two areas: 64 percent of all land holdings in landlord areas were classified as "marginal" (less than 1 hectare), while this figure was 50 percent in individual-based districts. Further, 48 percent of all holdings are small to medium-sized (1–10 hectares) in individual-based areas, but only 35 percent in landlord areas. There is no significant difference in the proportion of extremely large holdings, which is probably due to the impact of land ceiling laws passed after Independence.

The land and wealth distribution matters for public investment for at least three reasons: First, because it affects the kinds of private investment that people do, which in turn affects the demand for public investment—for example, those who grow sugarcane, a relatively capital intensive crop, will also demand irrigation. Second, because it affects the balance between those who cultivate mainly their own land and those who cultivate other people's land. Those who mainly cultivate other people's land probably care less about investments that make agriculture more productive, at least relative to programs that redistribute land to the landless. Their political energies may therefore be directed in a rather different direction. Third, the fact that the wealthy and therefore politically powerful in the landlord areas were often not themselves cultivators weakened the political pressure on the state to deliver public goods that were important to farmers.

It is also plausible that the nature of the settlement affected the nature of political power in the post-independence era. If one accepts the earlier argument about the landlords wielding extra economic power, it is easy to imagine that this would have created antagonistic relations between the peasants and the local elites. It is plausible that this limited their power to work together even after the basis for the conflict was removed. Indeed, if it created a culture of antagonism, it may even have ramifications outside agriculture, such as in their ability to demand schools, health centers, and so forth.

Finally, I have already noted that many landlord areas had permanently fixed revenue commitments and that it was more difficult to raise rents in landlord areas due to the greater political power of large landlords. This meant that the Colonial state had more stake in the economic prosperity of non-landlord areas, since this could be translated into higher rents. This is reflected in an increasing number of legislations trying to protect the peasants from money lenders and others in these areas starting in the second half of the nineteenth century. It also meant that the state had more reason to invest in these areas in irrigation, railways, schools, and other infrastructure.

This being India, one would also expect caste and religion to play a role. These might matter for three reasons: First because certain castes, such as the designated scheduled castes and scheduled tribes, have traditionally been discriminated against, and while such discrimination is now illegal, it is not hard to imagine that it persists in many places, making it harder for these groups to get their fair share. Moreover, a consequence of past discrimination is that these groups are now poorer and less educated than other groups that they have to compete against for the favors of the state, which may make it harder for them to get what they want. Second, because of a history of antagonism between different castes and between different religious groups, the potential for collective action may be relatively limited.[4] Third, even if they can work together, their priorities may be very different: The high castes, who have always had access to education, may care less about the adult literacy centers that the scheduled tribes want than about getting a new junior college.[5]

Finally, it is plausible that it is easier to deliver public goods in more densely populated areas. If people live far from each other and providing public goods access at any one location has a significant fixed cost, it is harder to justify trying provide public goods to all of them.

8.2   What Really Matters for Public Good Access?

One way to answer this question is to go back to AP and to try to see if I can explain away the large differences reported earlier. Figures 8.2 through 8.8 report the results of such an exercise, for six selected public goods representing the six categories of public goods reported by the Indian census—education, health, water, power, post and telegraph, and communication. All of these except communication should be self-explanatory: Communication covers roads, buses, trains, and related publicly provided services. The goods I chose are the fraction of villages that have access to middle schools, primary health care centers, tapped water, electrical power use, any post and telegraph facility, and metalled ("pucca") roads. The choice reflected my judgment about the kinds of goods within each category that seem to be in high demand—for example, I chose middle schools, rather than primary schools because by the 1990s, most villages (92 percent) in AP do have primary schools.

The first panel of each one of figures 8.2–8.8 shows the distribution of the particular public good variable for the twenty-two districts in AP (middle schools in figure 8.2, primary health care center in figure 8.3), centered around its mean. The second panel shows the distribution after controlling for the effects of two key geographical variables—being coastal and the average level of rainfall. The distribution tightens visibly in four of the six cases, but for electrical power use, if anything things get worse (there is no effect on the roads variable).

The third panel shows what happens if I also try to control for historical differences. The variables I use are the proportion of land that was *not* under the landlord-based system and an index that says whether or not the district was under British rule. To determine the former I used data from district-level Settlement Reports compiled by British administrators at various points of time, as well as other historical sources. Most of the Settlement Reports I use are from the 1870s and 1880s and were compiled after a fairly detailed survey of the

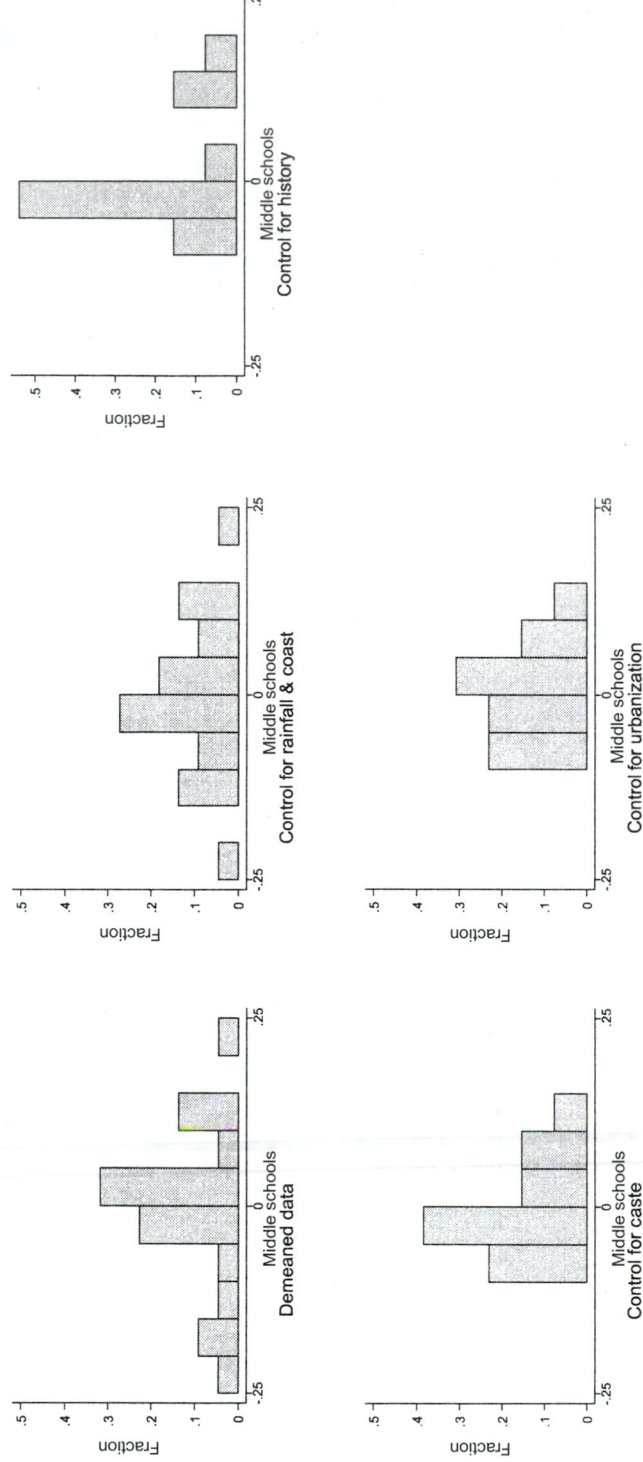

Figure 8.2
Andhra Pradesh. Proportion of villages with middle school.

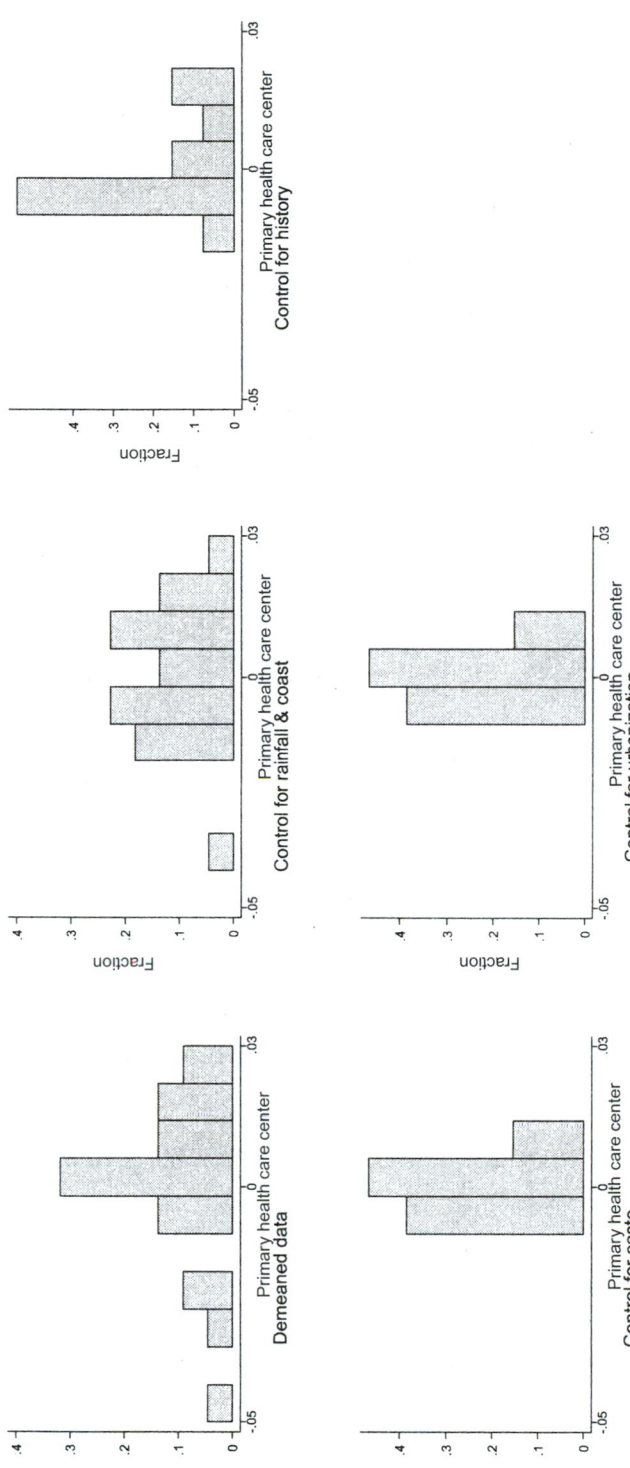

Figure 8.3
Andhra Pradesh. Proportion of villages with primary health care.

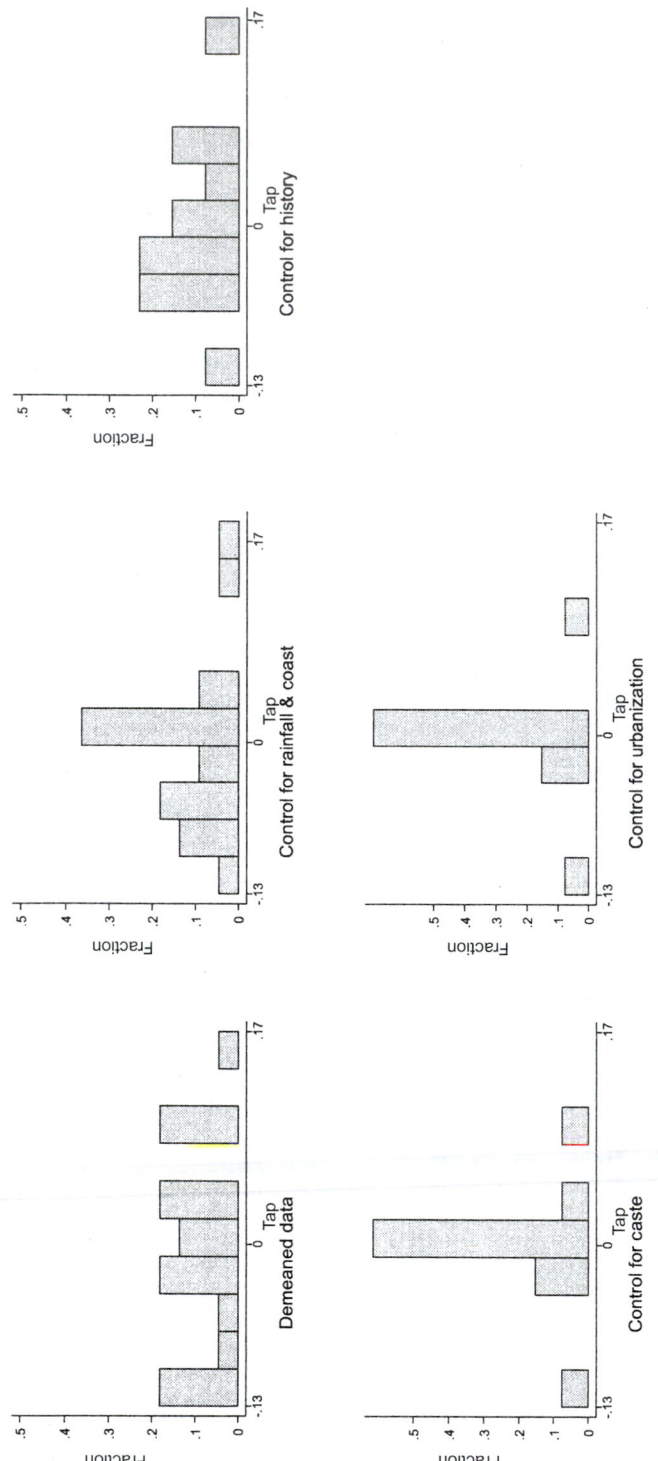

Figure 8.4
Andhra Pradesh. Proportion of villages with tap.

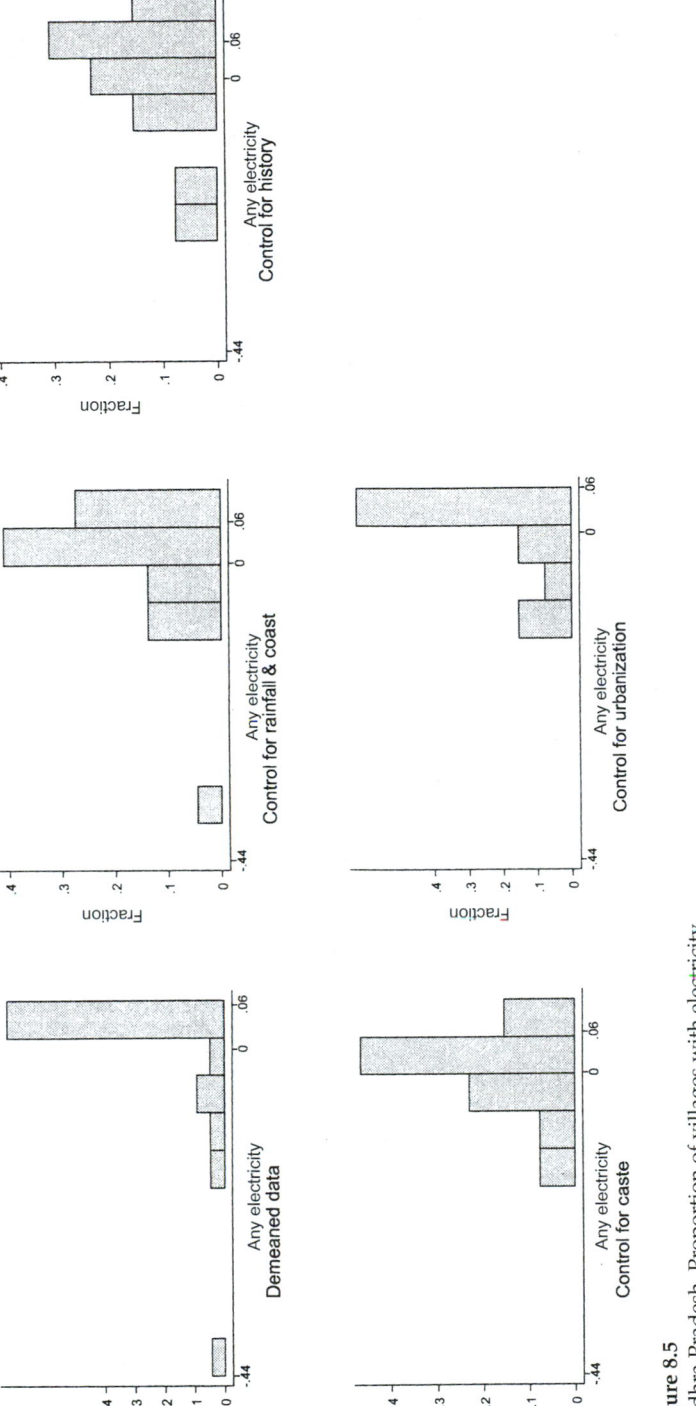

Figure 8.5
Andhra Pradesh. Proportion of villages with electricity.

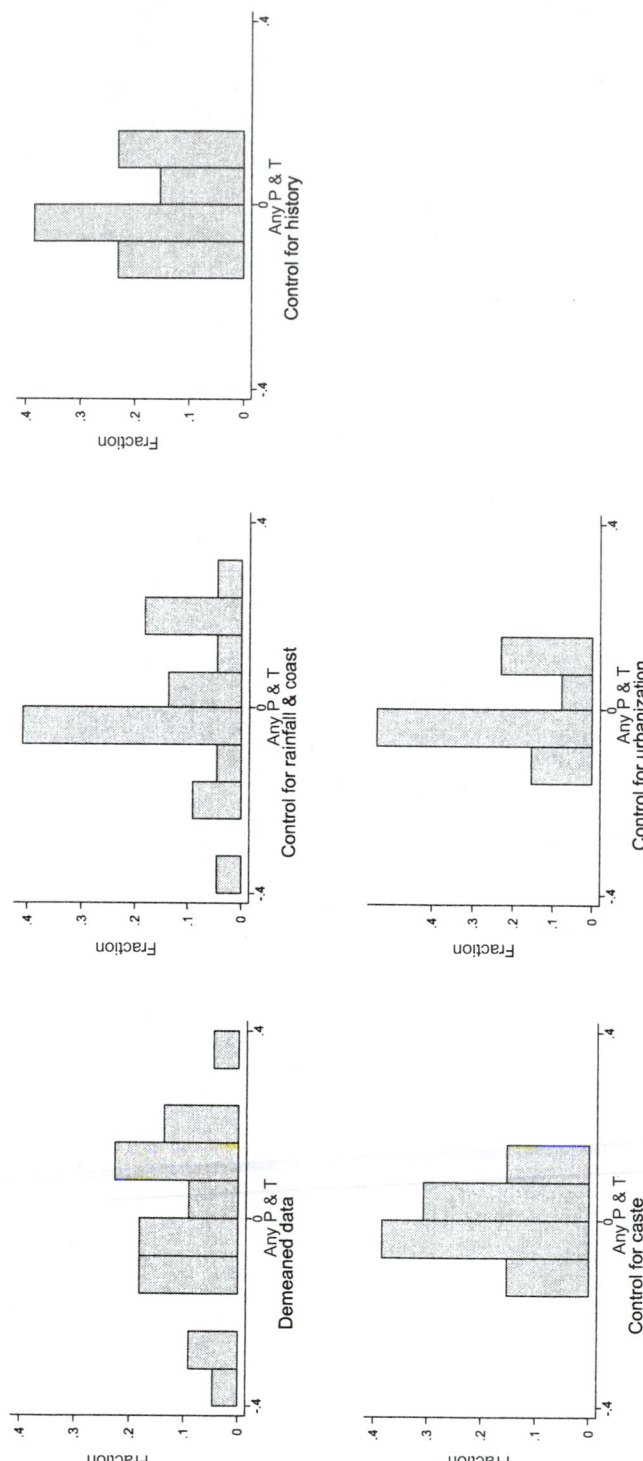

Figure 8.6
Andhra Pradesh. Proportion of villages with any P&T.

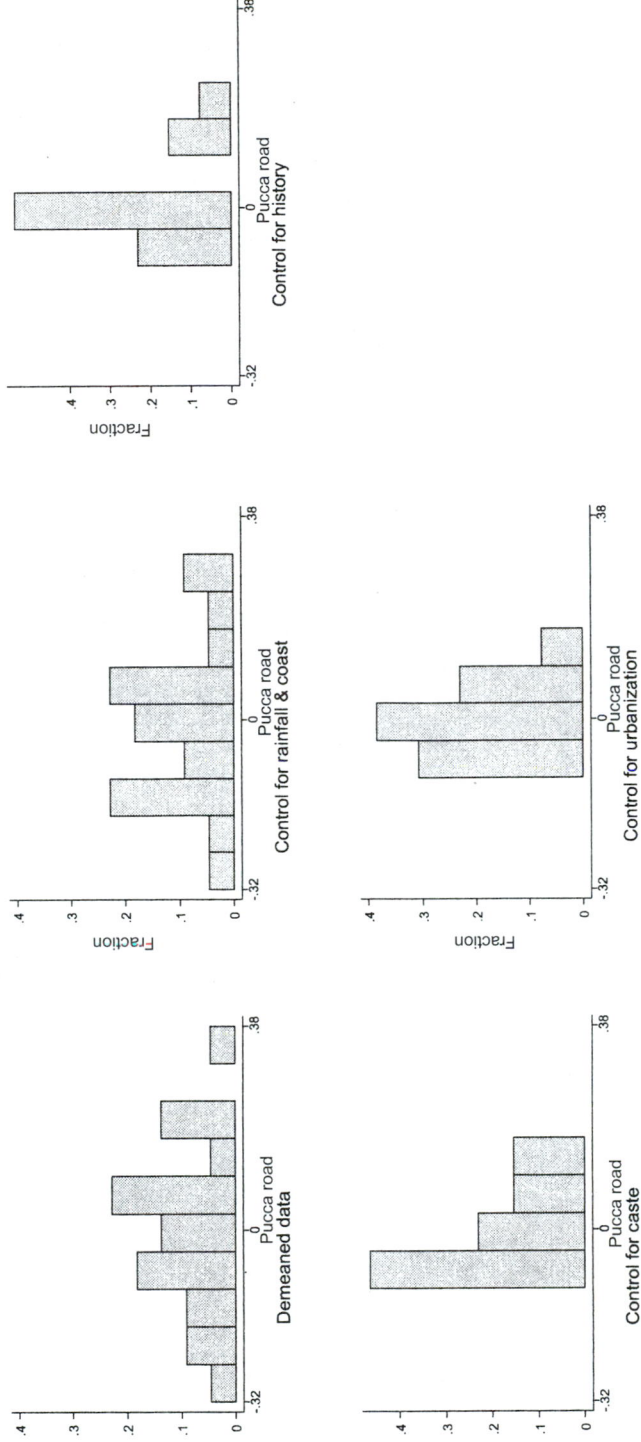

Figure 8.7
Andhra Pradesh. Proportion of villages with pucca road.

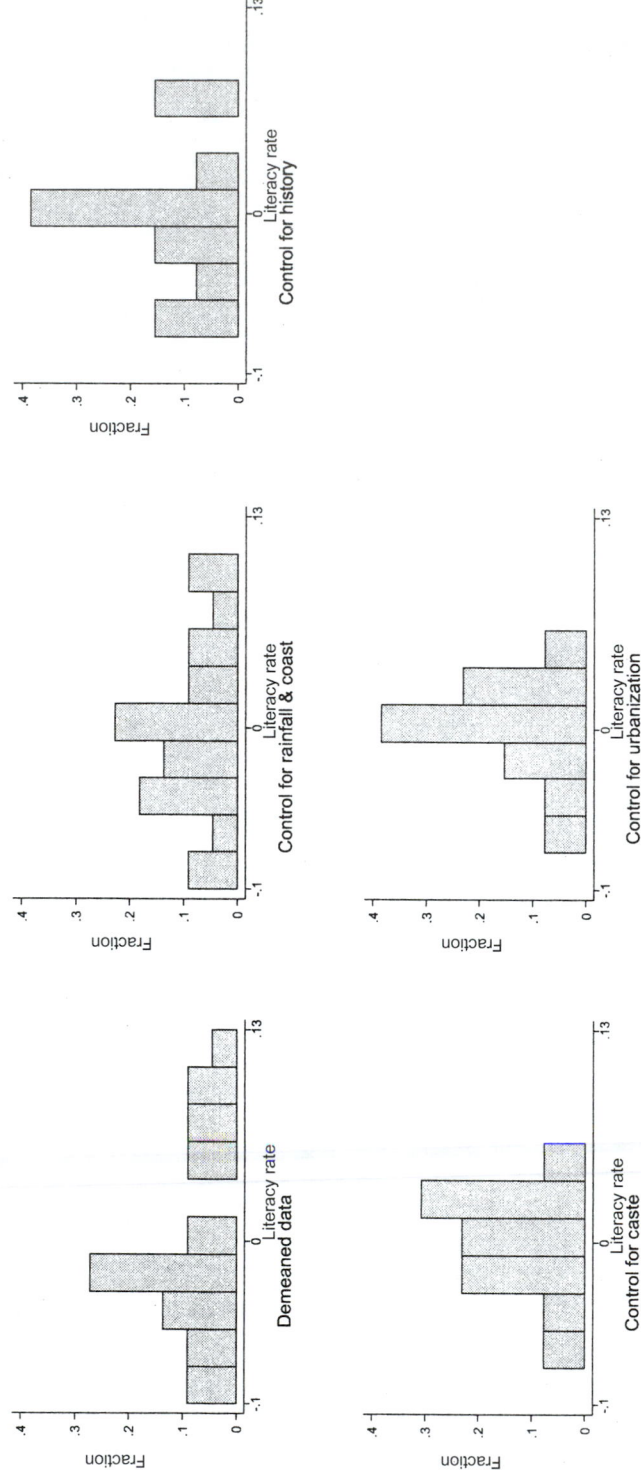

Figure 8.8
Andhra Pradesh. Literacy rate.

district. Depending on the historical information available, our measure of non-landlord control is either the fraction of villages or estates or total area not controlled by landlords.

Once I add these variables, the distribution tightens dramatically for middle schools, primary health care centers, post and telegraph facilities, and roads. There is no effect on taps and the effect on electrical power is hard to interpret.

The fourth panel shows what happens when I control for the caste differences as well: I control for the share of scheduled castes and scheduled tribes in the rural population and the index of ethnic fractionalization taken from Banerjee and Somanathan (2001). This index measures the probability that two people drawn at random from the population would belong to the same group. To calculate this index I had to go back to the 1931 census, which is the last census that gives really detailed caste information. The data is available by districts, separately for each of the British Indian provinces and Princely States. While state boundaries were redrawn after Independence, district boundaries remained more or less intact, and I can therefore use this data to construct caste shares for current districts. For new districts created by subdividing old ones, I weight the caste figures from the original district according to the area of the new district that was taken from them.

The number of castes listed in the 1931 census is large, and I restrict myself to Hindu castes that form more than 1 percent of the population of each state or province in 1931. Putting together data for different states produces a total of 185 caste groups. We make one major adjustment to this data to account for the increase in the proportion of Hindus after 1931. Some districts had significant Muslim populations that migrated to the newly created nation of Pakistan around the time of Indian independence in 1947. I scale up the numbers in each caste group, based on the population share of Hindus in the current census. This assumes that within Hindus, different castes grew at similar rates over time.

To complete the calculation, I need to decide how to treat other religious groups. There is no perfect way to do this, but I decided to ignore caste differences among non-Hindus and to treat each non-Hindu religious community—Buddhists, Christians, Jains, Muslims, and Sikhs—as a single homogenous group.

The results in panel 4 show that adding the caste variables does tighten the distribution in almost every case, with the impact in the case of taps being the most striking. Finally, panel 5 shows the effect of controlling for the extent of urbanization, as a way of measuring population density. Once again there seems to be a significant impact, except perhaps in the case of primary health care centers.

Figure 8.8 shows a parallel exercise, with the one difference that I am looking at rural literacy rates, which is an outcome of public investment rather than a measure of investment itself. The patterns I see are very similar.

Echoes of these results show up when I expand the list of public goods. If I start with the entire list of infrastructure measures that are reported in the census and eliminate the ones that are probably not man-made (rivers, fountains, etc.) and the ones that are almost surely private (nursing homes, registered medical practitioner, etc.), I end up with a list of thirty-three plausibly public goods. I then estimate a regression equation that combines all the variables already mentioned, for each of these thirty-three public goods, still using data from just the twenty-two districts in AP.

Rainfall almost never has a significant effect in these regressions, but being coastal has a positive effect for nine of the goods and a negative effect for two more. The proportion of land that was not under landlords has a significant effect for sixteen of the goods and is always positive, which is impressive given that I have twenty-two data points and have to estimate eight coefficients. Being non-British is also typically positive when it is significant (positive in 12 cases and negative in 1). The only other variable that shows up relatively often in the regressions is the share of the scheduled tribes, which is negative in seven cases and positive in two. Neither the share of the scheduled castes nor the fragmentation index shows up more than a couple of times.

Tables 8.1 through 8.7 present the results from an even more elaborate exercise where I estimate a similar relationship for the country as a whole. I still have the same list of thirty-three public goods, but my sample now is the 284 districts in the sixteen most populous Indian states. This allows me the luxury of using a much more elaborate set of geographical controls. I now also include latitude, altitude, an index of whether the district has a lot of steep slopes, the maximum and minimum temperature, and three indices representing soil types. I also add the share of Brahmins, Muslims, Christians, and Sikhs. A measure of the inequality of the land distribution is also included, in an attempt to pick up anything that the non-landlord measure has not.

Table 8.1
Education

	(1) Primary school	(2) Middle school	(3) High school	(4) Junior college	(5) Adult literacy center
Rainfall	−0.000	0.000	0.000	−0.000**	−0.000***
	(0.000)	(0.000)	(0.000)	(0.000)	(0.000)
Coast dummy	0.041	0.020	0.005	−0.002	0.083**
	(0.025)	(0.028)	(0.022)	(0.005)	(0.034)
Non-British	0.041**	0.038**	0.013	0.002	0.077***
	(0.019)	(0.015)	(0.010)	(0.003)	(0.020)
Proportion nonlandlord	0.036	0.031*	0.018	0.002	0.042**
	(0.026)	(0.018)	(0.014)	(0.005)	(0.021)
Fractionalization castes	−0.242**	−0.262**	−0.217**	−0.011	−0.069
and religious groups	(0.107)	(0.127)	(0.096)	(0.035)	(0.109)
Proportion of scheduled	−0.026	−0.245***	−0.138**	0.005	0.045
tribes/rural pop.	(0.052)	(0.057)	(0.060)	(0.016)	(0.054)
Proportion of scheduled	−0.082	−0.353***	−0.174**	−0.015	−0.051
castes/total pop.	(0.106)	(0.101)	(0.083)	(0.025)	(0.125)
Brahman	−0.645***	−0.255	−0.311*	0.043	−0.206
	(0.238)	(0.161)	(0.170)	(0.049)	(0.235)
Gini coeff. including	0.249**	0.001	0.124**	−0.005	0.015
agricultural laborers	(0.102)	(0.075)	(0.056)	(0.017)	(0.087)
Avpop.	0.000**	0.000*	0.000	0.000*	0.000
	(0.000)	(0.000)	(0.000)	(0.000)	(0.000)
Constant	0.965***	0.722***	0.325***	0.080**	0.071
	(0.143)	(0.171)	(0.118)	(0.041)	(0.130)
Observations	284	265	240	284	284
R-squared	0.52	0.66	0.64	0.60	0.29

Note: Robust standard errors in parentheses. *significant at 10%; **significant at 5%; ***significant at 1%.

The results, for the most part, conform to the patterns that I found before: Being non-landlord comes out positive, as does being on the coast, and to a lesser extent, being non-British. Having a large fraction of scheduled castes or tribes or Muslims looks like a disadvantage, as does being fragmented. More surprisingly, having a large fraction of Brahmins does not go with greater access to public goods, and inequality in the land distribution, while often statistically significant, is actually more often positive than negative. And population density clearly goes with improved access to public goods.

Table 8.8 presents the results on literacy: Being on the coast and having more rain go with higher literacy as does being in a non-

Table 8.2
Health I

	(1) Any medical facility	(2) Primary health care subcenter	(3) Primary health care center	(4) Health care center	(5) Hospital
Rainfall	−0.000**	−0.000*	−0.000	0.000*	0.000
	(0.000)	(0.000)	(0.000)	(0.000)	(0.000)
Coast dummy	0.048	0.054**	−0.001	−0.002	−0.006
	(0.057)	(0.022)	(0.004)	(0.003)	(0.004)
Non-British	−0.066*	0.002	0.009**	−0.002	0.004
	(0.036)	(0.010)	(0.004)	(0.002)	(0.003)
Proportion nonlandlord	0.170***	0.050***	0.015**	−0.006	−0.006*
	(0.052)	(0.016)	(0.007)	(0.005)	(0.004)
Fractionalization castes and religious groups	−0.235	−0.127	0.023	0.003	−0.059**
	(0.257)	(0.094)	(0.056)	(0.018)	(0.028)
Proportion of scheduled tribes/rural pop.	−0.229*	−0.050	−0.008	−0.008	−0.021
	(0.124)	(0.039)	(0.020)	(0.007)	(0.015)
Proportion of scheduled castes/rural pop.	−0.063	−0.151*	0.026	0.011	0.015
	(0.237)	(0.087)	(0.040)	(0.013)	(0.030)
Brahman	−0.567	−0.406***	−0.143**	−0.056	−0.047
	(0.477)	(0.143)	(0.068)	(0.035)	(0.050)
Gini coeff. including agricultural laborers	−0.611***	−0.028	−0.041*	−0.026	−0.016
	(0.199)	(0.061)	(0.024)	(0.018)	(0.013)
Avpop.	0.000***	0.000**	0.000*	0.000	0.000
	(0.000)	(0.000)	(0.000)	(0.000)	(0.000)
Constant	−0.011	0.031	0.165***	0.008	0.076*
	(0.346)	(0.111)	(0.056)	(0.017)	(0.039)
Observations	284	266	284	284	284
R-squared	0.47	0.40	0.59	0.44	0.65

Note: Robust standard errors in parentheses. *significant at 10%; **significant at 5%; ***significant at 1%.

landlord area, at least for men. Being in non-British or scheduled tribe-dominated areas makes one less likely to be literate, but being in scheduled caste-dominated areas has no significant effect.

8.3   What Should One Make of These Results?

The trouble with many of these results is that it is dangerous to take them at face value. The effects of geography are of course what they are, but none of the other measured effects need be what they say they are. For example, the effect of being a non-landlord area could simply be the effect of whatever made it appropriate for it to be a non-landlord

Table 8.3
Health II

	(1) Mother and child welfare center	(2) Child welfare center	(3) Family planning center	(4) TB clinics	(5) Child health care worker
Rainfall	−0.000**	0.000	−0.000	0.000*	−0.000**
	(0.000)	(0.000)	(0.000)	(0.000)	(0.000)
Coast dummy	−0.011	−0.007	0.025*	0.002	0.043
	(0.009)	(0.011)	(0.014)	(0.002)	(0.061)
Non-British	−0.012***	−0.001	0.012**	0.001	−0.080**
	(0.004)	(0.005)	(0.005)	(0.001)	(0.036)
Proportion nonlandlord	0.002	0.020***	0.018**	0.001	0.121**
	(0.007)	(0.007)	(0.008)	(0.001)	(0.048)
Fractionalization castes and religious groups	0.021	−0.023	−0.082*	−0.005	−0.232
	(0.040)	(0.052)	(0.042)	(0.007)	(0.232)
Proportion of scheduled tribes/rural pop.	−0.009	0.023	−0.050**	0.005	−0.067
	(0.020)	(0.033)	(0.024)	(0.005)	(0.117)
Proportion of scheduled castes/rural pop.	0.042	−0.007	−0.188***	0.010	−0.111
	(0.035)	(0.040)	(0.054)	(0.009)	(0.239)
Brahman	0.136	0.063	−0.169**	−0.017*	−0.230
	(0.085)	(0.075)	(0.079)	(0.009)	(0.454)
Gini coeff. including agricultural laborers	−0.096***	−0.043	0.028	−0.002	−0.634***
	(0.029)	(0.041)	(0.029)	(0.003)	(0.198)
Avpop.	0.000*	0.000***	0.000	0.000	0.000***
	(0.000)	(0.000)	(0.000)	(0.000)	(0.000)
Constant	0.052	−0.034	0.100**	−0.003	−0.040
	(0.059)	(0.041)	(0.047)	(0.006)	(0.305)
Observations	284	284	284	284	284
R-squared	0.55	0.20	0.39	0.22	0.45

Note: Robust standard errors in parentheses. *significant at 10%; **significant at 5%; ***significant at 1%.

area. Banerjee and Iyer (2002) argue at some length that this is in fact not the case as far as the non-landlord variable is concerned. At the heart of their argument are two observations: First, when one looks at agricultural yield data it becomes clear that the areas that became non-landlord were actually less productive at least until the first part of the last century. It is only after independence that these areas clearly start becoming more productive than the landlord areas. In other words, their current success, at least in agriculture, was not prefigured by their historical performance. Second, areas that were conquered later were much more likely to be non-landlord, both because the British were

Table 8.4
Water

	(1) Any water facility	(2) Well	(3) Handpump	(4) Tube well	(5) Tap	(6) Tank
Rainfall	-0.000	0.000***	-0.000***	0.000***	-0.000**	-0.000
	(0.000)	(0.000)	(0.000)	(0.000)	(0.000)	(0.000)
Coast dummy	-0.002	-0.100	-0.226***	0.010	0.082*	0.094*
	(0.002)	(0.071)	(0.077)	(0.069)	(0.043)	(0.050)
Non-British	-0.001	-0.032	-0.135***	-0.054	0.088***	0.013
	(0.001)	(0.033)	(0.045)	(0.037)	(0.023)	(0.027)
Proportion nonlandlord	0.001	-0.084*	-0.132**	-0.059	0.163***	-0.025
	(0.002)	(0.048)	(0.059)	(0.049)	(0.035)	(0.033)
Fractionalization castes and religious groups	0.019	0.630**	1.000**	-0.262	-0.820***	0.187
	(0.018)	(0.254)	(0.412)	(0.231)	(0.250)	(0.163)
Proportion of scheduled tribes/rural pop.	-0.003	-0.342***	-0.035	-0.016	-0.249***	-0.154**
	(0.004)	(0.105)	(0.150)	(0.103)	(0.086)	(0.069)
Proportion of scheduled castes/rural pop.	-0.015**	-0.926***	-0.350	0.401	-0.306*	-0.644***
	(0.007)	(0.265)	(0.286)	(0.277)	(0.180)	(0.178)
Brahman	0.004	-0.497	0.268	-0.087	0.476	-0.570
	(0.015)	(0.451)	(0.502)	(0.432)	(0.385)	(0.349)
Gini coeff. including agricultural laborers	0.007	-0.096	-0.117	0.347*	0.058	-0.237**
	(0.006)	(0.209)	(0.250)	(0.189)	(0.135)	(0.116)
Avpop.	0.000	-0.000	0.000	0.000	0.000	-0.000
	(0.000)	(0.000)	(0.000)	(0.000)	(0.000)	(0.000)
Constant	0.970***	-0.111	-0.352	-0.057	1.158***	0.300*
	(0.018)	(0.338)	(0.488)	(0.321)	(0.319)	(0.164)
Observations	284	284	284	284	284	284
R-squared	0.14	0.42	0.43	0.38	0.48	0.39

Note: Robust standard errors in parentheses. * significant at 10%; ** significant at 5%; *** significant at 1%.

Table 8.5
Electricity

	(1) Any electricity	(2) Electrified	(3) Electricity for domestic use	(4) Electricity for agriculture
Rainfall	−0.000***	−0.000	−0.000***	−0.000***
	(0.000)	(0.000)	(0.000)	(0.000)
Coast dummy	0.057	0.018	0.095***	−0.011
	(0.035)	(0.027)	(0.036)	(0.046)
Non-British	0.061**	0.016	0.110***	0.124***
	(0.028)	(0.026)	(0.028)	(0.034)
Proportion nonlandlord	0.059*	−0.008	0.077**	0.065
	(0.031)	(0.029)	(0.033)	(0.040)
Fractionalization castes	−0.506***	−0.189	−0.504***	−0.239
and religious groups	(0.160)	(0.144)	(0.173)	(0.198)
Proportion of scheduled	−0.197**	0.016	−0.141*	−0.394***
tribes/rural pop.	(0.077)	(0.064)	(0.080)	(0.085)
Proportion of scheduled	−0.284*	0.057	−0.322**	−0.164
castes/rural pop.	(0.166)	(0.145)	(0.156)	(0.197)
Brahman	0.369	0.041	0.673*	−0.167
	(0.323)	(0.281)	(0.376)	(0.387)
Gini coeff. including	0.420***	0.355***	0.621***	0.564***
agricultural laborers	(0.135)	(0.129)	(0.149)	(0.178)
Avpop.	0.000***	0.000**	0.000	0.000***
	(0.000)	(0.000)	(0.000)	(0.000)
Constant	0.853***	0.752***	1.023***	0.275
	(0.192)	(0.157)	(0.214)	(0.273)
Observations	284	259	284	284
R-squared	0.62	0.42	0.66	0.67

Note: Robust standard errors in parentheses. *significant at 10%; **significant at 5%; ***significant at 1%.

increasingly more comfortable with making their own deals with peasants and because of shifts in the ideology among the people ruling India. One can therefore look at the effects of variation in the nonlandlord share that are the result of being conquered later. Indeed one can even control for any direct effect of being longer under British rule by using the fact that areas conquered between 1820 and 1856 were much more likely to be non-landlord than areas conquered either earlier or later. This procedure has the additional advantage that the date of conquest is much more precisely measured than the share of land not under landlords, and therefore the estimates based on using this procedure are likely to be less affected by measurement error.

Table 8.6
Post and Telegraph

	(1) Any P&T	(2) Post office	(3) Telegraph	(4) Phone
Rainfall	−0.000**	−0.000**	0.000	−0.000
	(0.000)	(0.000)	(0.000)	(0.000)
Coast dummy	0.142***	0.145***	0.003	0.039
	(0.037)	(0.037)	(0.008)	(0.027)
Non-British	0.121***	0.114***	0.015***	0.073***
	(0.029)	(0.029)	(0.005)	(0.013)
Proportion nonlandlord	0.080***	0.076***	0.013**	0.066***
	(0.029)	(0.029)	(0.007)	(0.017)
Fractionalization castes and religious groups	−0.202	−0.168	0.024	0.081
	(0.254)	(0.257)	(0.053)	(0.127)
Proportion of scheduled tribes/rural pop.	−0.053	0.011	−0.046**	−0.128**
	(0.127)	(0.121)	(0.020)	(0.053)
Proportion of scheduled castes/rural pop.	−0.040	0.076	−0.023	−0.239**
	(0.163)	(0.155)	(0.045)	(0.118)
Brahman	−0.158	−0.047	0.021	−0.440***
	(0.301)	(0.285)	(0.053)	(0.141)
Gini coeff. including agricultural laborers	0.024	0.006	−0.007	0.061
	(0.115)	(0.116)	(0.027)	(0.071)
Avpop.	0.000*	0.000*	0.000*	0.000*
	(0.000)	(0.000)	(0.000)	(0.000)
Constant	0.638**	0.526*	0.081	0.253
	(0.293)	(0.282)	(0.071)	(0.159)
Observations	284	284	284	284
R-squared	0.50	0.42	0.64	0.52

Note: Robust standard errors in parentheses. *significant at 10%; **significant at 5%; ***significant at 1%.

A similar justification for the non-British variable can be found in Iyer (2002). She notes that certain parts of India were taken over because their ruler died without a natural heir under the so-called Doctrine of Lapse, but the application of the Doctrine of Lapse was suspended in 1858. As a result, the places where the ruler died without an heir after 1858 (and therefore were not taken over) constitute a legitimate control group for the places that did get taken over under the Doctrine of Lapse and the difference between the two groups gives the correct estimate of the effect of British rule. She shows that the true effect is always larger than what she would have got by naively running a regression with a non-British dummy in it. This implies that our estimates are also probably biased downward, that is, the non-

Table 8.7
Roads, Rail, etc.

	(1) Transport	(2) Bus	(3) Rail	(4) Pucca road
Rainfall	−0.000**	−0.000***	−0.000**	−0.000***
	(0.000)	(0.000)	(0.000)	(0.000)
Coast dummy	0.131***	0.130***	0.001	0.076**
	(0.035)	(0.035)	(0.005)	(0.032)
Non-British	0.154***	0.161***	−0.001	0.033*
	(0.023)	(0.023)	(0.002)	(0.018)
Proportion nonlandlord	0.194***	0.201***	0.000	0.154***
	(0.027)	(0.027)	(0.003)	(0.025)
Fractionalization castes	−0.437***	−0.445***	−0.049***	0.004
and religious groups	(0.154)	(0.155)	(0.017)	(0.163)
Proportion of scheduled	−0.267***	−0.260***	−0.019**	−0.138*
tribes/rural pop.	(0.083)	(0.083)	(0.009)	(0.072)
Proportion of scheduled	−0.486***	−0.475***	−0.012	−0.100
castes/rural pop.	(0.148)	(0.150)	(0.021)	(0.134)
Brahman	−0.410	−0.397	−0.069**	0.486*
	(0.271)	(0.272)	(0.028)	(0.257)
Gini coeff. including	0.204*	0.201*	0.021**	0.102
agricultural laborers	(0.114)	(0.114)	(0.010)	(0.093)
Avpop.	0.000	0.000	0.000	0.000**
	(0.000)	(0.000)	(0.000)	(0.000)
Constant	1.149***	1.156***	0.054**	0.264
	(0.231)	(0.231)	(0.024)	(0.223)
Observations	284	284	284	284
R-squared	0.75	0.75	0.57	0.74

Note: Robust standard errors in parentheses. *significant at 10%; **significant at 5%; ***significant at 1%.

British effect on public investment is, if anything, more positive than my results suggest.

I do not have a comparably tight justification for any of the other variables in the regression. The caste and religion variables, being measured in the 1930s, are presumably not subject to the reverse causation problem ("areas that have better infrastructure attract or retain more high castes"), given that most of the expansion of public goods happened after independence. However, one still needs to worry about whether these variables reflect some characteristic of the area that also affects the caste and religion variables, either through differential migration or differential fertility rates. The fact that I have detailed controls for a range of geographical characteristics does make this less

Table 8.8
Literacy

	(1) Rural male literacy rate	(2) Rural female literacy rate	(3) Rural literacy rate
Rainfall	0.000**	0.000***	0.000***
	(0.000)	(0.000)	(0.000)
Coast dummy	0.015	−0.003	−0.005
	(0.020)	(0.023)	(0.020)
Non-British	−0.027**	−0.053***	−0.042***
	(0.013)	(0.012)	(0.011)
Proportion nonlandlord	0.031**	−0.006	0.009
	(0.015)	(0.016)	(0.014)
Fractionalization castes and religious groups	−0.055	−0.009	−0.051
	(0.062)	(0.068)	(0.062)
Proportion of scheduled tribes/rural pop.	−0.214***	−0.142***	−0.187***
	(0.037)	(0.034)	(0.032)
Proportion of scheduled castes/rural pop.	−0.052	−0.110	−0.095
	(0.073)	(0.079)	(0.074)
Brahman	0.500***	0.381***	0.426***
	(0.137)	(0.127)	(0.126)
Avpop.	0.000	0.000	0.000
	(0.000)	(0.000)	(0.000)
Constant	0.563***	0.327***	0.422***
	(0.095)	(0.100)	(0.092)
Observations	304	284	284
R-squared	0.69	0.81	0.78

Note: Robust standard errors in parentheses. *significant at 10%; **significant at 5%; ***significant at 1%.

plausible, but in the end I have to make a judgment. This is, of course, all the more true when we come to things like the Gini coefficient and population density, which clearly reflect the way things are going in that area.

What, after this long caveat, do the results actually mean? The effect of being non-landlord is almost always positive, which tells us that landlord-dominated areas are the wrong places to grow up. The effect is often large. In Banerjee and Iyer (2002) I estimate a specification that includes only the districts of British India and uses the strategy, sketched earlier, of only comparing places that got different systems because they were conquered at different times. I find that, even after including the largest available set of geographical controls, being an entirely non-landlord district increases access to primary schools by 50 percent, access to middle schools by 75 percent, and access to primary health care centers by 100 percent. The corresponding increase in the average literacy rate is 50 percent, and infant mortality rates fall by two-thirds.

The effect of being non-British is, in effect, a comparison of an average district in a Princely State with an average district in British India that is totally landlord dominated. My results suggest that being in a former Princely State gives one more access to public goods than being in a landlord-dominated area, but not necessarily more than being in a ryotwari district.

That the effect of having a large proportion of scheduled tribes is negative will not surprise anyone familiar with India and may not therefore demand the same level of statistical scrutiny. The size of the effect is, however, striking: Using the estimated coefficients, an all scheduled tribe district will have 25 percentage points fewer villages with middle schools and tapped water than the average district, which just happens to have middle schools and tapped water in 25 percent of its villages. The effect of having a lot of Muslims is less strong but perhaps also not surprising, given all the other evidence on the relative disempowerment of Muslims in India. That the effect of fragmentation and that of having lots of scheduled castes are negative is also plausible, except that I do not find a corresponding pattern in the AP data. To understand better what is going on here, I ran the same regression with state fixed effects, in effect restricting the comparison to districts within the same state. The scheduled caste effect now more or less vanishes while the fragmentation effect is substantially diminished and about equally likely to be positive or negative. Most of the other effects persist, though to a lesser or greater extent. This suggests that the scheduled caste effect today comes from the fact that states where scheduled castes are more numerous function less effectively, but within each state, the scheduled castes are not doing substantially worse. The same is also probably true of the fragmentation effect, though, given that it is now positive in several cases, the interpretation is less clear.

The fact that Brahmin-dominated areas do worse than average is more puzzling. One possibility is that Brahmin-dominated areas have an elite (the Brahmins) that is particularly dissociated from the masses and only use their political energies to capture what may be called elite public goods (because they already have everything they could have obtained from the government in their own neighborhoods). This is consistent with the fact that the Brahmin effect is very strongly positive in the cases of metalled roads, electricity for domestic use, tapped water,[6] and colleges,[7] which are all "elite" goods, but mostly negative otherwise. Unfortunately, the effect on telephone connections is negative, which makes this theory somewhat less compelling.

The effect of the Gini coefficient here is not easy to interpret since I have already argued that being a non-landlord area was one reason why the land distribution would be different. Interpreting the effect of population density is equally problematic but it does conform very well to what everyone would expect.

Finally it is worth emphasizing that the regressions do rather well in predicting where the public goods are located: It explains up to three-quarters of the variation.

8.3.1   And therefore ... ?

If there is one thing that comes out of this data, it is the fact that access to public goods is substantially a matter of who can extract them from the political system. Most things that one associates with a lack of political effectiveness—class conflict as measured by landlord domination, high proportion of traditionally disempowered groups, ethnic fractionalization—are also good predictors of lack of access to public goods. I would not expect many to be surprised by this, but the magnitudes are still striking, given the fact that India is a democracy with a strongly egalitarian ideology.

It is not my intention to imply that this is the end of the story—that these differences are necessarily here to stay unless there is radical social change. Clearly certain types of intrastate differences are smaller than they used to be: In particular, scheduled caste areas do only marginally worse than the state average. And clearly there are agencies both within and outside the government that have the will and the opportunity to make a difference. The political economy of the Indian state has always allowed some space to those who have found the right language to challenge the system, as the Chipko movement eloquently testifies.

But it is difficult to be confident that the differences are all about to be erased. Scheduled tribe areas are not converging to the national average in any obvious way, nor are the landlord areas. In fact, Banerjee and Iyer (2002) shows that in terms of agricultural yields and investment (which includes public investment), the landlord areas have been falling behind the non-landlord areas over the last forty years.

As I see it, there are several reasons why this evidence should be taken seriously. First, it serves as an important warning against the view that one should not worry about the adverse distributional consequences of the recent shifts in policy. To the extent that it creates groups that are economically and/or politically disempowered, there is always the danger that when these groups eventually manage to acquire enough political power to try to reclaim what they see as their fair share of the pie, the process that this unleashes could derail the entire process of development. This is clearly one plausible interpretation of what went wrong in the landlord areas and the caste-fragmented districts—their problem may be that they are, in a manner of speaking, too busy righting all the wrongs of yesterday to focus on what would give them a better tomorrow. There is a little bit of direct testimony that supports this view: Banerjee and Iyer (2002) shows some evidence suggesting that the landlord districts do much better than the non-landlord districts in terms of redistributing land and yet end up doing worse on poverty reduction. Banerjee and Duflo (2000) shows that the cross-country evidence is also sympathetic to the view that the short-run effect of any major redistribution is to reduce growth. This is also perhaps what is behind the observation made earlier that scheduled castes are not doing too badly compared to the state average, but states with high proportions of scheduled castes are doing systematically worse. It is conceivable that the political movements that empowered the schedule castes unleashed a set of conflicts that have, for the time being, paralyzed governments in those states. This is not say that the process of empowerment is always going to lead to worse outcomes at the state level—it is entirely possible, for example, that the process of empowerment of currently disfavored groups will eventually lead to a politics where there is less waste simply because there is more competition. But the short-run effects can be dire, and there is no evidence that long-run effects are necessarily good. To the extent that the current process of growth is creating new marginalized groups and reinforcing the marginalization of groups that are already marginal, there is much to worry about and probably a lot to do.

Second, the fact that interstate differences are in many cases a big part of the story is worrisome given that a large fraction of state governments seem to be either bankrupt or totally paralyzed or both. It is true that state governments are becoming less important for some public goods with the movement to panchyati raj, but a lot still remains in their hands (including money), and in any case, what is to prevent the same pattern being reproduced at the level of the pan-chayats. In this context, it is worth revisiting the issue of decentraliza-tion: If the problem is that people have trouble working together, decentralization can help if it gives more authority to relatively ho-mogenous groups. If, however, the real conflict is at the village level—say, between the landless who still remember what the current land-lord's grandfather had done to their grandfather—then pushing the authority down to the village level might simply bring out the worst in both sides. Centralization, by forcing people to build broader coali-tions, may actually help: For example, it is entirely possible that the same landless may feel the need to ally themselves with the middle peasants in another village, and as a result may start taking a less nar-row view of their options. Moreover, there may be an important role for targeted initiatives to break the logjam that is holding back the state, district, or village. Ideally, such a program would offer enough new options to hitherto marginalized/embattled groups to make it attractive for them to refocus their energies away from simply fight-ing, and this could start a process of reintegration. Certainly this has been the thinking behind the recent national programs in Peru and Mexico (particularly in Chiapas) aimed at reintegrating indigenous peo-ple. Moreover, while centralization receives bad press these days, Chin (2001) shows that Operation Blackboard, the one large federal inter-vention in the education sector in India, was actually a moderate suc-cess: She concludes that between 3 and 7 million additional girls either became literate or completed primary school because of the program.

Third, the data that exists does not tell us much about the quality of the actual public services that are being delivered. However, where there is evidence, it seems to suggest that quality behaves in much the same way as the availability of public goods—literacy is also lower in the places where one expects greater conflict (see table 8.8) as is infant survival (not shown here but see Banerjee and Iyer 2002). Low quality of public goods has the potential to set off a vicious cycle: When public goods such as schools, colleges, hospitals, and power supply in rural India are not what the elite has come to expect, those who can afford it move to the city or at least make sure that they do not need to use the village infrastructure. As the elite exits from the system, two things happen. The rural population risks being left without leadership that can mediate the various conflicting interests and deal with the state bureaucracy, which makes it harder to improve the infrastructure. And the existing infrastructure may function less well, because the teacher and the doctor now live in the city and have to commute to the village: In particular, they may find it very tempting to be absent on occasion, now that most people with the social clout to kick up a fuss about absenteeism have already opted out. All of which makes it more tempting to try to opt out.

Of course, it is not clear that even those places where the existing mechanisms are working as well as they could be reasonably expected to are going to be able to retain their elites. But it is clear that if we are to have a chance we have to start dealing with the problem now—as more and more of the elite exit from the system, the problem gets harder to solve and it becomes increasingly likely that large chunks of rural India will turn into traps, with an infrastructure so bad that only those who are too poor to move and too powerless to challenge the system continue to be there.

There are of course many people who are trying to do something about it. The various nonformal education programs and health worker programs are being showcased as the prototype of a possible solution: By having teachers and health workers who are from the village and from the same social group as those they serve, they hope to cut down on absenteeism and strengthen local control over the programs. Unfortunately this comes at the cost of having to use teachers who have eight or ten years of education themselves and health workers who have a week's training. It is not at all clear that the quality of public services that are so generated is high enough to slow down the polarization process.[8]

One way to improve quality is to make the teachers and the doctors (and others like them) answerable to those who are supposed to benefit from their services. This is clearly the trend in India, but no state to our knowledge has as yet taken the politically difficult step of giving the panchayats or parents groups the power to fire delinquent government servants.[9]

The alternative is to rely more on market incentives. Going to a full-scale market-based system like Medicare/Medicaid in the United States, where the government pays private providers who bill them for services provided to private citizens, is not going to work because the scope for corruption and abuse is simply too large. It may be possible to try a more limited market-based scheme where reputed doctors are paid a large lump sum amount to compensate them for coming to a particular village (paid by the panchayat, on the spot) and thereafter are allowed to charge each patient what the market would bear. Given that even poor people do spend substantial amounts on health care,[10] the fact that they would have to pay a price may not be too much of a problem. On the other hand, it may exclude exactly those who need the help the most—the poorest and those least capable of judging the quality of the heath care they are getting.[11]

Similar concerns about alternative ways to improve the present system come up, of course, in the case of every single public good. It seems clear that at this point we need to innovate and indeed, there is a lot of innovation going on, mainly in the NGO sector. These innovations need to be evaluated rigorously and the best practice needs to be disseminated. Neither of these is easy: India lacks a culture where there is enough respect for what one might call the craft of social policy evaluation—mundane but vital things like how to measure success, how to set up the right control group.... And we seem not to recognize that perfection is the enemy of the scalable and the easily reproducible—if we insist that the programs be perfectly attuned to their environment, we will end up with programs that can never be imitated. This, for us social scientists, may well be where the next big fights are.

Notes

1. Based on the 1991 census.

2. Dreze and Sen (1995).

3. Dreze and Sen (1995).

4. Easterly and Levine (1997) have argued that a similar longstanding antagonism among tribes may explain the poor performance of most African states.

5. This is similar to the argument in Alesina, Baqir, and Easterly (1999).

6. Though in the specification reported here for tapped water, it is not significant.

7. Not reported here since I am not sure it is a public good.

8. Banerjee, Jacob, and Kremer (2000) find that doubling the number of teachers in nonformal education centers has very little effect on test scores, which suggests that the average teacher is not of the highest quality.

9. They have, however, taken the important step of requiring a certain fraction of powerful positions in the panchayats (including the position of pradhan) be reserved for women (one-third) and scheduled castes and tribes (in proportion to their share in the population). This will ensure that the effectiveness of the panchayat is not undermined by collusion between the typically high caste government officials and the higher castes in the village. (Chattopadhyay and Duflo (2001) provide some interesting evidence showing that the devolution of authority through this system does change the way the panchayats function.)

10. See Das (2001).

11. See Das (2001).

References

Alesina, A., R. Baqir, and W. Easterly. 1999. "Public Goods and Ethnic Divisions." *Quarterly Journal of Economics* 114(4):1243–1284.

Bagchi, Amiya K. 1976. "Reflections on Patterns of Regional Growth in India under British Rule." *Bengal Past and Present* 95(1):247–289.

Banerjee, A. V., and E. Duflo. 2000. "Inequality and Growth: What can the data say?" NBER Working Paper Series Number 7793.

Banerjee, A. V., and L. Iyer. 2002. "History, Institutions and Economic Performance: The Legacy of Colonial Land Tenure Systems in India." Mimeo., MIT.

Banerjee, A. V., and R. Somanathan. 2001. "Caste, Community and Collective Action: The Political Economy of Public Good Provision in India." Mimeo., MIT.

Banerjee, A. V., S. Jacob, and M. Kremer. 2000. "Promoting School Participation in Rural Rajasthan: Results from Some Prospective Trials." Mimeo., Harvard.

Chattopadhyay, Raghabendra, and Esther Duflo. 2001. "Women's Leadership and Policy Decisions: Evidence from a Nationwide Randomized Experiment in India." NBER Working Paper Series Number 8615.

Chin, Aimee. 2001. "Essays on the Economic Effects of Human Capital Investments." Ph.D. dissertation, MIT.

Das, Jishnu. 2001. "Three Essays on the Provision and Use of Services in Low Income Countries." Ph.D. dissertation, Harvard University.

Dreze, Jean, and Amartya Sen. 1995. *India: Economic Development and Social Opportunity*. Delhi and New York: Oxford University Press.

Easterly, William, and Ross Levine. 1997. "Africa's Growth Tragedy: Policies and Ethnic Divisions." *Quarterly Journal of Economics* 112(4):1203–1250.

Iyer, Lakshmi. 2002. "The Long-Term Impact of Colonial Rule: Evidence from India." Mimeo., MIT.

V   Technology and Takeoff

9 The Impact of Economic Reforms on Industry in India: A Case Study of the Software Industry

N. R. Narayana Murthy

The Indian economy, in the last decade, transitioned from an inward-looking, closed economy, to a liberalized, export-oriented one. The software sector witnessed unprecedented growth, with exports growing at a compounded annual growth rate (CAGR) of around 45 percent and domestic software sales at around 35 percent. In fact, before 1991, the Indian software sector was adversely affected by the restrictive economic policies. Thus, this sector provides an appropriate case study on how liberalization of the economy reduced friction to business and accelerated growth.

9.1   Growth of the Indian Software Services Industry

The Indian economy, especially the software sector, witnessed robust growth, post-1991. India's annual software exports increased from US$24 million in 1985 to US$164 million[1] in 1992 to US$7.8 billion[2] in March 2002. Similarly, India's domestic software sales increased from US$140 million[3] in 1992 to US$2.45 billion[4] in 2001–2002.

The economic reforms of 1991, introduced by the then Finance Minister Dr. Manmohan Singh, laid the foundation for this growth. A company such as Infosys exemplifies the benefits of these reforms. Infosys grew from US$0.13 million in revenues and twelve employees in 1982 to US$3.89 million and 300 employees in 1992, to US$545 million for the year ending March 2002, with 10,700 employees. Infosys, which started with one client in 1982, had eleven clients in 1992. By March 2002, the number of clients had increased to 293. Further, the total investment in business by Infosys increased from US$0.04 million in 1982 to US$2.16 million in 1992 to US$435.67 million by March 2002.

9.1.1   India before 1991

Before 1991, India adopted an inward-looking policy. There was distrust among the policymakers regarding the intentions of the private
sector. Further, imports were restricted. At one point of time, the marginal tax rate was 97 percent. In fact, wealth tax was as high as 8 percent and estate tax was 85 percent.

In addition, the corporate sector faced numerous bureaucratic hurdles. For instance, it took about twenty-five visits to Delhi, and nine to
twelve months, for approval to purchase a computer. A clerk in the
Reserve Bank of India (RBI) took five days to decide whether the managing director of a software firm could travel abroad for a day. Business faced difficulties in accessing even basic infrastructure such as
phones or data communication lines. For instance, retired government officers were given priority over private companies for phone
allotment.

9.1.2   The Economic Reforms of 1991

The economic reforms, introduced in 1991, laid the foundation for the
growth of the software sector in the country. The reforms abolished
many restrictive boundaries for business and increased the velocity of
decision making in organizations. It decentralized power to regional
and state offices. Further, it encouraged better industry orientation
among bureaucrats. Companies could now call on their local Software
Technology Parks of India (STPI) offices with requests, instead of con-
tacting Delhi each time. In addition, many bureaucratic processes were
removed.

The reforms resulted in availability of financing from the equity
route. Before the reforms were enacted, raising capital through equity
was an unattractive option, since pricing of initial public offerings
(IPOs) was controlled by the Controller of Capital Issues—a department under the government of India. For the first time, companies
were allowed to decide IPO prices, using market-driven price-earnings
ratios. This made equity a viable financing option, especially for software companies that did not have large fixed assets to secure debts.

Another important change was the introduction of current account
convertibility. The RBI eased restrictions on accessibility to foreign
currency. This made it easier to hire foreign consultants and establish
sales offices abroad. Further, it facilitated international brand-building
efforts and overseas travel. In fact, the number of overseas offices of
Indian information technology (IT) companies increased from 167 in

1995 to around 750 today. Infosys's overseas offices increased from 2 in 1992 to 31 in 2002.

Subsequent to the reforms, multinational companies were allowed 100 percent ownership of subsidiaries in India. This eased their entry; IBM, ORACLE, SAP, Microsoft, and Sun have since established presence in India. This created intense competition for talent. Indian software companies, under competitive pressure, adopted world-class quality processes, tools, and methodologies. Further, they invested in infrastructure and data communication facilities.

Duties and tariffs were reduced, and the tax structure was simplified and rationalized. Average tariffs fell by 70 percent between 1991 and 2000. Wealth tax is now 1 percent, and estate tax is abolished. The corporate tax rate was reduced from 45 percent in 1992 to 36.75 percent in 2002. Further, import procedures were simplified, and most items were brought under the Open General License Scheme. This facilitated their free import. In addition, duty on software was reduced to zero.

9.1.3   Post-1991: The Reform Process Continues

The reform process in India has thus benefited the nation tremendously and is now irreversible. Successive governments have continued this process, irrespective of their political affiliations. Some of the steps, which carried the reforms further, are discussed later.

9.1.3.1   Employee Stock Option Plan (ESOP)

Subsequent to the reforms, the government allowed Indian firms to offer stock options. Further, foreign currency–denominated stock options were introduced in 1998. Through ESOPs, employees got an opportunity for long-term wealth creation. This enabled companies to attract global talent. In fact, Infosys implemented its first stock option plan in 1994 and its dollar-denominated stock option plan in 1998. By June 2000, Infosys created 1,913 rupee and 235 dollar millionaires.

9.1.3.2   Capital Market Reforms

In 1993, the government introduced guidelines that allowed Indian companies to list on foreign exchanges. In fact, in 1998, Infosys became the first India-registered company to list on an American exchange (the NASDAQ). Further, two-way fungibility was introduced, facilitating greater liquidity. Over the past three years, norms for investments and acquisitions abroad were eased. In 2000, the condition that firms had to be profitable for three consecutive years before they could go in for an IPO was relaxed.

Further, minimum public float for IPOs was reduced to 10 percent. In addition, foreign institutional investment limits in various sectors were increased. Presently, it is 100 percent in many sectors including software, petroleum refining and exploration, roads, tourism, and film industry. All these reforms have enabled companies to access capital markets in a more efficient manner.

9.1.3.3 Communication STPI started providing satellite-based data communication facilities for software companies. This led to easier and cheaper availability of data communication facilities. For instance, the price of 2MB bandwidth decreased from US$1.2 million per month in 1984 to US$3,800 in 2002. In fact, there has been a decrease of 40 percent in the price of 2MB bandwidth over the last three years. In addition, basic telephony was opened to allow private-sector participation. Reforms also increased competition in cellular telephony; in most places, four operators are now allowed. This has led to an explosion of the cellular population in India, with the number of cellular phones increasing from 0.3 million in March 1997 to 8.5 million by 2002. In fact, recently, VOIP (Voice Over Internet Protocol) was introduced.

9.1.4 Benefits from These Reforms
The reforms reduced the interference of the bureaucracy on the industry. In addition, it raised the confidence of Indians in exploring global markets. For instance, in 1991, India's overall exports totaled US$18.14 billion; in March 2001, the figure reached US$44.5 billion.[5] Further, software accounted for less than 1 percent of India's exports in 1991; in the year ending in March 2002, it accounted for 17 percent.

The reforms proved several bureaucratic dogmas wrong. For instance, it was believed that introducing current account convertibility would lead to a large-scale flight of capital. Further, people believed that reducing import duties would lead to a decrease in the foreign exchange reserves, because of large-scale imports. However, foreign exchange reserves actually increased from US$1.2 billion in June 1991 to US$55.8 billion[6] in June 2002.

It was also believed that protectionism was the only way to help the Indian industry grow. On the contrary, the entry of multinationals into India created a competitive environment that forced Indian companies to successfully adopt world-class infrastructure, quality processes, human resources practices, and so forth. For instance, Hindustan Motors and Fiat produced the same cars, for the Indian market, for forty years. However, they are now forced to produce new and better models in order to keep pace with the competition.

The traditional Indian mindset believed that it is not possible to create wealth legally and ethically. However, companies like Infosys disproved this. Infosys started with US$250 in seed capital in 1981; the company's market capitalization, as of June 28, 2002, is US$6.78 billion. In fact, post-1991, equity became a viable financing option. This encouraged entrepreneurship in India.

Postreforms, India emerged as an attractive destination for foreign institutional investors (FIIs). Investments by FIIs increased from US$6 million in 1991 to US$244 million in 1993 and to US$1.8 billion[7] for the year April 2001–March 2002. In fact, the establishment of the Securities and Exchange Board of India (SEBI) in 1992 increased regulation and, hence, improved the confidence of investors.

9.2   Second-Generation Reforms

It is important for India to understand the lessons from the success of the reform process and to continue the reforms. In this context, some of the areas where further reforms are needed are discussed here.

Reforms are needed in the field of education. For instance, licensing of education must be abolished. India has one of the largest education systems in the world, with 237 universities, 46 deemed universities, and 10,600 colleges, employing more than 330,000 teachers. Despite this, total enrollment in India for higher education forms only 6 percent of the relevant population (17–23-year-olds). In this context, educational institutions must be allowed to function as corporations. There should not be subsidies for higher education. Moreover, meritocracy must be introduced among faculty by implementation of pay-per-performance system.

The government should focus on basic education. Presently, only around 60 percent of the children study up to grade 5. Subsidies must be restricted to basic education. However, basic education must also function in a free-market environment. In fact, the government can give vouchers to people below a certain income level as an incentive for schooling.

The labor market must be flexible enough so that Indian companies can compete with their foreign counterparts. This is crucial to implementing meritocracy within organizations. At the same time, the country needs to create a social security mechanism for those who do not have jobs.

India should enact reforms to improve the interfacing between the state governments and corporations. Presently, apart from a few industry-friendly states such as Karnataka and Andhra Pradesh, states still experience friction while interacting with business. For instance, even now, some states have recruitment quotas for domiciles and force corporations to hire from state employment exchanges. Hence, there is a need to make interfacing with state governments easier for corporations.

9.3   The Road Ahead

Finally, India must not be afraid to dream—bold dreams that are accompanied by actions. Fear and suspicion will only retard India's growth. In fact, Indians can create world-class companies in India that compete with the best from around the world. All it requires is that an enlightened political leadership, bureaucracy, corporate leadership, and academia work collaboratively.

Notes

1. NASSCOM, "The Software Industry in India, 1996: Strategic Review." New Delhi: National Association of Software and Service Companies.

2. NASSCOM-McKinsey Report 2002. New Delhi: National Association of Software and Service Companies.

3. NASSCOM, "The Software Industry in India, 1996: Strategic Review."

4. NASSCOM.

5. Economic Survey of India 2001–2002. Ministry of Finance, Government of India.

6. RBI's weekly statistical supplement, May 24, 2002.

7. SEBI.

10

Information Technology and India's Economic Development

Nirvikar Singh

10.1 Introduction

The success of India's software industry on the global stage has captured the imagination of Indians in a way that only cricket and hockey successes could in the past. Indians (or people of Indian origin) have become leaders of, as well as contributors to, the information technology (IT) revolution in the United States, reinforcing the impression that India is world class in IT. At the same time, India remains an extremely poor country, with levels of human development for the masses that put it in the same league as sub-Saharan Africa. From this perspective, India's IT success represents the emergence of another elite enclave, with increased inequality the result.

In this chapter, I examine the question of whether IT can do more than fuel an enclave-based export boom. Can IT contribute to India's economic development in a broader, more fundamental way? What are the potential mechanisms by which this can occur? What is the likelihood of IT accelerating India's growth, and what are the potential roadblocks or bottlenecks where government policy can make a difference between success and failure? This chapter assumes a basic familiarity with the general structure and performance of the Indian economy, and the economic reform process that has been taking place in the last decade and will continue to do so in the future. In section 10.2, therefore, I begin my analysis directly by examining the performance of India's IT sector, discussing the role of software versus hardware, the growth pattern of the software industry and software exports, the rapid emergence of IT-enabled services, and the role of the domestic market.

Section 10.3 turns to a consideration of the resource needs of the IT sector, and possible constraints and bottlenecks. These include the supply of IT-skilled labor to support future growth, telecommunications and other aspects of infrastructure, and possible financial constraints. Section 10.4 uses a range of economic ideas to map out the possibilities for broad-based IT-led development, going beyond the IT sector. I draw on recent analyses of the process of economic development that emphasize factors such as innovation, complementarities in technologies and in demand, and pecuniary externalities. In terms of the mechanisms for development, I discuss examples such as increasing value added, using better telecom links to capture more benefits domestically through offshore development for industrial country firms, greater spillovers to the local economy, broadening the IT industry with production of telecom access devices, improving the functioning of the economy through a more extensive and denser communications network, and improving governance at all levels.

Section 10.5 examines the policy environment, which interacts with resource availability, in the light of broader developmental possibilities. Issues raised here include the provision of education, labor market distortions, infrastructure development in areas such as telecommunications, and tax and subsidy policies. Section 10.6 provides a summary conclusion, with an assessment of possibilities and recommendations for policy.

10.2   The IT Sector

Information technology essentially refers to the digital processing, storage, and communication of information of all kinds.[1] Therefore, IT can potentially be used in every sector of the economy.[2] The true impact of IT on growth and productivity continues to be a matter of debate, even in the United States, which has been the leader and largest adopter of IT.[3] However, there is no doubt that the IT sector has been a dynamic one in many developed countries, and India has stood out as a developing country where IT, in the guise of software exports, has grown dramatically, despite the country's relatively low level of income and development. An example of IT's broader impact comes from the case of so-called IT-enabled services, a broad category covering many different kinds of data processing and voice interactions that use some IT infrastructure as inputs, but do not necessarily involve the production of IT outputs. India's figures for the size of the IT sector typically include such services, which are discussed in this sec-

Table 10.1
India's GDP and IT Sector

Year	GDP at current prices (Rs. billion)	IT sector (Rs. billion)	IT sector (US$ billion)
1994–1995	9,170	63	2.0
1995–1996	10,732	99	2.9
1996–1997	12,435	137	3.8
1997–1998	13,900	187	5.0
1998–1999	16,160	248	6.1
1999–2000	17,865	371	8.7
2000–2001	19,895	554	12.2

Sources: GDP: ⟨www.adb.org⟩. IT sector: ⟨www.nasscom.org/it_industry/indic_statistics.asp⟩.

tion. I begin with a review of the overall industry size, then discuss software versus hardware, exports versus domestic sales, and, finally, IT-enabled services.

Table 10.1 provides statistics on the overall size of GDP, and on the size of the IT industry, in billions of current rupees. The IT industry figures are not necessarily as accurate as the GDP figures, and they are based on revenues rather than value added, so they are not conceptually directly comparable. Nevertheless, table 10.1 gives an idea of the growing importance of the IT sector in India's economy. The IT sector grew over this six-year period by a factor of 9, whereas GDP slightly more than doubled in the same period. Table 10.1 also gives dollar equivalents for the IT sector figures: These reflect the changing exchange rate over the period, though again there appear to be some discrepancies. With the rupee falling against the U.S. dollar over this period, the dollar value of the IT sector grew by a factor of 6.

Even with its spectacular growth, India's IT sector in 2000–2001 was less than 3 percent of GDP (even if one treats all sales as value added), suggesting that there is considerable room for further growth. For example, if India's nominal GDP were to double over the six years subsequent to 2000–2001, while the IT sector were to increase by a factor of 6, and if one assumes that value added is about two-thirds of total sales, the resulting ratio of the IT sector to GDP would be in the range of 8 percent, or not dissimilar to that in the United States today. This calculation assumes slower growth than in the 1999 McKinsey-NASSCOM projections, but may be a more likely figure.

10.2.1 Software versus Hardware

The basic distinction in IT is between hardware and software. The former refers, of course, to the physical components of processors, storage devices, and communications devices. The latter refers to the instructions that govern the flow and processing of information in digital form, within and between hardware devices and components. The design of hardware actually involves the development and use of appropriate software code, so there are definite overlaps in the two categories. It is also possible to substitute software for hardware in the basic design of circuits. The actual production of hardware is classified within the manufacturing sector and is more distinct from the development of software. The profitable manufacture of semiconductors and other sophisticated hardware components typically requires infrastructure, large-scale investments in capacity, and accumulated experience that India does not possess and is not in a position to acquire easily. India's development path, despite its emphasis on import-substituting industrialization, has not supported the growth of a robust, world-class manufacturing industry, such as has arisen in many East Asian countries.

Nevertheless, India does perform many hardware assembly tasks internally, almost entirely for the domestic market. Components in such cases typically come from East and Southeast Asia. The ability to organize this aspect of production may be the basis for further development of hardware capabilities. Several East Asian countries also began mainly as assemblers of sophisticated components produced elsewhere and extended their presence in the value chain backward as they learned by doing. While being late to the game may make entry more difficult, the fact that manufacturing of components becomes increasingly standardized, and the cost of these components falls, works in favor of late entrants. For example, the production of most memory chips has become commoditized, and moved to developing countries, where twenty years ago it was the core of Intel's business.

The example of firms like Dell and Cisco may also be useful to keep in mind when evaluating the hardware industry in India. Dell outsources most, if not all, of its component manufacturing. It is, in fact, an extremely sophisticated assembler. Its value creation is based on organizing this assembly as efficiently as possible, doing so on demand, and keeping its inventories absolutely minimal. Strong customer service plus management of communications and logistics at both ends of the value chain are also keys to Dell's success. Dell's positioning to

Table 10.2
India's IT-Sector Decomposition (Rs. billion)

Year	Hardware	Software	Other*	Domestic**	Export**
1994–1995	23.8	26.1	13.6	34.6	21.1
1995–1996	36.8	41.9	20.2	59.0	26.6
1996–1997	48.1	63.1	25.8	68.4	49.8
1997–1998	52.4	100.4	33.8	88.5	73.4
1998–1999	42.5	158.9	36.4	105.4	110.3
1999–2000	65.7	243.5	61.6	152.7	176.3

Sources: ⟨www.nasscom.org/it_industry/indic_statistics.asp⟩.
*Includes peripherals, training, maintenance and networking; **Hardware, software, peripherals.

take advantage of strengths in infrastructure and closeness to a growing customer market is an important lesson for India. The point here, which I develop subsequently in this chapter, is that a hardware industry in India is feasible, building on India's experience in assembly, but it will require significant improvements in infrastructure and careful attention to market needs. Our earlier discussion of hardware design is relevant here, since this is an area where software expertise matters more and manufacturing infrastructure does not. Therefore hardware design may be a promising area for Indian IT. Table 10.2 gives some basic statistics on the decomposition of India's IT sector.

India's software industry is more robust than its hardware industry, at least in certain areas. While selling packaged software to consumer (and most business) markets requires economies of scale and scope, as well as marketing and customer support muscle, project-oriented components of software development do not, to quite the same degree. The software development and use life cycle includes analysis and specification of requirements, design, coding, testing, installation, maintenance, and support. Many of these activities, particularly coding and testing, involve *relatively* routine IT skills that India's workforce has in large absolute numbers (though small relative to the total population).

The existence of the Indian Institutes of Technology (IITs), the ubiquity of Unix in academic environments, and the relatively low infrastructure demands of learning to use and create software all worked in India's favor on the supply side. The use of English in India's higher education system, the increase in the use of Unix and related operating systems due to the rapid rise of the Internet, and the large number of Y2K-related projects in the late 1990s all contributed to demand for

India's software industry services, in addition to the general growth of IT in the 1990s. Much of this demand came from abroad, as I discuss in section 10.2.2. However, the software industry's domestic revenues also grew rapidly in the last few years, at over 30 percent per annum, on average.

Despite the even faster growth of software exports, domestic software revenue still represents about 30 percent of software industry gross receipts. The National Association of Software and Services Companies (NASSCOM) projects domestic sales to grow substantially faster than export sales in the next decade, enough to make domestic sales over 50 percent of the industry's sales, and this seems to borne out by recent growth in domestic software (31 percent annual growth from 1998–1999 to 2000–2001; NASSCOM 2002a,b), and IT overall (42 percent growth in 1999–2000). Much of this growth was driven by demand from state governments, which have been introducing e-governance initiatives. The second largest sector in terms of domestic IT demand is financial services. In the domestic market, products and packages make up almost half of revenues, with projects accounting for over a quarter, while professional services, support and maintenance, IT-enabled services and training each make up less than 10 percent (Singh 2002). This pattern is quite different from that of exports, as I discuss in this chapter.

10.2.2 Software Exports

India's software exports went from a few million dollars in the 1980s to over a billion dollars by 1995–1996 and $6.2 billion in 2000–2001. Despite the global slowdown, software and services exports exceeded the 2000–2001 figure by 31 percent in dollar terms, exceeding $8 billion.[4] While growth has slowed from the earlier 50 percent rate, the dollar increases are as big. While the NASSCOM-McKinsey target of $50 billion in software export revenue by 2008 may be overoptimistic,[5] the resilience of software exports in a difficult economic climate has proved pessimists wrong.

The pattern of activities that generates software export revenue is somewhat different from the sources of domestic revenue. In particular, professional services accounted for 44 percent of export revenue in 1998–1999, followed by projects at 36 percent. Products and packages were only 8 percent of the total compared to nearly half for domestic revenue. Desai (2000) suggests that the difference in the patterns of domestic and export sales is overstated, because domestic sales of packages are by resellers of packaged software licensed from foreign software vendors. However, this appears to be changing, as Indian firms develop packages for the home market in areas such as financial services.

Coding and testing appear to form a significant proportion of the skills used in the Indian software industry. Some have expressed concern[6] that the Indian software industry is "programmer heavy," and therefore unable to move up to higher value-added segments of software. Related issues that reinforce these concerns are the brain drain of the most talented or experienced IT people, the lack of sufficient managerial skills for more sophisticated contract work, and the lack of domestic spillovers from the "body shopping" of programmers for on-site work in developed countries. Again, the latest trends suggest that Indian firms have begun to overcome these roadblocks.[7]

Indicators of the strength of India's software export capabilities include the depth of its base and the breadth of its global reach. There are over 2,000 Indian software exporters, and while only the top five (TCS, Infosys, Wipro, Satyam and HCL) are—or are approaching the status of—global brands, they together account for only about 30 percent of software exports.[8] While the United States remains by far the largest market for India's software exports, its share of India's software exports has fallen slightly, to 62 percent, with Europe coming in at 24 percent, and Japan and the rest of the world accounting for the remaining 14 percent.[9] Individual firms and organizations such as NASSCOM have shown themselves to be adept at targeting markets with substantial growth potential, such as Germany, and the reputations built in exporting to the United States are proving important.[10]

10.2.3   IT-Enabled Services

IT-enabled services are not necessarily related to the production of software or IT in general, but use IT to make the provision of services possible. Customer call centers are one example, where Indians have been training to speak with American accents, in order to deal with customer queries from the United States. Accounting services are a second example. Yet another, longer-standing market segment is that of medical transcription. NASSCOM categorizes ten different types of IT-enabled services, varying widely in terms of skills required and value added.[11] The ten categories overlap to some extent, but they give a good idea of the scope of the industry.

- Customer Interaction Services
- Business Process Outsourcing/Management; Back Office Operations
- Insurance Claims Processing
- Medical Transcription
- Legal Databases
- Digital Content
- Online Education
- Data Digitization/GIS
- Payroll/HR Services
- Website Services (NASSCOM 2002c)

In terms of potential, the first category in table 10.3 is projected to reach $60 billion worldwide in 2003. Other categories may be similar in size or smaller, but Indian industry is making inroads into all of them. According to NASSCOM, revenues from IT-enabled services in India in 2000–2001 were over $800 million, up 70 percent from the previous year. Customer interaction services were the highest growing segment within this sector, with over 100 percent growth in 2000–2001 and generating 20 percent of the sectors' revenue. Back office operations' revenues grew over 40 percent in the same period and provided a third of the sector's revenues. NASSCOM projects IT-enabled services to generate revenues of $17 billion and provide employment for 1.1 million people by 2010, while a report submitted to the Indian government's Electronics and Computer Software Export Promotion Council sees IT-enabled services exports growing from their estimate of $264 million in 2000 to over $4 billion in 2005.[12]

The rapid growth of the sector illustrates that many of the early problems have been overcome. These included firms that were too small to market to or deal directly with clients and too small to make investments in adequate training and infrastructure.[13] Success has generated attention, and NASSCOM, the government, and others are working on providing incentives, venture funding, training, and infrastructure. Good communications links are obviously important for the success of IT-enabled services. An additional bottleneck in the past may have been the lack of managerial and marketing skills and of reputations for quality. Part of the solution includes the import of such skills by multinationals such as GE and Citigroup shifting some of their back-office operations to India. There is no doubt that there have been positive reputational and resource spillovers from the software export sector to IT-enabled services.[14]

10.3   Resource Considerations

As in any industry, the availability of adequate supplies of inputs is critical for growth. Much of the caution about the prospects for India's IT industry has focused on potential bottlenecks in the supply of skills and on the quality of the infrastructure. I add financial constraints to this combination and discuss each of these briefly.

10.3.1   Supply of Skills

A major reason for the success of India's software industry is the large supply of labor with some IT skills. India graduates perhaps about 125,000 engineers a year, second only to the United States worldwide.[15] However, not all these engineers go into the IT industry, and not all IT professionals have engineering or computer science qualifications—this being true in the United States as well.[16] India's stock of IT professionals is estimated at over 400,000,[17] so that IT industry revenues per IT professional (assuming that all of them work in the industry, which is unlikely) are about $30,000.[18] Government targets and others' optimistic projections imply that IT industry revenues will increase by a factor of 15. The breakdown of this growth could be something like a doubling in revenue per IT professional, and therefore almost an eightfold increase in numbers. However, to the extent that much of this future growth will come in IT-enabled services, the additional employment may come in areas where different, easier-to-acquire skills are needed.

Whether growth comes in revenue per employee or number of workers, there are implications for training. Increasing revenue per IT professional requires improvements in managerial and marketing skills,[19] as well as the production of more highly trained IT people. Training more people in IT requires investments to increase the capacity of this component of the higher education sector. This is a thorny problem, given the poor state of India's higher education system. Even at the elite IITs, faculty are poorly paid relative to industry, and the physical infrastructure has deteriorated from lack of investment. Increases in government expenditure to fix these problems are difficult in an environment of large budget deficits and long-term neglect of basic education. Interestingly, the task of training workers for

IT-enabled services such as call centers is much easier, since the universities produce large numbers of graduates with some familiarity with the English language and Western culture. In all areas of IT and related services, however, increased private and public investment has occurred.[20] One potential problem is that of maintaining standards and quality, but industry-determined certifications exist, and reputations can be established quite quickly in practice in a competitive environment. IT industry investment itself plays a role, since the industry has a strong interest in growing the available supply of IT professionals.[21]

A further problem besides sheer numbers is the issue of level of training, and even the IITs are hard-pressed to provide postgraduate education comparable to what is available in the United States. Here, the brain drain, initially severe, can be beneficial, as the current slowdown in the United States sends back thousands of Indian IT professionals with valuable training and experience.[22] Desai (2000) uses this issue to suggest that India may actually be better off by continuing to specialize in the lower end of the market, for coding and testing, as well as in IT-enabled services, at least in the next few years, but this argument may miss the point that sustained success requires the simultaneous use of workers with many complementary skills at different levels.[23] Which route is most profitable is best left up to the players, with the government's role being to avoid excessive policy distortions that create imbalances across different segments within the IT sector. The last two years have suggested that the education industry can respond quite well to a situation where the benefits of certain kinds of education are clear and immediate.

10.3.2 Infrastructure

Government failure in the realm of infrastructure provision has been a major characteristic of Indian economic development. Of the various infrastructure constraints, probably that of electric power is the most fundamental, and the most difficult one to tackle. I do not address it here, because the subject is too large, and it is not central to my analysis, though electric power is clearly necessary for an IT industry.[24] Other infrastructure constraints, such as water, roads, and ports, have served as greater bottlenecks for manufacturing. In fact, one of the reasons software exports were able to take off in India was their lack of dependence on these latter kinds of infrastructure. The development of software parks by eager governments has helped relax physical infrastructure constraints where they did exist. However, a severe potential constraint is the poor overall state of India's telecom infrastructure. The benefits of well-functioning telecommunications are much broader than just in IT, but the Internet and the associated IT boom have made India's telecom bottleneck a greater concern. At the same time, rapid technological change and the success of India's IT industry are together leading to solutions.

The basic technological driving force for telecoms is the IT revolution itself. The ability to digitally encode all kinds of information, whether voice, data, or video, makes it possible to send all this information over a single network with digital capabilities. This combined network may include copper wires, fiber-optic cables, and wireless transmission. This is the essence of "convergence." The implication of convergence is that telecoms are receiving more attention than in the past. While India began to encourage setting up Public Call Offices (PCOs) throughout the country in the 1980s, teledensity remains very low, between two and four per hundred (well below other developing countries such as China). The quality of lines and exchanges is poor, and most telecoms remained a government monopoly until very recently, failing to follow quickly on the path of liberalization begun in 1991. It has been the rise of India's software industry that has focused attention on the benefits and feasibility of dramatic change in the telecom sector.

The software industry uses international data links for accessing clients' hardware, communicating by e-mail, exchanging files among joint development teams, and carrying out remote diagnosis and maintenance work.[25] IT-enabled services use voice lines for call centers, and data lines for transmitting electronic files back and forth. Internet-based media companies also require data links. While all economic activity requires good communications infrastructure, the rapid rise of the Internet has increased such needs.

International links are an obvious area for improvement if the Indian software industry is to realize its lofty growth projections. Belated, but now rapid, deregulation is likely to remove international bandwidth constraints.[26] Several problem areas remain, which will require attention. These include the system of interconnect charges, licensing fees, and deposit requirements for entry, restrictions on franchising, bandwidth allocations, and so on. The challenge of building a financially viable, robust, and extensive telecom infrastructure still exists.[27] It appears that government regulators still have a tendency to overregulate, one prominent example being the requirement for new private telecoms to meet old-style quotas for installing village telephones, without adequate regard to financial viability.

With appropriate policy adjustments, technological progress (including domestic innovation) may be an important factor in removing current telecom infrastructure constraints. Ashok Jhunjhunwala (2000) gives the example of cable services in India, which are priced at $2 to $4 per month and have 35–40 million subscribers. At this kind of price point, however, a rural telecom operator in India cannot recover setup costs for access, which are about $800 using conventional technologies. The goal of innovations by Jhunjhunwala's team, therefore, has been to bring the cost of combined Internet and voice access down to $200. The latter figure would make access affordable to 50 percent of Indian households at current income levels. Without such innovations, government targets of increasing India's teledensity fourfold (from 4 to 15 per hundred) and Internet access tenfold are empty rhetoric.

The bottom line is that bringing down the cost of access through innovation targeted at the domestic market is a critical component of any dramatic increase in telecom connectivity in India. Economically combining Internet and voice access also has the benefit of increasing the value of connecting to the network. The benefits accrue not just to the poor, but also to the tens of millions of lower-middle-class households who are currently outside the affordability radius. A denser domestic network not only increases the value of international network links, but also provides opportunities for increasing the rate of training of IT personnel. Finally, the development of an indigenous hardware industry for low-cost access devices and network components has the potential to fill in gaps in India's IT capabilities on the manufacturing front.[28]

10.3.3 Financial Constraints

A striking feature of the Indian economy prereform was its inefficient use of capital. Relatively high savings rates were associated with relatively low growth rates. Financial-sector reform in India has focused on making the country's organized capital markets more efficient. Simple institutional improvements such as electronic trading and settlement, guidelines for corporate governance, and so on have been introduced. However, the nature of the financial system overall still involves "financial repression," with the banking sector and a large number of other financial institutions subject to parking of government and state enterprise deficits and to directed lending.[29] Hence, substantial inefficiencies remain in the financial system. This has negative implications for industry overall,[30] but particularly for a fast-growing sector such as IT.

Clearly, broader reform of the financial sector is required. While such reform has, as noted, been taking place in areas such as the functioning of Indian stock markets, corporate governance, regulation of banking, and central government borrowing procedures, the constraints imposed by the web of government-controlled financial institutions and their "bad" loans to the public sector are a severe hurdle to further reform. For IT start-ups, venture capital has been extremely important, and this should be the case for India also. While the initial lack of a venture capital industry in India may have been positive, in the sense that the policies to create one could be considered from scratch, efforts to do so have tangled with existing mazes of financial regulations and legal restrictions, including tax and corporate law. An important beginning was made by a committee on venture capital appointed by the Securities and Exchange Board of India (SEBI), India's chief financial regulator. SEBI adopted the committee's report in June 2000, but many of the changes required are beyond SEBI's jurisdiction.[31]

Despite policy hurdles, which are still receiving attention, venture capital in India is starting to take off. A government-sponsored venture capital (VC) fund, the National Venture Fund for Software and IT industry (NFSIT), was launched in December 1999. States such as Andhra Pradesh, Karnataka, Delhi, Kerala, Gujarat, and Tamil Nadu have also set up their own venture funds. It is not clear how effective government-sponsored funds can be, since venture capital involves high risks that are not normally associated with government activities, and government intervention may be subject to other incentive problems. Putting aside these issues, it is true that venture capital funding in India's IT sector increased from $80 million in 1997–1998 to $500 million just two years later.[32] If a venture capital industry can flourish, and stock market institutions can continue to develop, the growth of India's IT sector can be fueled, but the problems of the rest of the financial sector still cast a shadow.

10.4   IT and Development

The case for IT as an engine of growth and development must rest mainly on standard economic criteria, such as comparative advantage, complementarities, and the dynamics of the global economy. The IT sector can be an important source of growth for India if the country has a comparative advantage in providing certain kinds of IT-related products and services, if the global demand for these products and services is likely to grow rapidly, and if the growth of the sector has positive spillover benefits to the rest of the domestic economy. The first two of these conditions seem to be well established, though they merit some discussion of future possibilities, particularly with respect to the reasons for and the dynamics of India's comparative advantage in this sector. One of the most interesting issues, which we wish to emphasize here, is the third condition, of spillover benefits. This is the area where the IT sector may be special, and not just another export enclave. Furthermore, IT may have a role to play in broader human development, beyond just economic growth. This is a contentious issue, with sharply opposing views expressed. I proceed in this section as follows. First, I outline some theoretical ideas that are relevant for thinking about the role of IT in growth, and that will inform my consideration of different aspects of this role. Thus, I sequentially examine issues of comparative advantage in software and services, the development of a domestic market, spillovers to the economy as a whole, and the potential impact on governance.

10.4.1   IT and Growth Theories

The starting point for considering the role of IT in development has to be theories of growth that give endogenous innovation a central role. The ingredients of these models typically include differentiated capital inputs, monopolistic competition, production of new inputs through R&D, and ultimately economy-wide increasing returns that allow sustained growth to occur. Hence these models shift away from the exclusive focus on capital accumulation that characterized the neoclassical growth model and the core of Indian postindependence economic policy. The work of Grossman and Helpman (1991) and Rivera-Batiz and Romer (1991a,b) incorporates international trade and the evolution of comparative advantage into endogenous growth models. In these analyses, the economy is typically divided into manufacturing, R&D, and traditional sectors, so IT does not necessarily fit neatly into any one category. Design and development of software may have characteristics of R&D, while IT-enabled services are more like manufacturing in their use of established techniques for production. The general message of these models, however, is that externalities associated with monopolistic competition may give policy a role in influencing the evolution of comparative advantage.[33]

The general models of endogenous growth leave open the issue of what makes IT special. Here, the concept of general-purpose technologies (GPTs) seems very useful. The idea of GPTs was introduced by Bresnahan and Trajtenberg (1995), who define them in terms of having three key characteristics: pervasiveness, technological dynamism, and innovational complementarities.[34] Examples of GPTs include writing and printing (both earlier advances in IT), modern digital electronic IT, steam and electricity (both advances in power delivery systems), and synthetic materials. Helpman and Trajtenberg (1998a,b) have developed a model of growth led by GPTs, in which sustained growth comes from the periodic, exogenous introduction of new GPTs. Other mechanisms that would give endogenous growth are ruled out, but otherwise, the framework consisting of endogenous R&D, monopolistic competition, and the introduction of new intermediate inputs as the mechanism of g.⁀wth is similar to endogenous growth models. In these models, any GPT has similar abstract effects. Dudley (1999), using a different theoretical approach, but the same overall idea, makes a case for information and communication technology as a particularly influential or fundamental GPT. He constructs a simple model of innovation working through falling costs of communication in networks.

I can say a little more about the characteristics of GPTs in the context of IT in particular. Pervasiveness seems to be potentially a natural property of IT. In the Indian context, doubts are centered on issues of cost and access. I have touched on those briefly earlier in the chapter, and I return to them later in this section. Table 10.3, however, illustrates the important positive trends that support pervasiveness. Technological dynamism refers to the potential for sustained innovation that comes with new GPTs and is again illustrated by the dramatic fall

Table 10.3
Falling costs of computing ($)

Costs of computing	1970	1999
1 Mhz of processing power	7,601	0.17
1 megabit of storage	5,257	0.17
1 trillion bits sent	150,000	0.12

Source: Chart 1 from Woodall (2000).

in costs shown in table 10.3. Complementarities of GPTs are vertical complementarities, because GPTs spur innovation and lower manufacturing costs in downstream sectors, with positive feedback effects to the GPT itself. There are also horizontal complementarities, since the downstream sectors may face a coordination problem in expanding sufficiently to encourage the improvement of the GPT. Note that international trade with a more advanced country may be one way to overcome some of these externality problems. That seems to be the lesson of India's IT-sector development.

The importance of complementarities in understanding growth processes has been described in most detail by Matsuyama (1995) (see also Ciccone and Matsuyama 1996; Basu 1997). Matsuyama makes three useful observations. The first is the identification of the differing roles played by horizontal and vertical complementarities, such as I discussed in the previous paragraph. The second is the difference between technological complementarities, emphasized by writers such as Kremer (1993) and Milgrom, Qian, and Roberts (1991) and the demand-based complementarities and pecuniary externalities that drive models such as those of Matsuyama and his coauthors. The third point is the difference between the effects of history and of expectations in affecting equilibrium outcomes and growth. Either or both may work against development and growth, by preventing coordinated movement out of a "bad" equilibrium.

Matsuyama examines a range of models, showing how growth may be arrested or sustained and what kinds of inefficiencies might arise. In particular, the externalities generated by the structure of complementarities can lead to inefficiencies that are best characterized as coordination failures. This set of problems also arises in the GPT models of Helpman and Trajtenberg, discussed earlier. Without going into detail, I suggest that this literature has some relevance for thinking about the role of IT in Indian development. In particular, while the success of IT so far may be the result of factors that have to do with initial comparative advantage, the fortuitousness of freedom from government controls (see Kapur 2002) and integration with the world economy during the boom of the 1990s, the kinds of problems that IT may face as an engine of growth in the future, have to do with potential coordination failures in providing other inputs along with IT, or in the downstream sectors that use IT. For example, if Indian manufacturing remains moribund because of the government's fiscal problems and their effects on the financial sector, a significant market for India's IT sector may be stifled. I investigate some of these issues in the remainder of this section.

10.4.2 Comparative Advantage

The static theory of international trade is based on comparative advantage, determined by relative factor endowments and/or technology differences. Empirically testing this theory is difficult, since other influences may also be at work. For example, intra-industry trade driven by product differentiation and economies of scale may involve different trade patterns than those based on traditional comparative advantage. However, in the case of software exports, attributing the export boom to comparative advantage seems reasonable.[35] We have noted India's pool of workers with software and language skills that are valued in the international market: They are the source of India's comparative advantage in at least some segments of the software industry. As Kapur (2002) emphasizes, the lack of explicit government restrictions on this sector allowed this comparative advantage to assert itself, whereas manufacturing has not enjoyed the same benefits.

While India missed the boat with respect to the labor-intensive manufactured exports that contributed to the East Asian miracle, it is now in a position to replicate this phenomenon with labor-intensive software services and (even more labor-intensive) IT-enabled services. Even if exports of this nature cannot sustain earlier growth rates, they can make a substantial contribution. For example, 20 percent growth in a sector that is 5 percent of the economy adds 1 percentage point to overall economic growth. In the very short run, therefore, moving up the ladder of value added (or establishing a broader hold on the value chain) may not be a critical issue.

There are two reasons for not stopping here, however. The first is a defensive one: greater automation of software development and the emergence of other low-cost labor sources of competing IT skills may lead to export growth falling or even reversing, as global demand for Indian programming services slows or falls due to automation. The second reason is that it may be possible to do even better. Comparative advantage is not fixed, and countries can move toward producing higher value-added goods and services as they grow, with favorable consequences for long-run growth. Applying endogenous growth models is not an automatic proposition, since results are sensitive to assumptions. For example, learning by doing in manufacturing (including software production in this abstract conception) gives different outcomes than does the assumption of a separate R&D sector that competes with manufacturing for skilled labor.

If one accepts the potential theoretical benefits of moving up the value-added ladder, what does this mean in practice for India's software industry? One possibility is offering higher value-added component services, involving design and strategy. Another is offering more complete packages or bundles of services. The latter differs from the former in that a higher management component is included in the package than in particular aspects of software development, even if those require more technical skill. While the global economic slow-down that began in 2001 will hamper these developments in India, there is no reason why Indian software firms cannot enter such markets. The availability of a growing number of professionals with combinations of engineering and management skills will help in this area.[36]

Companies such as TCS have long-standing domestic and developing country consulting expertise, but they may be less suited to compete in a crowded U.S. market than India's new software giants such as Infosys and Wipro, or smaller newcomers.[37] What is the possible competitive advantage of these firms? Certainly lower costs will help, but these may be better used to provide upgraded or broader services, rather than in competing on price alone. In particular, empirical research (Banerjee and Duflo 2000) shows that reputation effects are quite important for Indian software exporters.[38] Such companies may also develop a strong niche in other developing countries, where lower prices may be more important. A high-tech slowdown in the United States may actually aid the development of such firms in India, if it leads to some reversal of the brain drain.[39] Otherwise, managerial and high-level technical skills may constrain movement up the value-added ladder. In some cases, including consulting as well as IT-enabled services, multinational firms have relaxed some of the managerial constraints through their own entry, importing managers as well as training local ones.

10.4.3 The Domestic Market

The domestic market for IT products and services is not independent of the export market. The nature of information goods in general is that they involve high fixed costs of production and low marginal costs. While customization and service provision mitigate this property, they do not negate it. Reputation and experience effects, on the other hand, enhance the importance of economies of scale and scope. Hence it is important for Indian software firms to compete simultaneously in domestic and export markets, in order to take advantage of these economies. This is true even though the product-service mix that is being sold in different markets is going to be somewhat different. Since Indian software firms can compete successfully abroad, they should also be able to succeed in their own backyard.[40] In fact, they have advantages in the domestic market, including knowing their customers better and being closer to them. On the other hand, a poor domestic infrastructure, dependence on imported hardware, late mover disadvantages, and lack of both economies of scale and learning by doing can all reduce or eliminate any advantage that Indian software firms might have over foreign competitors.

Two mitigating factors operate on potential disadvantages of Indian firms. First, some of the problems are faced by all firms, irrespective of location: For example, entering the market for desktop operating systems in the face of Microsoft's dominance is difficult, if not impossible, for any firm anywhere in the world. Second, the boundary lines between domestic and foreign can be blurred when multinationals have Indian subsidiaries, particularly for IT or IT-enabled services. In such cases, the effects on the local economy are not that different from when these services are provided by Indian firms. Two differences in the case of multinationals, however, are in profit repatriation and in the creation of another brain-drain channel, if Indian employees of multinationals can be assigned to other countries.

At the level of business software and software services, therefore, it seems that issues for the domestic market boil down to the same concerns as for export markets. These are availability of the key inputs— namely, various types of skilled IT personnel and managerial and marketing skills. Location and ownership are not of direct importance, but are only proxies for whether the IT software and services provider has the right combination of people, knowledge, experience, and reputation to compete successfully. Liberalization in general means that all Indian firms face the challenge of building such combinations of assets. The software industry happens to be significant because it has developed independent of India's traditional business houses, and hence mostly free of the bad habits those business groups developed over many decades of operating in noncompetitive environments.

I have focused the discussion so far on software. Hardware may offer additional opportunities to Indian IT firms in the domestic market. In developed countries, the establishment of the PC market occurred before the Internet took off. In a good example of complementarities, however, the growth of the Internet has increased the demand for PCs and other access devices. Internet access is probably the most attractive use for many potential consumers of IT in India, but Internet penetration may not go far enough with hardware designed for developed countries. Internet kiosks, with shared access, are a solution that has emerged for urban and rural areas, with the start-up cost for a basic kiosk having been brought down to under $2000. While Internet use is beginning to grow rapidly, the number of subscribers remains minuscule, estimated at 1.8 million in December 2000. The main reasons for this backwardness have been the long-standing government monopoly, through VSNL, of the country's Internet gateways, as well as the general poor state and high cost of the telecom infrastructure. The removal of the VSNL monopoly in 2002 marks a process that began a few years earlier, with NASSCOM lobbying resulting in private ISPs being allowed to set up their own international gateways starting in 2000.

The possibility of designing and building lower-cost access hardware in India may represent an opportunity for the domestic IT industry. While India has tried to develop a domestic hardware industry since the 1980s, it has not succeeded in establishing an industry that is efficient and globally competitive.[41] Much of the problem has been due to a lack of scale and infrastructure (as well as general restrictions on Indian business). For components such as sophisticated chips, this will continue to be the case, but, as noted earlier, Indian industry can build on existing capabilities in the assembly of standardized components. If some of these components are designed specifically for the broader Indian market—for example, to go into low-cost Internet and telecom access devices, as envisaged by the IIT Chennai group (Jhunjhunwala 2000)—where they are built may not be crucial.[42] I note once more that Dell is a profitable company because it serves targeted markets efficiently, not because it manufactures sophisticated components. Instead, management and infrastructure are the key inputs that are required.

10.4.4 Broad-Based Growth

Are a software industry that serves the domestic market as well as exports, a hardware industry that can produce low-cost access devices, and IT-enabled services for foreign markets together enough for broad-based economic growth? The IT sector can directly contribute 1 or 2 percentage points to India's growth rate, and this is not insignificant. The possible concern is that it will remain an enclave, exacerbating inequality and doing little for long-run growth. These concerns arise even in developed countries.[43]

The argument for broad positive impacts is based on the kinds of models discussed at the beginning of this section. To the extent that IT can have significant effects on the efficiency of operations in other industries, there are strong complementarities between the IT sector and the rest of the economy. Examples of areas where increased efficiency may be possible include accounting, procurement, inventory management, and production operations.[44] This is, of course, the standard argument in the United States for the virtues of the "new economy" based on IT. To connect my observations to the usual e-commerce jargon, I note that these benefits are situated in the B2B arena. The difference for India is that it is starting from a much lower level of IT adoption, and the potential gains may be higher. In fact, developing countries have the opportunity to leapfrog over older, more expensive approaches such as Electronic Data Interchange, which represent significant legacy investments in countries such as the United States. This is also a positive indicator for the future.[45] The argument of Kapur (2002), that India's success in software exports has increased the confidence of Indians, may also be couched in terms of a positive shift in expectations helping to overcome a potential coordination failure.

A general concern with IT adoption is job loss, and there is certainly the potential that certain kinds of clerical jobs will be eliminated or reduced in numbers. Unions in Indian industries such as banking have opposed "computerization" for this reason. However, the evidence suggests that increases in other kinds of jobs as a result of IT use more than make up for job loss, so that total employment is not a significant issue. In particular, IT-enabled services promise to directly generate employment much more significantly than activities such as software development. This leaves the issue of adjustment costs, and here severance pay rules or government job adjustment assistance can be more effective and efficient than the current morass of detailed restrictions embodied in India's labor laws. This is why Desai (2000) is right to stress the importance of broader labor law reform if the benefits of growth in India's IT sector are to be fully realized.

In the context of complementarities, it is also important to recognize that these effects are not just in terms of cost savings. IT implementation may enhance the quality of service beyond anything that is feasible through other methods. Furthermore, depending on who the "customers" are, the benefits may accrue to a broad cross-section of the population. Improved efficiency in the stock market as a result of automated trading and settlement may benefit a small section of the population (though the indirect benefits of greater capital market efficiency may be broader). The use of IT in rural banking and micro finance, however, can impact a much broader cross-section of the population. The evidence of pilot schemes such as the SKS InfoTech Smart Card project is encouraging. Handheld computers and smart cards can substantially reduce the costs of making loans, as well as monitoring them. Reducing these transactions costs may turn out to be critical for the scalability and sustainability of microfinance schemes. This and similar examples provide evidence against the enclave view of the IT sector in India.

Of course potential benefits do not necessarily translate into actual ones. Firms and managers can make mistakes in their IT investment decisions, but this is no different from any other kind of investment. In a reasonably competitive industry, with sufficient information available, there is always pressure to make the right decisions, rewards for those who do, and punishments for those who do not. Indian industry must be allowed to follow this model to realize the potential benefits of IT. If it is discouraged from making such investments, the domestic market for Indian IT will not grow, with negative consequences for the IT sector as a whole. This line of thought argues in favor of a sound competition policy, rather than any specific incentives, but I explore this issue further in the next section.

I have focused mainly on the formal sector in assessing the impact of IT. Even if the growth of the IT sector has positive spillovers for other industries, this leaves out the substantial nonindustrial sectors of the economy. I postpone a discussion of government use of IT to a separate section, turning now to an examination of the truly broad-based impacts of IT. There are several possible areas of impact. First, information processing may enhance efficiency in agriculture as well as in manufacturing. While individual farmers cannot make IT investments, agricultural cooperatives can provide the institutional framework that allows farmers to benefit. For example, Chakravarty (2000) gives the example of IT use at milk collection centers in cooperative dairies. This permits faster and safer testing, better quality control, quicker and more accurate payments to farmers, and time savings for farmers in their deliveries. The falling cost of information processing means that such success stories can potentially be widely replicated.

The second impact is in the communication of information. Here the case studies are legion. Farmers and fishermen can receive weather forecasts, market price quotes, advice on farming practices, and specific training. Offers to buy or sell livestock, or other two-way communications are also possible. Some of this information dissemination and exchange is best done through voice media such as fixed or mobile telephones, while other types require the capabilities of the Internet.[46] Some evidence suggests, not surprisingly, that richer farmers and fishermen, as well as middlemen, are faster adopters of such technologies (*The Economist* 2001a), but falling access costs, through innovations such as those of the IIT Chennai group, should broaden information access and its benefits. Broad-based benefits of IT require broad-based access to the network, as I discussed earlier.

A third area of impact is closely related to the second, but it involves communication of information in a more fundamental way. It is possible that IT-based delivery mechanisms can overcome traditional barriers to widespread delivery of education at all levels. I have noted the importance of IT training itself. However, even basic education may be enhanced by the use of IT. While it may seem paradoxical that delivery of basic education should rely on "high tech," there is nothing new in this. The radio and television have been very successful distance-education media in the past, and computers and the Internet offer several advantages, in terms of the potential for interactivity, customization, and sheer volume of material. Given the poor state of basic education,[47] while improved incentives for teachers and school administrators (either in the public or private sector) will help, technology can play an important complementary and even substitutive role. For example, TARAhaat (a semi-commercial subsidiary of a nongovernmental organization, or NGO), in attempting to develop a network of rural Internet centers in a district in Punjab, found that even in the absence of reliable connectivity that would allow access to a variety of Internet-based services, it was able to tap into an underserved market for education in the vernacular medium in the basics of computers and the English language.[48]

The TARAhaat example illustrates several general points. First, in all attempts to introduce IT to rural India in a manner that promotes development, sustainability is a key issue. The TARAhaat franchisee model offers important promise in this regard with respect to incentives and scalability, though there have been difficulties in implementation. Second, the experiment validates the idea that IT costs have come down sufficiently to make rural IT services financially viable. Third, there is the issue of complementarities, both technological and pecuniary. One major roadblock for TARAhaat has been the poor quality of the existing telecom infrastructure. This has severely limited the scope of services that its franchisees could offer[49] and is an example of government failure. On the other hand, the provision of complementary inputs such as financing and physical infrastructure, through subsidized loans from nationalized banks and the use of local government buildings, have been important in reducing start-up as well as operating costs. The most important complementarity emerged when the Punjab Technical University quickly piggybacked on TARAhaat's efforts, enhancing the franchisees' initial financial viability through its own offerings of college-level IT education. This example suggests how the kinds of coordination failure identified in the work of Matsuyama and others may be overcome.

10.4.5   Governance

One area where government can provide indirect support for the IT sector is by boosting the domestic market though its own purchases. Initially, this seemed to follow the pattern of the introduction of PCs in the United States, with purchases of sophisticated equipment and software that sat underutilized on desktops. However, falling costs, increased understanding of what IT can do, and greater domestic expertise are starting to take the role of IT in government beyond this beginning.

There are two broad uses of IT for improved government functioning. First, back-office procedures can be made more efficient, so that internal record keeping, flows of information, and tracking of decisions and performance can be improved. Second, when some basic information is stored in digital form, it provides the opportunity for easier access to that information by citizens. The simplest examples are e-mailing requests or complaints, checking regulations on a Web page, or printing out forms from the Web so that a trip to pick up the forms from a physical office can be avoided. More complicated possibilities are checking actual records, such as land ownership or transactions. Still more complicated are cases where information is submitted electronically by the citizen, for government action or response.

The numerous examples of successful pilot e-governance programs include the following:

• Computer-aided registration of land deeds and stamp duties in Andhra Pradesh, reducing reliance on brokers and possibilities for corruption

• Computerization of rural local government offices in Andhra Pradesh for delivery of statutory certificates of identity and landholdings, substantially reducing delays[50]

• Computerized checkpoints for local entry taxes in Gujarat, with data automatically sent to a central database, reducing opportunities for local corruption

• Consolidated bill payment sites in Kerala, allowing citizens to pay bills under seventeen different categories in one place, from electricity to university fees

• E-mail requests for repairs to basic rural infrastructure such as hand pumps, reducing reliance on erratic visits of government functionaries[51]

As in the broader case of using the Internet for communications and transactions, sustainability of e-governance initiatives is a significant issue. Since governments at all levels are financially strapped, the initial investments and ongoing expenditures for IT-based service delivery may act as a barrier to adoption as well as to long-run sustainability. However, my initial investigations suggest that the franchise model can be successful here. Low-cost rural Internet kiosks, a tiered franchising model, and a suite of basic government access services for which users are willing to pay are key components of what Drishtee, an outgrowth of the Gyandoot project in Madhya Pradesh, is implementing in several parts of India.[52] Cooperation of local governments and subsidized financing have been important elements for Drishtee, as in the case of TARAhaat, with the former being obviously critical in the case of Drishtee. It is important to note that once Internet access is available, its benefits are not restricted to e-governance. Individuals can obtain market information, training, job information, advice on farming techniques, and so on, as discussed earlier in this section. This is certainly part of Drishtee's long-run model.

Given the poor quality of governance in India, it seems that e-governance initiatives can provide direct benefits to citizens, particularly those who are less well off (the rich in any case hire intermediaries to collect information, make payments, etc.). The preliminary evidence suggests that the use of IT can increase transparency and accountability, simply by requiring information, such as basic complaints, to be logged completely and systematically. In this respect, the use of a non-governmental intermediary such as Drishtee may have advantages over purely internal government initiatives, beyond that of financial viability.

10.5   Policy Environment

The overall goals of economic policy in India are standard: high growth together with macroeconomic stability and poverty reduction. Balancing these goals is the difficult part. For example, incentives for exports, such as tax breaks, are designed to spur growth, but may adversely affect the government's fiscal deficit. As quantitative controls have receded in importance, such tax subsidy policies have become more significant policy components. The growth of India's IT sector, and the success of the software industry in particular, has tended to skew policy toward the industry, with targeted incentives being implemented or recommended.

Targeting incentives to the software industry is not necessarily the best method to promote the industry, nor to achieve broader goals of growth and human development. Providing implicit or explicit subsidies to the industry can introduce distortions, and it involves forgoing other uses of funds, given the severe budget constraint that the government faces. Broader promotion of the IT sector also suffers from some of the same problems. Investing heavily in government-sponsored IT-related training is problematic when basic education in India is so poorly provided by the public sector. Policy goals for the IT sector might be better met by focusing on infrastructure provision, enabling the private sector to play a role here as well. The telecom sector is a case in point.

The historical case for regulation or nationalized provision in telecoms was based on economies of scale, implying that competition would be unstable or inefficient. Technological change has removed this justification in significant portions of the telecom value chain by lowering fixed costs and adding new technological options, allowing competition to become feasible. Since monopoly may persist in portions of the value chain (i.e., portions of the network), regulation of interconnection charges may still be required to maintain a level playing field. However, directly managing technology choices and competition is not easily justified on economic grounds. The broad policy goals of promoting competition and innovation in the provision of telecom infrastructure and services are moving in the right direction.

Broad-based growth of India's IT sector will depend on improving the telecom infrastructure, as well as on training enough people for the sector and using them effectively and efficiently. For telecoms, the regulatory framework is crucial, whereas for human resource development and use, the labor laws matter greatly. It may also be noted that laws that directly constrain manufacturing remain on the statute books and adversely affect areas such as manufacturing or assembling hardware—the problem here is one that still affects Indian manufacturing in general.[53]

In India the regulatory institution for telecoms is the Telecom Regulatory Authority of India (TRAI), which was established in 1997 and given greater and clearer authority in 2000.[54] The scope of the TRAI includes establishing quality of service parameters, monitoring compliance, examining technology choices, and so on.[55] It is supposed to establish a level playing field and encourage competition, but it has lacked clear authority precisely where it is needed the most, in setting entry fees and some interconnection charges. Unfortunately, bringing quality of service, technology choice, and universal service obligations (USOs) into the regulatory mix only serves to muddy the waters and divert attention from the central task of enabling effective competition.

USOs are being built into licensing deals for private service providers. These take the form of quantitative targets for installing rural telephones and funds created through a form of tax on basic service, to be used for proposed subsidies for rural users. It is not clear that numerical targets have any use at all, when licensing and interconnection fees make it uneconomical for local access providers with lower-cost technology to enter. The distinction between rural users in general, and shared access through Internet kiosks, is crucial but has not been accepted by majority vote in a TRAI committee that reported on the USO.[56] Our own investigation of the start-up problems of TARAhaat and Drishtee suggests that a narrowly targeted subsidy for enabling reliable telecom access (including solutions such as that of the IIT Chennai group) to Internet kiosks makes most sense.

Desai (2000) examines the problems of labor laws, using the report of the Subject Group on Knowledge-Based Industries (2000) as his starting point. The report calls for exemption for the IT sector from a broad set of rules relating to labor, including provisions relating to overtime, working conditions, restrictions on contract labor, and dismissal of workers. Interestingly, if IT workers are in short supply, they should be able to negotiate terms that are attractive enough to make the labor laws redundant. Desai suggests that the main function of the labor laws in this sector is to enable government labor inspectors to demand bribes. He also argues for broader reform of labor laws and rightly points out the potential for distortions if one sector is given an exemption. He also acknowledges the political difficulties of more comprehensive reform. In this case, the IT sector may usefully serve as the thin edge of the wedge that begins cutting down some of the worst problems with India's labor laws, in particular the lack of permitted flexibility in contracting. The development of IT-enabled services will be a litmus test of the changing role of labor laws in India.

My examination of the role of the IT sector in broad-based development also suggests the importance of the financial sector. While it seems that large IT firms can rely on retained earnings or the stock and bond markets for growth, start-ups need a venture capital industry that is just beginning to emerge. As in the case of labor laws, one can argue that the policy environment must be geared toward industry in general, and not just the IT sector. Kapur and Ramamurti (2001), for example, note that industries such as biotech, chemicals, media and entertainment, and construction all require knowledge services that go beyond the basic definition of IT-enabled services. In all these cases, venture capital may be a significant fuel for entrepreneurial energy.

Some of the greatest difficulties face small-scale entrepreneurs, who have been protected by reservations, but who do not necessarily have easy access to the right kinds of help they need as start-ups. Again, my research on the experience of the local franchisees of TARAhaat and Drishtee suggests that the nationalized banking sector, with its system of directed credit and simultaneous forced holdings of government and PSU loans, which have left bank portfolios in bad shape, is not well placed to provide small-scale financing of this kind. In particular, in the case of TARAhaat, difficulties in obtaining start-up capital from banks appeared to be a major impediment to rapid expansion of the franchising scheme, even within a small geographic area.[57] This is where the overall macroeconomic problem of the fiscal deficit appears to trickle down all the way to the village, with a negative impact on development.

Our general assessment of the policy environment is therefore that, with one exception, the policy problems are mostly general ones, and not specific to IT. Problems in financial market institutions, labor laws, and regulation in general are best dealt with from an economy-wide perspective, as I elaborate on in the conclusion. The exception is the case of rural telecoms and Internet access, where it seems that narrow targeting of limited subsidies (through waiving certain fees rather than explicit payments) for start-up costs may be worthwhile in generating growth of communications and of enterprises that use communications.

10.6   Conclusion

To conclude, I briefly consider general microeconomic and macro-economic policy issues, along with implications for the IT sector. The central areas of India's policy reforms have been replacing quantitative trade restrictions with tariffs, lowering effective levels of protection, removing an area of discretionary controls on private-sector invest-ment, and creating modern financial markets. Standard examples of where these reforms can be built upon, to further stimulate growth, include removal or relaxation of obsolete "small-scale sector" reser-vations and size restrictions, privatization of inefficient state-owned enterprises, rationalization of tax-subsidy policies and tax administra-tion, and relaxation of severe labor market restrictions. This list can be characterized by its emphasis on improving the efficiency of the mech-anisms with which the government directly affects the private sector. The entire Indian economy, not just the IT sector, can presumably ben-efit from such reforms, which will reduce distortions of private-sector behavior.

A second area where attention is required may be characterized as enabling reforms. These include reforms of contract law and judicial institutions; financial-sector regulatory institutions; telecom-sector reg-ulatory institutions; infrastructure such as electric power, roads, and ports; and systems of education and training in general. Again, the benefits of such reforms are potentially quite general, and not re-stricted to any one sector of the economy.

A third area of policy is macroeconomic management. While India's record here is quite good, it needs to make a transition in its policy institutions here as well, since removing detailed microeconomic con-trols requires changes in the regulatory modes of macroeconomic management. Perhaps the area that has received the most attention is policies toward international capital flows and their implications for exchange rate management. Desai (2000) has suggested that large projected increases in software exports could create a "Dutch disease" phenomenon,[58] in which a resulting exchange rate appreciation hurts other sectors, and revenues from exports are wastefully spent. Several factors mitigate this concern: the likelihood that export revenue growth will slow down; the potential linkages that exist between software, the IT sector as a whole, and the broader economy (unlike natural resource extraction enclaves); and a better understanding of exchange rate management than existed twenty-five years ago, when the phenomenon first was identified and labeled. Thus, while exchange rate policy is certainly important in general, the growth of the IT sector will not necessarily raise special concerns.

Given that there is plenty that remains to be done in terms of overall economic policy reform, are there areas where the IT sector deserves special attention? The answer I have given in this chapter, with one exception, is no. Special subsidies or export incentives are likely to be inefficient ways of stimulating the growth of the IT sector, or of positive spillovers for the rest of the economy. Similarly, special central government initiatives to increase the availability of IT training and related education are also likely to represent a mistargeting of scarce government resources. The same stricture applies, to some extent, to state government policies to encourage the IT sector.[59] The government may be better off removing general restrictions to doing business, as well as providing an enabling institutional infrastructure (appropriate laws and regulations), rather than attempting to target the IT sector through a form of industrial policy.

The exception lies in the telecom sector, which has particularly strong complementarities with the broader IT sector. Policies to achieve development goals would do better to emphasize removing barriers to innovations that will support lower-cost access to telecom networks of all kinds (wireless and fixed, voice and data). Very specific, targeted, start-up subsidies to enable widespread, shared access to telecoms and Internet in rural areas are likely to have high social returns, since it appears that financially sustainable franchise models exist. These high returns include better governance, as well as knowledge that is an important input into "empowerment," or "development as freedom" (Sen 1999). In this respect, I would argue that rural IT access is an important complement to and enabler of local government reform in India (Rao and Singh 2000).

My goal in this chapter has been to assess the possible role of India's IT industry as a driving force of higher economic growth in India, without exacerbation of inequalities or creation of instability. My conclusion is cautiously positive. While projections for software exports may be overly optimistic, complementarities or spillovers in the domestic market, including increased government and business use of IT, are likely to be strong. For this rosy scenario to play out, however, continued broad economic reforms will be important, as well as reforms in the telecom sector that promote competition and innovation in providing last-mile access.

Acknowledgments

This chapter is a revision of one presented at a conference on the Indian Economy, held at Cornell on April 19–20, 2002. I am grateful to Kaushik Basu, Yale Braunstein, Ashok Desai, Atanu Dey, Rafiq Dossani, Kyle Eischen, P. D. Kaushik, and Vini Mahajan for helpful discussions and comments on related work. I am particularly grateful to Devesh Kapur for his comments as a discussant at the conference and to Gayatri Koolwal for detailed suggestions on the previous version. None of them is responsible for any remaining shortcomings. I have learned about aspects of this topic from numerous people, in addition to the ones named. I have tried to reference their works as much as possible and regret any inadvertent omissions.

Notes

1. A popular alternative is ICT, for information and communications technology. The World Bank, for example, favors this term.

2. In this sense, it is an exemplar of what is called a general-purpose technology in economic modeling of growth processes. See Helpman (1998) and Kapur and Ramamurti (2001). I take up this idea in detail in section 10.4.

3. To give a sampling of research in the United States, David (2000) emphasizes the lag with which any new technology affects productivity; Gordon (2000) offers a skeptical view of the impact of IT on productivity, arguing that the empirical evidence indicates that the impact is narrow and limited; Jorgenson (2001), in the most comprehensive analysis, finds that IT has contributed significantly to total factor productivity growth (TFPG) in the United States. Of course, higher TFPG implies higher overall growth, ceteris paribus.

4. Data from Electronics and Computer Software Export Promotion Council, reported in *Business Standard*, April 9, 2002. Hardware export figures, while much smaller, also showed robust growth.

5. See ⟨http://www.nasscom.org/it_industry/sw_export.asp⟩.

6. See, for example, Heeks (1996, 1998) and Desai (2000).

7. See, for example, Tschang (2001) and Kapur (2002).

8. These figures are taken or constructed from ⟨http://www.nasscom.org/it_industry/top20_exporters.asp⟩. See also ⟨http://www.nasscom.org/it_industry/top20_sw_cos.asp⟩ and ⟨http://www.nasscom.org/it_industry/sw_export.asp⟩.

9. The figures are from ⟨http://www.nasscom.org/it_industry/export_destinations.asp⟩. Similar figures are given by *Dataquest* (2001), Heeks (1998), and Desai (2000).

10. For example, see ⟨http://www.tcs.com/news/tcs_media/htdocs/sh01/nov01_FT_article.htm⟩.

11. Raman Roy, CEO of Spectramind, suggests five categories of "teleworking": data entry and conversion, rule-set processing, problem-solving, direct customer interaction, and expert "knowledge services," ranked in terms of increasing sophistication and value added. See *The Economist* (2001b, 60).

12. See the *Economist* (2001b).

13. See *DQ Week* (2001).

14. See Kapur and Ramamurti (2001) for a more detailed argument, including the role of Indians with experience of working in Silicon Valley and other global IT centers.

15. See *Business Week* (2001). However, Aggarwal (2001) gives a substantially lower figure of 55,000 engineering graduates annually, excluding private institutes and Masters of Computer Applications (MCA). Arora et al. (2000) estimate an overall figure, including MCAs and graduates of informal training institutes, of close to 140,000 per annum. Kapur (2002) quotes World Bank estimates of 160,000 graduates and diploma holders in engineering and technology in the late 1990s. See also Arora et al. (2001) and Arora, Gambardella, and Torrisi (2001), and Saxenian (2001).

16. See Arora et al. (2000), as well as Heeks (1996) and Desai (2000) for further discussion.

17. Data from NASSCOM, reported in *CCI Business Bulletin*, February 23–March 1, 2002, available online at ⟨http://www.ccindia.com/bulletin.html⟩.

18. This uses the revenue figure from table 10.1, for the Indian IT industry, and is overstated to the extent that it excludes some types of employees. Arora et al. (2001) construct a lower estimate of $15,600 for 1998–1999 (their table 1).

19. The implication is that changes in the product-service mix toward that involving higher value-added tasks would be associated with these improvements, resulting in increased productivity.

20. See Arora and Athreye (2002) and Kapur (2002) and the references therein. The former paper emphasizes the regional concentration of engineering colleges in India.

21. IT industry figures include over $400 million of IT training revenues, for example.

22. Kapur (2002) argues that this process has begun and has been important in India, though perhaps not to the same extent as in countries like Taiwan (Saxenian 2000).

23. This idea has been formalized in the "O-ring" theory of production, developed by Kremer (1993). See also Basu (1997, chap. 2).

24. See Dossani and Crow (2001) for an excellent survey and analysis of power-sector reform in India.

25. See Heeks (1996, 1998).

26. See Singh (2002) for further details and additional references.

27. Two sources for tracking policy issues and broader concerns are ⟨www.trai.gov.in⟩, the Web site of the Telecom Regulatory Authority of India, and ⟨http://www.tenet. res.in/Papers/papers.html⟩, which features the work of the IIT Chennai group headed by Ashok Jhunjhunwala. The most recent of these is ⟨www.tenet.res.in/Papers/techolo. html⟩. See also Jhunjhunwala (2000).

28. This does not mean trying to do it all in-house; again Dell is a useful example to bear in mind.

29. See Singh and Srinivasan (2002) for a more detailed discussion in the context of federalism and reform.

30. It is arguable that the problem of low growth in India's manufacturing is substantially attributable to difficulties in financing investment.

31. Important overviews of the issues appear in Dossani and Saez (2000) and Dossani and Kenney (2001). Rafiq Dossani was one of the members of the SEBI committee.

32. The data, and other information on India's VC environment, can be found at ⟨http://www.nasscom.org/business_in_india/vc_scenario.asp⟩.

33. Other, more recent treatments of endogenous growth and trade that may be useful in thinking about IT in India include Basu and Weil (1998) and Chuang (1998).

34. See Lipsey, Becker, and Carlow (1998) for a detailed survey and examination of the concept, as well as the other pieces in Helpman (1998). The idea of complementarities is discussed in greater detail later; it is closely related to the older idea of linkages; see Basu (1997) and Ray (1998) for references and discussion.

35. Note that, to the extent that India is providing intermediate goods or services in its software exports, the situation is more complex than that of standard trade theory, where only final goods are traded. Monopolistic competition models such as those of Matsuyama are then relevant. For an attempt to calculate India's possible comparative advantage, see Arora and Athreye (2002, table 4).

36. Similar considerations apply to IT-enabled services; see note 11.

37. See Das (2001) for a discussion of the Indian e-business consulting market.

38. Arora et al. (2000) and Arora and Athreye (2002) discuss Indian firms' efforts to signal quality by hiring engineers, and through international certification of their processes. They document the positive impact of the latter on value added per employee.

39. For a description of how Infosys is struggling with the tech slowdown, trying to "transform itself ... from a great code-writer to a one-stop technology services provider," see Bjorhus (2002).

40. The reverse need not be true, as Arora and Athreye (2002) emphasize in their discussion. They also suggest that there are strong potential spillovers from the IT sector to other services industries, in the form of improved managerial practices that have developed in IT and are easily applied to a range of services.

41. See Hanna (1994), for example, for further details.

42. Another example is the "Simputer," designed by scientists from the Indian Institute of Science. The portable $200 device will use some parts manufactured in Singapore, Linux-based software developed in India, and run on three AAA batteries. See Khoo (2002).

43. See, for example, Pohjola (1998) and Woodall (2000), as well as the references in note 3.

44. These are all examples of what are also known as "forward linkages," since IT adoption has positive impacts on the operations of a range of industries. The effect of the growth of the IT sector on the provision of technical education would be an example of a "backward linkage." In either case, there is a complementarity at work. Evidence of some forward linkages in the informal IT sector is provided by Kumar (2000).

45. See also Miller (2001) for a further discussion of the potential for B2B e-commerce in India.

46. Eggleston, Jensen, and Zeckhauser (2002) provide some quantitative evidence for the market efficiency effects of improved communications and information transfer, using data from rural China.

47. See Dreze and Gazdar (1997) and the PROBE report (PROBE Committee 1999). One can also make a case for access to IT based on broader notions of development, such as Sen (1999). That the poorest of the poor can benefit is borne out by instances such as the famous in the hole-in-the-wall-computer ⟨http://www.niitholeinthewall.com/home.htm⟩.

48. See Kaushik and Singh (2002) for more detail on the TARAhaat effort.

49. An example from field research in Bathinda district of Punjab in December 2001 illustrates: A farmer told us he had taken computer lessons at the TARAhaat kiosk, bought a home computer, and signed an Internet service contract so that he could exchange email with his brother in Toronto, Canada, as well as look for information on agricultural practices. All three IT-related products and services depended on basic telecom availability. See also Prahalad and Hart (2002).

50. These two examples are from Bhatnagar and Schware (2000), which also provides broader examples, including ones driven more by the efforts of NGOs than governments.

51. These three examples are from *India Today* (2000), which also lists several other similar projects.

52. Further details of Drishtee's efforts are in Kaushik and Singh (2002).

53. I am grateful to P. D. Kaushik (personal communication) for this point. By his count, there are over 400 central government statutes governing manufacturing, as well as numerous state laws. He also notes that the software industry escaped these constraints partly by not being recognized by the government as an "industry."

54. See Dossani and Manikutty (2000) for details.

55. See for example, the paper by M. S. Verma, Chairperson of the TRAI (Verma 2000) and Telecom Regulatory Authority of India (2000).

56. See the report at ⟨http://www.trai.gov.in/recom.htm⟩, and especially the two appendixes, which are a dissenting comment by Rakesh Mohan and the rest of the committee's response. See also Dey (2000) and Singh (2002).

57. Drishtee was able to avoid this problem to some extent, with smaller-scale kiosks that allowed poorer entrepreneurs to avail of targeted government loan schemes.

58. An excellent explanation of Dutch disease is by John McLaren, at ⟨www.columbia. edu/~jem18/teaching/pepm/dutchdis.pdf⟩. McLaren clarifies the source of concerns that are associated with Dutch disease, including exacerbation of *prior* distortions and of inequality.

59. Bangalore in Karnataka is well known as a regional IT center in India, having developed initially without much explicit government support. The governments of Andhra Pradesh (Eischen 2000) and Tamil Nadu (Bajpai and Radjou 1999; Bajpai and Dokeniya 1999) have led in attempts to establish IT-based industries with conscious government policies. Other state governments, such as Punjab (see www.dqindia.com/mar1599/news.htm) are following suit, with mixed success.

References

Aggarwal, Balaka B. 2001. "Faculty scarcity at IITs threatens knowledge capital." March 19. Available online at ⟨http://www.ciol.com/content/news/trends/10103902.asp⟩.

Arora, Ashish, and Suma Athreye. 2002. "The Software Industry and India's Economic Development." *Information Economics and Policy* 14:253–273.

Arora, Ashish, V. S. Arunachalam, Jai Asundi, and Ronald Fernandes. 2000. "The Globalization of Software: The Case of the Indian Software Industry." A report submitted to the Sloan Foundation. Carnegie Mellon University, Pittsburgh, PA. Available online at ⟨http://www.heinz.cmu.edu/project/india/publications.html⟩.

Arora, Ashish, V. S. Arunachalam, Jai Asundi, and Ronald Fernandes. 2001. "The Indian Software Service Industry." *Research Policy* 30:1267–1287.

Arora, Ashish, Alfonso Gambardella, and Salvatore Torrisi. 2001. "In the Footsteps of the Silicon Valley? Indian and Irish Software in the International Division of Labour." Paper presented at the Conference on Silicon Valley and Its Imitators, Stanford Institute for Economic Policy Research, July 2000.

Bajpai, Nirupam, and Anupama Dokeniya. 1999. "Information Technology-Led Growth Policies: A Case Study of Tamil Nadu." Development Discussion Paper no. 729, Harvard Institute for International Development, October.

Bajpai, Nirupam, and Navi Radjou. 1999. "Raising the Global Competitiveness of Tamil Nadu's Information Technology Industry." Development Discussion Paper no. 728, Harvard Institute for International Development, October.

Banerjee, Abhijit V., and Esther Duflo. 2000. "Reputation Effects and the Limits of Contracting: A Study of the Indian Software Industry." *Quarterly Journal of Economics* 115, no. 3:989–1017.

Basu, Kaushik. 1997. *Analytical Development Economics*. Cambridge, MA: MIT Press.

Basu, S., and D. N. Weil. 1998. "Appropriate Technology and Growth." *Quarterly Journal of Economics* 113, no. 4:1025–1054.

Bhatnagar, Subhash, and Robert Schware. 2000. eds. *Information and Communication Technology in Development: Cases from India*. New Delhi: Sage Publications.

Bjorhus, Jennifer. 2002. "India's Infosys Struggles through Transformation." *San Jose Mercury News*, February 11, 1E.

Bresnahan, Timothy, and Manuel Trajtenberg. 1995. "General Purpose Technologies: 'Engines of Growth.'" *Journal of Econometrics* 65:83–108.

Business Week. 2001. "India 3.0: Its Software Outfits Take on the World." February 26, 44–46.

Chakravarty, Rupak. 2000. "IT at Milk Collection Centers in Cooperative Dairies: The National Dairy Development Board Experience." In Information and Communication Technology in Development: Cases from India, ed. Subhash Bhatnagar and Robert Schware, 65–75. New Delhi: Sage Publications.

Chuang, Y. C. 1998. "Learning by Doing, the Technology Gap, and Growth." *International Economic Review* 39, no. 3:697–721.

Ciccone, Antonio, and Kiminori Matsuyama. 1996. "Start-up Costs and Pecuniary Externalities as Barriers to Economic Development." *Journal of Development Economics* 49:33–59.

Das, Shyamanuja. 2001. "The Indian Challenge: Will They . . . Or Won't They?" March 7. Available online at ⟨http://voicendata.com/content/top_stories/101030703.asp⟩.

Dataquest. 2001. "SW INDUSTRY: Working around the Slowdown." February 14. Available online at ⟨http://dqweek.ciol.com/content/search/showarticle.asp?artid=21244⟩.

David, Paul A. 2000. "Understanding Digital Technology's Evolution and the Path of Measured Productivity Growth: Present and Future in the Mirror of the Past." In *Understanding the Digital Economy*, ed. Erik Brynjolfsson and Brian Kahin, 49–98. Cambridge, MA: MIT Press.

Desai, Ashok V. 2000. "The Peril and the Promise: Broader Implications of the Indian Presence in Information Technologies." Working paper, CREDPR, Stanford University, August.

Dey, Atanu. 2000. "New Telecom Policy 1999: A Critical Evaluation." Paper presented at the Conference on Telecommunications Reform in India, Asia/Pacific Research Center, Stanford University, November 9–10.

Dossani, Rafiq, and Robert T. Crow. 2001. "Restructuring the Electric Power Sector in India: Alternative Institutional Structures and Mechanisms." Working paper, Asia/Pacific Research Center, Stanford University.

Dossani, Rafiq, and Martin Kenney. 2001. "Creating an Environment: Developing Venture Capital in India." Working paper, Asia/Pacific Research Center, Stanford University.

Dossani, Rafiq, and S. Manikutty. 2000. "Reforms in the Telecommunications Sector in India: An Institutional View." Paper presented at the Conference on Telecommunications Reform in India, Asia/Pacific Research Center, Stanford University, November 9–10.

Dossani, Rafiq, and Lawrence Saez. 2000. "Venture Capital in India." *The International Journal of Finance* 12, no. 4:1932–1946.

DQ Week. 2001. "Medical Transcription: Not in the Pink of Health." February 2, Available online at ⟨http://www.ciol.com/content/search/showarticle.asp?artid=21128⟩.

Dreze, Jean, and Haris Gazdar. 1997. "Uttar Pradesh: The Burden of Inertia." In *Indian Development: Selected Regional Perspectives*, ed. Amartya Sen and Jean Dreze, 33–128. Delhi: Oxford University Press.

Dudley, Leonard. 1999. "Communications and Economic Growth." *European Economic Review* 43:595–619.

Economist, The. 2001a. "Another Kind of Net Work: Mobile Phones in India." March 3, 59.

Economist, The. 2001b. "Outsourcing to India: Back Office to the World." May 5, 59–60.

Eggleston, Karen, Robert Jensen, and Richard Zeckhauser. 2002. "Information and Communication Technologies, Markets and Economic Development." Working paper, Economics Department, Tufts University, and John F. Kennedy School of Government, Harvard University.

Eischen, Kyle. 2000. "National Legacies, Software Technology Clusters and Institutional Innovation: The Dichotomy of Regional Development in Andhra Pradesh, India." University of California, Department of Sociology.

Gordon, Robert J. 2000. "Does the 'New Economy' Measure Up to the Great Inventions of the Past?" *Journal of Economic Perspectives* 14, no. 4 (fall):49–74.

Grossman, Gene, and Elhanan Helpman. 1991. *Innovation and Growth in the Global Economy*. Cambridge, MA: MIT Press.

Hanna, Nagy. 1994. "Exploiting Information Technology for Development: A Case Study of India." World Bank Discussion Paper 246.

Heeks, Richard. 1996. *India's Software Industry: State Policy, Liberalisation and Industrial Development*. New Delhi: Sage Publications.

Heeks, Richard. 1998. "The Uneven Profile of India's Software Exports." IDPM Working Paper no. 3, University of Manchester, October.

Helpman, Elhanan, ed. 1998. *General Purpose Technologies and Economic Growth*. Cambridge, MA: MIT Press.

Helpman, Elhanan, and Manuel Trajtenberg. 1998a. "A Time to Sow and a Time to Reap: Growth Based on General Purpose Technologies." In *General Purpose Technologies and Economic Growth*, ed. Elhanen Helpman, 55–84. Cambridge, MA: MIT Press.

Helpman, Elhanan, and Manuel Trajtenberg. 1998b. "Diffusion of General Purpose Technologies." In *General Purpose Technologies and Economic Growth*, ed. Elhanen Helpman, 85–120. Cambridge, MA: MIT Press.

India Today. 2000. "Is e-Governance for Real?" December 11, 70–75.

Jhunjhunwala, Ashok. 2000. "Unleashing Telecom and Internet in India." Paper presented at the Conference on Telecommunications Reform in India, Asia/Pacific Research Center, Stanford University, November 9–10.

Jorgenson, Dale W. 2001. "Information Technology and the U.S. Economy." *American Economic Review* 91, no. 1 (March):1–32.

Kapur, Devesh. 2002. "The Causes and Consequences of India's IT Boom." *India Review* 1, no. 1:91–110.

Kapur, Devesh, and Ravi Ramamurti. 2001. "India's Emerging Competitive Advantage in Services." *Academy of Management Executive* 15, no. 2:20–31.

Kaushik, P. D., and Nirvikar Singh. 2002. "Information Technology and Broad-Based Development: Preliminary Lessons from North India." Working paper, University of California, Santa Cruz.

Khoo, Ernest. 2002. "The Simputer: A Handheld for the Masses?" CNET News.com, January 11. Available online at ⟨http://news.com.com/2100-1040-808321.html⟩.

Kremer, Michael. 1993. "The O-Ring Theory of Economic Development." *Quarterly Journal of Economics* 108, no. 3:551–575.

Kumar, Nagesh. 2000. "New Technology Based Small Service Enterprises and Employment: The Case of Software and Related Services Industry in India." International Centre for Development Research and Cooperation, New Delhi.

Lipsey, Richard G., Cliff Becker, and Kenneth Carlaw. 1998. "What Requires Explanation?" In *General Purpose Technologies and Economic Growth*, ed. Elhanen Helpman, 15–54. Cambridge, MA: MIT Press.

Matsuyama, Kiminori. 1995. "Complementarities and Cumulative Processes in Monopolistic Competition." *Journal of Economic Literature* 33, no. 2:701–710.

Milgrom, Paul, Yingyi Qian, and John Roberts. 1991. "Complementarities, Momentum, and the Evolution of Modern Manufacturing." *American Economic Review* 81, no. 2 (May):84–88.

Miller, Robert R. 2001. "Leapfrogging? India's Information Technology Industry and the Internet." IFC Discussion Paper no. 42, The World Bank, Washington, DC, May.

NASSCOM. 2002a. "Domestic IT Market." New Delhi: National Association of Software and Service Companies. Available online at ⟨http://www.nasscom.org/it_industry/domestic_it_market.asp⟩.

NASSCOM. 2002b. "Domestic Software." New Delhi: National Association of Software and Service Companies. Available online at ⟨http://www.nasscom.org/it_industry/domestic_sw_services.asp⟩.

NASSCOM. 2002c. "IT-Enabled Services Types." New Delhi: National Association of Software and Service Companies. Available online at ⟨http://www.nasscom.org/it_industry/spectrum.asp⟩.

Pohjola, Matti. 1998. "Information Technology and Economic Development: An Introduction to the Research Issues." WIDER Working paper no. 153, United Nations University, November.

Prahalad, C. K., and Stuart L. Hart. 2002. "The Fortune at the Bottom of the Pyramid." Available online at ⟨http://www.strategy-business.com/media/pdf/02106.pdf⟩.

PROBE Committee. 1999. "Public Report on Basic Education in India." Centre for Development Economics. New Delhi: Oxford University Press.

Rao, M. Govinda, and Nirvikar Singh. 2000. "How to Think about Local Government Reform in India: Incentives and Institutions." Paper presented at the International Conference on Second Generation Reforms in India, Madras School of Economics, Chennai.

Ray, Debraj. 1998. *Development Economics*. Princeton, NJ: Princeton University Press.

Rivera-Batiz, Luis A., and Paul M. Romer. 1991a. "Economic Integration and Endogenous Growth." *Quarterly Journal of Economics* 106, no. 2:531–555.

Rivera-Batiz, Luis A., and Paul M. Romer. 1991b. "International Trade with Endogenous Technological Change." *European Economic Review* 35, no. 4:971–1004.

Saxenian, AnnaLee. 2000. "The Bangalore Boom: From Brain Drain to Brain Circulation?" Forthcoming in *Bridging the Digital Divide: Lessons from India*, ed. Kenneth Keniston and Deepak Kumar. Bangalore: National Institute of Advanced Study.

Saxenian, AnnaLee. 2001. "Bangalore: The Silicon Valley of Asia?" Working paper no. 91, Center for Research on Economic Development and Policy Reform, Stanford University, February.

Sen, Amartya K. 1999. *Development as Freedom*. Oxford, Oxford University Press.

Singh, Nirvikar. 2002. "Information Technology as an Engine of Broad-Based Growth in India." In *The Future of India and Indian Business*, ed. P. Banerjee and F.-J. Richter, 24–57. London: Palgrave Macmillan.

Singh, Nirvikar, and T. N. Srinivasan. 2002. "Indian Federalism, Economic Reform and Globalization." Paper for comparative federalism project, CREDPR, Stanford.

Subject Group on Knowledge-Based Industries. 2000. *Recommendations of the Task Force on Knowledge-Based Industries*. Prime Minister's Council on Trade and Industry, Prime Minister's Office, New Delhi. Available online at ⟨http://www.nic.in/pmcouncils/reports/knowl/⟩.

Telecom Regulatory Authority of India (TRAI). 2000. "Consultation Paper on Issues Relating to Universal Service Obligations." TRAI, New Delhi, July 3.

Tschang, Ted. 2001. "The Basic Characteristics of Skills and Organizational Capabilities in the Indian Software Industry." Working paper no. 13, ADSB Institute, Tokyo.

Verma, M. S. 2000. "TRAI's Objectives and Policy Focus in a Changing Environment." Paper presented at the Conference on Telecommunications Reform in India, Asia/Pacific Research Center, Stanford University, November 9–10.

Woodall, Pam. 2000. "The New Economy." *The Economist*, September 23, 6 (survey).

VI   Grassroots and the Globe

11 India's Informal Economy: Facing the Twenty-First Century

Barbara Harriss-White

11.1 Introduction

India's economy is roughly the size of Belgium's, but with one hundred times the population. Eighty-eight percent of them live in settlements with fewer than 200,000 people.[1] Their economy is dominated by agricultural and food-related goods and services. In 1997, an average of something over 10 percent of total consumption expenditure in this part of the economy was estimated to be on the output of the corporate sector.[2] The other 90 percent was spent on the output of the informal economy, in which most of the 88 percent worked.

The informal economy either lies outside the scope of state regulation, or is officially subject to state regulation but nevertheless does not operate according to the rules that state regulation officially prescribes. In the former sense it is also known as "unregistered," and defined as consisting of firms with electricity but under ten workers or without electricity and over twenty workers (very rare outside agriculture). Although this second definition is clear enough on paper, in practice most firms with labor forces in excess of the threshold for registration have a substantial casual labor force that is undeclared under the Factories Act and hence not state-regulated. Indeed, one study of corporate capital put the proportion of unorganized labor in various corporations at between 40 percent and 85 percent.[3] Moreover out of India's labor force of over 390 million, only 7 percent are workers on regular wages and salaries—and of this small proportion, only half are unionized. And between 1989 and the mid-1990s the unregistered workforce *increased*, from 89 percent to 93 percent.

The informal economy was recently estimated as comprising 60 percent of net domestic product, 68 percent of income, 60 percent of savings, 31 percent of agricultural exports, and even 41 percent of

manufactured exports.[4] There is no evidence that the informal economy is shrinking and plenty that it is the shock absorber of the reform
period.[5] But shock absorption is but one of the many roles of this, the
greater part of the Indian economy, and not the most important.

The fathers of modern India, not least Nehru, and early development
economists such as Myrdal were well aware of the forms of social
organization that regulated the economy and considered them "a tremendous force for inertia" (Myrdal 1968, 103) to be reduced by the
rationalities of big business, the state, and planned development.[6]
Some thirty years later in the 1990s, the era of liberalization once again
provoked predictions that the rationalities of contract would replace
custom and that acquired characteristics would replace ascribed ones
as the basis for market transactions.[7] Just as the economy would be
released from political influence, so also would traditional social institutions, or "primordial identities," become increasingly irrelevant to its
operation. The aim of this chapter is to explore why these predictions
are regularly disappointed.

I use for this purpose the concept of social structures of accumulation developed by Gordon, Kotz, Reich, and their colleagues in the
United States. Their key insight was the central importance of the regulative environment to the creation and stability of productive wealth.[8]
Unlike them, however I am not proposing a thesis about the role of
these structures in the historical evolution of India's economy, but
instead use it as a framework for an analysis of the principal socioeconomic relationships involved. Among other advantages, the development of this analytical approach avoids the tendency of so many
scholars to limit attention to legal-institutional structures established
by or linked to the state. Although the state influences the social structures I am chiefly concerned with in this chapter, they lie overwhelmingly outside it.

The main arguments advanced in this chapter are that the larger part
of the Indian economy is regulated in significant ways by social structures that are resistant or immune to change by means of macroeconomic policy. These regulative structures are fields of power that
also operate outside the economy. In its regulation of the informal
economy, the Indian state is not proof against the influence of these
structuring identities, as a result of which it does not work as one
would expect a modern developmental state to work and as institutions like the World Bank are portrayed as doing. The implication is
that standard prescriptions for reform under structural adjustment and

liberalization fail to address Indian reality. Their implementation is filtered through these structures. They will produce, if not the opposite of what is expected, at least some complicated surprises, ones not necessarily beneficial to most Indians. Liberalization increases the contradiction between solvent forces and forces that are reworking forms of social regulation and intensifying their economic content.

To study the informal economy seriously means relying on innumerable more or less localized pieces of evidence, obtained for the most part from field research. Our generalizations are therefore to be taken as cautious and provisional. All-India-wide generalizations, however, including every aspect of macroeconomic policy, are really subject to the same proviso. Anyone who doubts the wider significance of the claims made here about the social structures under review must be willing to provide a mass of counterevidence at the same level of detail. In any case, whatever the answers, the need to ask questions about social regulation is not in doubt.

11.2   The Social Regulation of the Indian Economy

In this section I examine the ways in which the most significant social structures of accumulation—religions, caste, space, classes, and the state—regulate India's informal economy. I start however with gender. There are two reasons for its priority. First, gender regulates the basic building block of the Indian economy: the family firm. Second, gender matters to the development of the economy, as well as being an issue of human rights.

11.2.1   Gender

Gender relations persist in being a pervasively important structure of accumulation in India. The informal economy is for the most part a matter of family businesses ("combat unit(s) designed for battle in the market" (White 1993)). These are the prime sites for the control of workers (of whom the most commonly oppressed and exploited are casual female labor). Family businesses are also structures of hierarchical authority between men—patriarchy in its oldest sense. Irrespective of living arrangements, men negotiate authority based on the division of tasks and skill among them, while also deferring to authority based upon age. Men divide tasks among themselves: accountancy, purchase, sales (and the negotiation and enforcement of contracts and credit relations), and the supervision of labor. "It is usual for a man to recruit his partners, managers and technical experts from among his close kindred," observed M. N. Srinivas of industrial entrepreneurs near Delhi over thirty-five years ago, and this has changed little, if at all.[9]

Accumulation is therefore the result of an intensely male, concentrated, and specialized set of relations of *cooperative control* for the production of the managerial labor. These managers also own the capital, sometimes in substantial conglomerates based on kinship networks. As firms grow in size, the demand for male family labor increases; but as fertility declines, the number of male agnates decreases. Yet instead of drawing women family members into these firms, local elite women tend to be deprived of productive work and live fairly secluded lives based on the home. Male affines seem to be preferred to the recruitment of professional managers.

Marriages and alliances are carefully controlled to create and protect the resource flows crucial to capital accumulation. There are "business families" as well as "family businesses."[10] Laidlaw's description of Jain practice is worth quoting because it is widely relevant. A family's "credit" in business "is its stock in the broadest sense, which includes social position, its reputation and the moral and religious as well as the business conduct of all its members. . . . When a family contracts a good marriage, its credit increases . . . (t)he potential impact on business confidence of particular potential alliances are explicit factors for consideration . . . because business practice depends . . . so much on trust, moral conduct and financial standing. . . . This means that a family's credit lies not only in the hands of the men who are actually engaged in business, but in that of its women too. When sons succeed automatically to their father's position in the family firm, the future of the business enterprise is, quite literally, in the women's hands" (Laidlaw 1995, 355–356). The conduct of their women then has implications for business.

These patriarchal arrangements affect allocative efficiency. Competition between firms (which are superficially independent entities but actually based on kinship networks) is frequently suppressed. Collusive oligopolies can be enforced. A small but vivid illustration is the manufacture and marketing of sweets in a South Indian town. Five large separate shops exist that belong to a father and his four sons. Sweets are prepared to some extent separately, but working capital is shared, prices are fixed, and entry to the sector is resisted. From the returns from sweets this joint family has invested in a large agricultural estate and also in a legal training for one of its scions.

Other economic consequences follow from keeping strong family control over young male property owners. They are often educated only to the level compatible with continuing to live at home or with close kin, namely, within the social and cultural limitations of small towns. The impact on economic performance is ambivalent. On the one hand, the edge of competitive innovation is thereby blunted and since most technical change is capital biased, the economy is more labor intensive than it otherwise might be. On the other hand, rates of accumulation are kept high by lack of competition.

The reinforcement of patriarchal relations in the class controlling local capital also has contradictory effects on the welfare of women. These have been theorized as positive for the female work force or for upwardly mobile subaltern social classes but negative in the heart of the local business class itself. Their most extreme impact is on life itself. Economic explanations focus on the consequences of what Ester Boserup called "productive deprivation" together with the diffusion from its North Indian heartland of the dowry, not vested in the bride but taking the form of a transfer from bride givers to bride receivers. As the economic costs of women rise and their economic benefits fall, so does their relative status. Recent research in South India where the relative status of women has been high confirms what Satish Agnihotri found, India-wide, for the 1980s: namely, that as household wealth rises the relative survival chances of women drop.[11] Whereas the juvenile sex ratio for landless agricultural households in 1994 was 930, that for children under 15 in the local agro-commercial and business elite was 784.[12] This is extremely low. The 2001 census reveals that whereas the aggregate sex ratio is improving, the child sex ratio is deteriorating to quite alarming proportions in certain states in North India.[13] An economic explanation for this phenomenon would emphasize the implications of economic growth for the expansion of small-scale property ownership, and then the implications of petty property for inheritance by men.

In the end however the relatively low and deteriorating life chances for women in the families of business elites has to be accounted for by a male supremacist culture. For although gender bias can be explained by low relative female status arising from lack of earned income, by the costs of dowry, and by the demand for male family labor in firms, business families are relatively wealthy and not bound by material constraints. In the business elite I studied in 1994, the ratio of dowry per daughter to business assets net of dowry per son was estimated at

1:12. Dowry is in no sense a burdensome pre-mortem inheritance. It can be concluded that wealth creation and property accumulation benefit men disproportionately.

11.2.2   Religious Plurality

Although Indian religions have coevolved over the centuries, practically no research has been done on the economic impacts of this coevolution, whether on the impact of ideas and doctrines about right behavior in the public sphere, and in relation to "others," or on the impact of their respective forms of social organization. My argument here therefore consists of preliminary hypotheses. The roles of religions will always be specific. Religions can be found supplying collective identities that in turn provide indispensable conditions for capital accumulation. In India, religious affiliation can govern the creation and protection of rent, the acquisition of skills and contacts, the rationing of finance, the establishment and defense of collective reputation, the circulation of information, the norms that regulate the inheritance and management of property, and those that prescribe the subordination of women. In addition, religious groups are often found regulating and distributing livelihoods, and providing insurance and last-resort social security. In these ways the distinction between the private and the public sphere is blurred and forms of noneconomic and divine authority may still be found to govern economic behavior. A single simplified example must stand for many. The economic significance of the Jain religion is far greater than the share of Jains in India's population (0.4 percent). With a religious philosophy involving nonviolence and the renunciation of worldly passion and with a claim to be caste-free and ritually egalitarian, Jains are commonly found to be wealthy local merchants, moneylenders, and pawnbrokers and are actually divided by subsect and lineage. The Jain mercantile diaspora began under the Mughals and was consolidated under the British (under whose rule *bunias* laid the foundations of Indian manufacturing industry and banking). In the informal economy, Jain business and kinship is tightly structured along the lines described earlier. Outside the set of core-ligionists, money is lent but not borrowed (other than from commercial banks).

In the few instances where religious groups have been studied (e.g., *Baniyas* by Fox, *Jains* by Laidlaw and Ellis, *Marwaris* by Timberg, and *Muslims* by Mines and Wright and *Kaikkoolar* merchants by Mines[14]), and depending on the relative size and power of the minorities locally, transactions between economic actors belonging to different religions have been observed to be more exploitative than within-group ones.[15] The coexistence of economic groups based on religion sustains and stabilizes rates of return.

This is not to argue that collective preconditions to competition cannot be found in organizations that straddle groups defined by religion—as in the case of chambers of commerce—or be marked by groups within a given religion—as indeed they are with caste, which I discuss next. The proliferation of sects and denominations has non-economic causes and, conversely, other forces also limit competition and protect rents, as already shown. But actually existing religious plurality in contemporary India has meant that the deepening division of labor and the proliferation of new and technologically upgraded commodities and services are easily, commonly, and sometimes exclusively aligned with religious subcastes and sects.[16] Satish Saberwal, following Marx, refers to it as India's social "cellularity" (1996, 39) onto which are mapped many "communities of accumulation." The consequences of such tessellation include the social patterning of residential areas, the spatial patterning of economic activity, the sometimes very profitable occupation by minorities of sectors of the economy formerly deemed to be defiling by Hindus (e.g., the tanning and recycling industries and the *bidi* labor force all dominated by Muslims) or of crafts produced for former aristocratic patrons (e.g., in Uttar Pradesh: brassware, glassware, cotton and silk embroidery, and the making of perfume—all also dominated by Muslims). While there is evidence that the exclusive links between guilds based on religion and occupation have long been contested and are dissolving, there is nevertheless a surprising amount of continuity in the Indian economy. Its general implication is a social resistance to the mobility of capital and labor; but the outcomes of this resistance are not determinate, depending as they do on local historical circumstance. For Jains this may mean great indirect power over the local rural economy through webs of credit. For other religious groups, such as the Muslim traders of Pallavaram,[17] the scale of their accumulation may be limited by lack of access to finance or long-distance trade contacts.

But religions also owe their roles in the economy in part to the secular aspirations of the state. First, in setting out "constitutionally" to be independent of all religions, and by establishing a legal regulative framework for the economy (which has been implemented very patchily), the Indian state has left the economy vulnerable to religious competition in a great range of ways, from the provision of infrastructure (such as educational facilities—open to one and all) to communal conflict fanned by economic rivalry.[18] In so doing, they reinforce the conditions that make religious organization necessary in the economy. In this gentle to fierce competition, groups identified by religion become increasingly objectified sets of moral agents with locally contested rankings and power.

Yet the Indian state has not been able to remain unaffected and indeed has been penetrated by religions—by the routes of political patronage, by the consequences for minority politics of reservations, and by unequal treatment of the religions in the amendments of diverse bodies of religious personal and family law. As a result of this penetration and the tesselation of the economy, apparently neutral development policy will have differential impacts on people of different religions. Further, not acknowledging the relation between the private sphere (to which it was assumed religion would be increasingly relegated) and the public sphere, which includes the economy, meant ignoring the impact of personal and family law on the economy. These bodies of divinely authorized law affect the building blocks of the economy through their differing impacts on property ownership and transfer on partition and inheritance and on the rights of individuals to (joint) property.

11.2.3   Caste

Andre Beteille writes of metropolitan India: "Caste is no longer an important agent of social placement or control" (1996, 450). But in a small town in South India (which I think does not differ much from most other regions in this respect), field research shows that Beteille's conclusion does not hold. Here, the remnants of occupation-based castes are organized in several loose hierarchies based on work, diet, religion, language, land-based versus network forms of organization, and the politico-administrative categories of the state. Thus all the work connected with the public health infrastructure, without which the economy cannot function, is left for Scheduled Castes. Most Backward Castes and Scheduled Castes form 80 percent of the labor force. Backward Castes are gaining ground as owners of businesses, but Forward Castes dominate the concentration of capital. A third of all firms use family labor alone while a further 15 percent will not employ labor not of their caste. So nearly half the firms are caste-homogeneous.

The local economy is increasingly organized in corporatist forms based directly or indirectly on caste. "Caste is the strongest trades union."[19] Yet the regulative roles played by caste are complex. They vary with the position of individual castes in this loose hierarchy—and no doubt with the distribution of castes in different states.

Caste structures the creation and disposal of waste without which markets do not work. Rubbish marks the boundary between domestic and public space. Caste males do not generally handle this waste. Its disposal is part of a paradigm of service and subordination where caste and gender still reflect rank and stigma.[20] Scheduled Caste laborers do this sanitary work, but they have also entered trade in commodities with certain physical properties, such as foodstuffs with skins, or things that have to be transformed by cooking prior to consumption, or that need recycling, or that are traded in physically dirty surroundings. Entry into such markets has been a matter of the seizure and legitimation of physical public space—fruit and vegetable sellers have encroached onto the platforms of some shops or set up stall or sack-space on the roadside. The local state, in the form of the municipal market, has allowed freer entry to Scheduled Caste traders than have existing marketplace businesses, which have reacted with hostility to this particular disturbance to the local market order.

Although party politics, religion, philanthropy, and redistributive obligations all play a part in the way the local economy is organized and regulated, by far the most significant structures are caste-cum-trade associations. Caste has been reworked as an economic institution, and it is least flexible at the base where social disadvantage is most entrenched. While some caste/trade associations are intermittent and called into life only when the trade is threatened, many, especially those of business sectors in which (Most) Backward Castes operate, are playing increasingly important roles in regulation. These include the rationing of entry to a trade, the definition of proper contracts, the settlement of disputes, collective insurance, collective representation to the state, the organization of the spatial territory of the marketplace, the monitoring of rent seeking and the way rents are shared with state officials and politicians, the control of labor disputes, the fixing of the wage and other terms and conditions of work, the control of prices in derived markets (e.g., for transport, porterage, sweeping and even certain raw materials), and last but not least collective security.[21]

The organizations of the local business elite differ from lower caste-cum-trade associations by being more mixed-caste, better networked, and more ambitiously federated. Reinforcing patriarchy and the rhetoric of "town unity," caste ideology works to support the economic interests of the local business class in exactly the manner Gramsci thought to be the essence of civil society.[22] Ideology, not usually considered a social structure of accumulation, is in fact a significant shaper of it. It supplies the institutional structures on the back of which corporate organizations have evolved. It also helps create the overlap between economy and society that is necessary to any corporatist project. The Indian economy has a distinctive propensity for this form of regulation, by means of which the antagonism between business and labor is suppressed. The welfare and security of labor is at the bottom of the agenda of such institutions. Labor is often found to be admitted to these associations only to be managed by owners in the interests of the owners' accumulative strategies.[23]

11.2.4   Space—Clusters

All these determinant structures of accumulation are mapped onto distinctive patterns of economic *space*. Capital is accumulated in towns and cities, yet India is weakly urbanized and its urbanization displays a distinctive pattern of specialized clusters. Taking Tamil Nadu again, the Palar Valley specializes in leather goods, Cheyyar in reed mats, Arni and Kanchipuram in silk, Tiruchengode in drilling equipment and lorry bodies, Tirupur in hosiery, Salem, Coimbatore, and Bhavani in textiles, Tiruchirapalli in gems, Sivakasi in matches, Palladam in chewing tobacco, and so on—this list is very far from complete. Clustered development is thought to be a distinctive form of modern capitalism, one capable of generating two kinds of mutually beneficial collective efficiency. Passive collective efficiency is obtained from spatial proximity. This provokes the circulation of information, the consolidation of networks of contacts, subcontracting, and process specialization as well as access to services and infrastructure. Active collective efficiency is obtained from trade associations through which R&D, training and even export contacts may be engineered. But only a small minority of India's clusters are of this sort. Most clusters are low-tech, with highly exploitative labor arrangements; some are the disguised and outsourced production units of one or two big companies hellbent on escaping the pincer of unions and Factories Acts. Further, while the voluminous literature explores the high- and low-level trajectories of specialized clusters, another kind of clustered development, which is neglected, is to be found in almost every urban settlement—gold ornament crafting along with pawnbroking is one such example, and foodgrains processing another. The character of each cluster varies, it can be hypothesized, according to local structures of property ownership and agrarian accumulation, and according to the varying roles played in each cluster by castes (particularly but not exclusively mercantile castes) and by the state. The spatial distributions of these three social structures of accumulation strongly influence the kinds of commodities produced in a given area. They keep accumulation highly localized, shape the way labor is controlled, limit competition, and permit—and legitimate the persistence of—environmental hazards such as the contamination of underground water and the ubiquity of solid waste.

In most regions the local agrarian structure stratifies rural society sufficiently to let a range of technologies of transformation coexist, each with different labor and factor requirements, creating a finely differentiated range of products for markets which are socially and geographically segmented.[24] The agrarian structure also shapes the terms of resource transfers between the major sectors of the economy, the supply of surplus labor (mainly but not exclusively from agriculture), and the terms on which it works—and may even accumulate—in the nonfarm economy. Clusters are shaped by path dependency originating from local land tenure, land use, and cropping patterns, but are perpetuated by other factors (such as the lock-in of processing technologies and the development of nonlocal trade) when land use changes.

Although commerce is increasingly cosmopolitan, investments do not follow a simple logic of profitability because caste is often still the preferred basis for business partnerships, repeated contacts, and credit. Private capital is not fungible and "capital contra-flows" may be observed in which urban capital-exporting castes investing in villages (e.g., in weaving) are unable to invest in the sectors open to migrant agricultural caste capital investing in town (e.g., in grain processing). Mercantile castes have a political and economic field based on networks independent of the agrarian castes. Nevertheless these networks are divided into small localities that are distinctively marked by specialization.[25] (The one major exception to this rule is the nineteenth-century *marwari* diaspora to regions weak in merchant castes where they still control the processing and trade in basic commodities—

including gold.) In cases where a cluster has involved many castes, it has been found that the cooperation needed for collective efficiency is harder to organize and the transition from a low-level equilibrium cluster to an Emilia Romagna type of industrial district is less likely.[26]

If there is a secularizing solvent for this clustered economy, it is undoubtedly the state, not only via its interventionist control over strategic sectors that provide raw and intermediate materials but also via the provision of infrastructure and subsidies. There are two ways, however, in which the state tends to act to reinforce clustering rather than erode it. The checkered histories of small industrial estates shows that the state tends to complement capital in existing central places rather than substituting for it on new sites, and there is a marked "distance decay" in the quality and quantity of provision. Second, the state tolerates nontrivial environmental externalities by its negligent enforcement, or complicitous nonenforcement, of environmental standards. Exceptions to this (such as the degree of success of state-enforced, state-subsidized collective treatment plants for tanning effluent in the Palar valley leather cluster) only prove the general rule.[27]

11.2.5 Classes

11.2.5.1 Labor Most of the Indian workforce has no formal written contracts with their employers. Their livelihoods come from (casual) wage labor (30 percent of the workforce) and from self-employment—dispersed and fragmented petty production and trade (56 percent of all livelihoods).[28] Right after Independence, labor was systematically demobilized and made to depend on the state for mediation with employers.[29] Only about 3 percent of the workforce is unionized and even this degree of labor organization has long been under attack from corporate capital (so it can hardly be the sole reason for the mediocre developmental performance of the corporate sector).[30] The other 97 percent of workers are hardly regulated by the state; they lack enforceable rights at work and rights to social security. Migration notwithstanding, labor markets tend to be small-scale and fragmented. The Indian labor force is regulated not only through the compulsions of assetlessness, clientelage, beck-and-call contracts, and debt-mediated labor attachment, but also through the social structures of gender, religion, caste, and the local corporatist occupation-based organizations.

Apart from the domestic sphere, women's work is heavily concentrated in rural sites and in agricultural work, on casual contracts, and at wages bordering on starvation—on the average only 70 percent of the wages paid to men.[31] In nonfarm work, women are likely to be concentrated in the lowest grades and stages, on piece rates rather than daily wages, and with earnings even lower than those of men than in agriculture proper. Caste still shapes ideologies of work; it makes for compartmentalized labor markets "with non-competing groups whose options are severely constrained" (Harriss 1989). Few Brahmins will undertake heavy manual work, while to be Scheduled Caste (29 percent of the population) makes a person twice as likely as otherwise to be a casual laborer, in agriculture and poor.[32] Technologies reinforce the contempt meted out to *dalits* through demeaning and physically damaging work: Enormous weights are still carried by headloading rather than by wheelbarrow or conveyor belt; brooms and brushes require women to work stooping rather than standing. Caste also screens out *dalit* recruits for entry into jobs in the rural nonfarm economy. Workers themselves sometimes enforce the stratification of occupations so as to maintain their hold over enclaves of the labor market. In cases when owners and employees belong to the same caste (e.g., in the diamond cutting industry in Surat (Gujarat) or the hosiery industry in Tirupur (Tamil Nadu)), laborers often emphasize their solidarity with employers, thereby ensuring the exclusion of other caste groups. Caste also provides an idiom in which many sections of the laboring poor organize themselves politically, though not always in the context of work or labor relations. Social movements and the political mobilization of *dalits* have gained momentum in their search for respect and social status. Caste-based social movements have developed in synergy with the workplace-based politics of lower castes. In rural Bihar and elsewhere, the struggles of Scheduled Caste landless labor, at times in alliance with radical left-wing political organizations, have led to violent confrontations, with caste battles reflecting class conflict.[33]

Labor is also controlled through the supply of infrastructure, in public spaces and in domestic life as well as at work. Not only is life outside work socially regulated but also the state actively regulates the reproduction of labor, through workers' *lack* of housing, water, education, their *lack* of social security, and their *lack* of space for living and leisure—perhaps more comprehensively that it regulates their work. Caste-based political organization is often focused on their needs.

11.2.5.2 Capital—The "Intermediate Classes" Outside India's metropolitan cities, the greater part of the economy is still dominated by a loose, awkward coalition of what Michal Kalecki called "intermediate classes" and what Aijaz Ahmad calls "non-polar classes"[34]: a grouping of rich peasants, working commercial capitalists (family businesses), and the collusive fraction of the bureaucracy that implements state regulations—some of which protect local business and some of which they sabotage. The income of the rich peasants and family businesses can "neither be classified as a reward for labor nor as a payment for risk-taking (i.e., profit) but is an amalgam of the two. The self-employed lie midway between the large-scale, professionally managed capitalist enterprises of the private sector, and the working classes" (Jha 1980, 95). The intermediate classes do not correspond to the Marxian definition of class, being essentially defined by occupying a "contradictory class location," in between workers and capitalists proper.[35] They have the strength of numbers. In 1980 P. S. Jha's estimate came to 30 million with eight to ten dependants apiece—namely, a total of some 250 million or about one-third of the entire population. In relation to big business they appear small and dispersed, but in relation to labor they present a mighty front; they are the "masters of the countryside."[36] These classes have conflicts of interest with labor as well as with corporate capital. They are in tension with labor over their control of the supply and prices of essential wage goods in which workers have a vital interest. However, while they may align themselves politically with corporate capital, they do not do this consistently because they reap direct opportunistic returns from the control of scarcity and from rents, whereas corporate returns are mediated by managers and by shareholder interests. Intermediate classes are able to control scarcities by markup price formation, through oligopolistic collusion in markets, and through structures of regulation and of partial state intervention that remain little touched by liberalization. In sectors where they compete head on with big business, intermediate firms may undercut big business by using family labor, by depriving wage labor of costly rights, and by operating smaller-scale technology with lower fixed costs at higher-capacity utilization. And big business, despite its notorious delinquence, is still easier to tax than are the intermediate classes.

Evidence from long-term field research on agricultural merchants in West Bengal and Tamil Nadu, together with that from a long-term study of the economy of a town in Tamil Nadu, reveals that while markets look crowded, much initiative is used to take the edge off competition, by means of which market shares are defended.[37] Exclusive, repeated network transactions are a common ploy. Oligopolies coexist with petty traders. The latter often depend on the former for information, contacts, and access to transport and credit. The vertical integration of a joint firm may be disguised by being divided up into apparently independent components. Wherever their activities have been examined in detail, agro-processing and trading firms have been found to tend toward uniqueness, complexity, and diversity in the business activities they comprise and combine. Not only does this endow the entire system with plasticity in the face of shocks, for the individual firm it also is a form of "branding" and an invitation to loyalty.

The mode of accumulation of the intermediate classes depends centrally on politics, though local capital does not have to enter party politics directly to ensure its power. Intermediate classes connive with local officials to secure the protection both of the rents they create in markets and of the state's resources that they capture. They seek state subsidies but, more important, they secure concessions by influencing policy in its implementation rather than its formulation. Nowhere are the concessions and collusion more important than in the evasion of tax.

The intermediate classes have survived and are surviving an unprecedented threat from several quarters: from MNCs, from the dismantling of some of the structure of state regulation, and from the abandonment of its developmental mandate (which began in the 1980s with the erosion of fiscal discipline and the havoc caused to public-sector capital expenditure by interest payments and foreign exchange markets, and continued after 1991 under the reforms);[38] and the rise of a new middle class with a stake, through insurance and share ownership, in the corporate economy. The means of their survival are threefold. First, there is the productive investment of resources hitherto tucked away in the black economy. Second, unreformed state regulation of prominent heights of the economy (food, electricity, kerosene, fertilizer, liquor), some involving large subsidies to business, much involving bribery, protects market-based rents and tax evasion. Tax evasion is the biggest disguised subsidy such classes have received and it defrauds the state, with serious consequences for the state's capacity and legitimacy. Third, the intermediate classes have been regenerated by a new, dispersed wave of accumulation on the part of the lower agrarian castes. The process involves disorderly relations with consumers, labor, and the state. A sharp struggle over the surplus is under way, since, at 10.24 percent over the *decade* of the 1990s, the rate of agricultural growth has been mediocre and less than that of population growth.[39]

11.3   State Regulation

How does the state fit into this socially regulated economy? Although the Indian state is a significant actor in the informal economy, much of it lies beyond the state's direct control, either because its units (small firms) are under the size threshold for regulation, or because the state neglects to regulate it—or is actively prevented from regulating it.

Just as the informalized markets in which the intermediate classes operate create their own institutions to regulate and protect them, so the state by its interventions creates many informal, socially regulated markets. For instance, the public distribution system of food grains, extremely resistant to deregulation, has long created price margins which draw in unlicensed and non-state-regulated processing and trade. Leakages from its stores and lorries still supply parallel markets for stolen grain. There are even standard prices for the exercise of influence and markets in bureaucratic postings.[40]

At the same time as the state shapes socially regulated informal markets, it is shaped reflexively by nonstate social structures of accumulation. It is the ambivalent agent of gender empowerment—a far more progressive employer in this respect than private enterprise. It is a formal initiator of development projects to empower women and an implementer of reforms to expand female representation and political participation. At the same time, by making it very difficult for women to qualify for licenses or development credit, the state effectively reinforces male property rights. It does little to counter a prevailing anti-female bias in education and has not proved able or willing to resist the alarming deterioration in the relative status of girls.

As we saw, it is also a distinctly ambivalent agent of secularization in the economy. Acts of Hindu religious observance have long been incorporated into state office routines and state development expenditure is being channeled through NGOs and trusts that are "fronts" for religious organizations. Through the policy of job reservations the state is at the frontline of social transformation as the important yet flawed champion of the social and economic emancipation of oppressed castes and tribes.

Yet the international lending institutions see the state only as a technique of governance. They have called for it to downsize employment.

As a result competition between castes has been reinforced, and an informal system of job reservations has been developed through patronage practiced by all castes. At the local level it is deeply permeated by private status. Its effective capacity depends on the social identities of the officials who happen to be in post—landed, male, upper-caste officials are better tax gatherers for instance—as well as by private interest (officials use their powers of discretion both to extract rents for themselves and to protect the rents of others). A "shadow state" is created—a penumbra of people living from intermediation and corruption, with a strong interest in its perpetuation. The further it is from capital cities, the less the state seems to have been able to regulate, redistribute, or subsidize accumulation. Its monopoly of coercion, never complete, is being challenged by the proliferation of new mafia forces and private protection services.

11.4   Real Structural Adjustment

For the international development agencies, structural adjustment and liberalization consist of rafts of policies to remove distortions caused by protection and by domestic subsidies, in effect to adjust the domestic price structure to that of the world market, to let the structure of production reorganize itself, and to extract the economy from politics. The state is no longer itself to be a structure of accumulation.

It is true that the results of planned development differ from those produced by market forces, as the politically determined locations of steel plants and heavy industry in India clearly show. Liberalization ought therefore to generate spatial dislocations as it replaces non-market allocations by those of markets. Indeed this is predicted, unintentionally, by the advocates of liberalization, who maintain that liberalization is capable of *reversing* regional disparities, which have been in part the unintended consequence of the Indian Finance and Planning Commission's bureaucratic controls over production, investment, and trade. If markets respond to relative factor scarcities with greater allocative efficiency, if regions with lower capital-labor ratios have a higher marginal productivity of capital and therefore offer higher rates of return to capital, then regional disparities ought to be reversed by deregulation and replaced by regional convergence. But, as Jeffrey Sachs observes, what appears to be happening is the opposite: an accentuation not only of regional disparities but also of disparities within regions.[41] In general accumulation is increasingly specialized and spatially clustered and is driving intensified regional as well as social and labor market differentiation. Whereas Kanbur and Jhabvala argue in chapter 12 that this is due to technology, I contend that this is due in good measure to social structures of accumulation.

The adjustment of structures of prices and production is also accompanied by adjustments in social structures of accumulation and in ideas and practices of accountability. If Indian capitalism is a *social solvent*,[42] it works sluggishly (to say the least) at the local level that has been my focus. In fact if anything the reverse seems true: Because capital accumulation relies on social structures of accumulation (which liberalization does not address at all), the effect of liberalization is not to abolish or transform those in which markets are embedded but to encourage them to rework themselves as economic institutions and to persist. In the era of liberalization and globalization, not only is the structural adjustment that is taking place the replacement of state-planned development, and "custom," by market and contract. It is also *the intensification of the relations between markets and the "nonmarket" institutions without which markets cannot operate. Gender* relations are the most resistant to change and operate to favor men quite disproportionately over women in the class that accumulates; there is no reason to see liberalization as capable of transforming them. *Caste* and *religion* are much more flexible. They are emerging as structures that may generate exclusive, networked forms of accumulation and corporatist forms of economic regulation and that tend to operate to control labor to the advantage of capital. In practice, moreover, far from dissolving religious bonds, liberalization has been associated with an upsurge in religiosity. The real fluidity lies not in the solvent force but in the speed with which such collective identities are intensified. Though never theorized in this way, *Hindutva* itself might even be explored as an attempt to carve and consolidate a moral space for Hindu accumulation at the expense of accumulation by adherents of other religions.

Instead of a drastic reduction in the premium for political power predicted by the theory of liberalization, one sees a new phase of mass political assertion of this power. In the meantime the state structures aimed at promoting the livelihoods for and upward mobility of lower castes are completely at loggerheads with the objectives of liberalization; but, even if they are constrained, their abolition is not an option. The state cannot avoid its role for low and sceduled caste aspiration.

And as I noted earlier, in the economy in which 88 percent of Indians live, the state is so riddled with fraud and corruption that an enormous "shadow" has grown up around it that depends on and feeds off it. Long ago Myrdal called the Indian state a "soft" state. If anything it has become softer—Weber's "steel cage" has rusted—while the social structures around it have hardened. It looks less and less like the instrument of market rationality that the advocates of liberalization envisage.

Reforms—however liberalizing in intent—that depend on the formal legal infrastructure thus face three contradictions. First, while development requires the rule of law, in India regulative law is often unimportant—since much of the economy is not regulated by law and since locally influential and respectable people frequently appear to be convinced that they are entitled to be above the law.[43] Law is at best compromised by a mass of unintended and unforeseen consequences; at worst it is a mere base for extortion, formally counterproductive but informally very productive—for legislators and bureaucrats. Second, any attempt to "downsize" or even shed inappropriate laws means a capitulation to those already breaking them, which delegitimizes the state. Third, attempts to shed laws that are inappropriate because impossible to implement results in looser laws that are easily abused.[44] And what is true for the law is likely to be true more widely for the institutions that implement the law.

Another kind of unorthodox structural adjustment, and one long preceding that of the World Bank and the IMF, is that caused by underfunding the state. The leaching of taxable resources into the rapidly expanding black economy deprives the state of resources.[45] Black wealth is laundered abroad, or stored in real estate, finance, (retail) inventory, and a relatively small amount in the form of gold. According to one careful estimate this leakage is some twenty times greater than leakages due to corruption.[46] The state responds to this famine of resources by protecting salaries at the expense of equipment and investment,[47] producing for example the phenomenon of a fire brigade with firemen but without water or diesel fuel, whose functioning is completely dependent on a local private economic patron. Freezes on staff recruitment play havoc with lines of reporting accountability, enforcement capacity, the time taken to achieve objectives, and the quality of goods and services.[48] Low-quality provision encourages informal private or black alternatives. The loss of legitimacy resulting from this kind of structural adjustment is self-reinforcing.

Likewise corruption is not reduced when the sites for the corrupt privatization of public goods and services are removed by state compression or privatization. Quite the opposite appears to have happened. The reasons are not hard to find. Partial changes in ownership may decentralize and multiply sites for corruption by complicating accountability and diluting enforcement capacity. Some business interests may use bribes to dilute enforcement or to maintain privileged access to resources or to exemptions while other interests will bribe to enforce deregulation. Officials may seek bribes against promises of future economic rents, given that their tenure outlives that of their political masters.[49]

Although liberalization invites a change in the character of the control of the economy, not a release from it, still there is considerable continuity in the structure of regulation nurturing the intermediate classes. The largest subsidies—for fertilizers, food, agricultural electricity, and to a lesser extent credit—have proved extremely hard to reduce.[50] The intermediate classes remain potent players. The capacity to accumulate has now spread from castes and classes that have hitherto resisted paying tax to lower agrarian castes that have never before been required to pay them—at least not directly. A new wave of small capital is reinforcing and expanding the informal and black economy, intensifying the casualization of labor and transferring the risks of unstable livelihoods to the workforce.

11.5   The Implications for Development Policy of the Real Structural Adjustments

"Policy" is then best understood as the outcome of the way political resources have been deployed in the struggles for rents that take place at all stages—discursive, procedural, and allocative—of the so-called "policy-making process." Liberalization does not destroy these rents but simply intensifies the struggle for them.

To ask, as students of Indian development are so often invited to do, whether what exists is "inefficient" implies that some alternative set of social structures of accumulation is imaginable with which those that actually exist in India might be compared. Nothing in the relationships and trends one can currently observe seems to suggest that this is possible. India's social structures of accumulation are deeply entrenched.

The relations between the formal state, the formal economy, the shadow state, and the informal economy are the outcomes of political struggles. The state's convection system of taxation and distribution is shorn of civic egalitarianism. The possession of nuclear weapons cannot compensate for this kind of failure in nation building. Unless and until there is a strong public mandate for tax compliance and against corruption—both of which are essential first steps toward accountability, and have been invoked as "solutions" for decades[51]—the prospects for the intermediate classes still look good. Fraud and tax evasion are part and parcel of Indian capitalism. In order for both noncompliance with the state and the flouting of the constitutional entitlements of labor to be so widespread and persistent, people's moral world—the units of accountability—must be immediate or restricted to levels well below the nation—or even the local state. Countering this socially regulated but fundamentally antisocial economy calls for the emergence of a much more robust and active culture of collective accountability in which the legitimacy of the state also needs to be renegotiated.

If a point of leverage for change exists at all, it lies in mechanisms that might make capital more accountable to the state, and the state to other parts of civil society. These are urgent questions of *development policy* that are *prior* to exercises of technical choice and *prior* to the listing and evaluation of policy options and sequences that are the stock-in-trade of conventional development policy. These questions are at a considerable remove from the World Bank's adoption of, at best, a narrowly electoral and formal concept of democracy, together with the abstract and unreal conceptions of economy and polity that currently prevail in mainstream economics and in much of the other social sciences.

Acknowledgments

I would like to thank the participants at the Indian Economy Conference, Cornell University, especialy Alaka Basu, and also the Seminar at the Department for Economics and International Development, Bath University and the Cambridge Advanced Programme on Development Research in Economics for their stimulating responses.

Notes

This is a summary of part of my book *India Working* (Cambridge: Cambridge University Press, 2003).

1. From the 1991 census less than 12 percent of the population lived in metropolitan cities. Over 74 percent were rural and a further 14 percent lived in towns under 2,00,000: a total of 88 percent.

2. From raw data in Centre for Monitoring the Indian Economy, 1997. The proportion varies from 6 percent in Assam to 17 percent in Punjab and Rajasthan. Corporate and public-sector enterprise is estimated to produce about 20 percent of GDP (Sinha, Sangeeta, and Siddiqui 1999).

3. Davala (1992) and Bhowmik (1998). Jhabvala and Kanbur (chapter 12) find that 50 percent of workers in unregistered garments firms do not have contracts.

4. Sinha, Sangeeta, and Siddiqui (1999).

5. See Ghose (1999).

6. Nehru, quoted in Madan (1987).

7. Jayaram (1996), Lal (1988), Mendelsohn (1993); Panini (1996, 28, 60).

8. Gordon, Edwards, and Reich (1982) and Kotz, McDonough, and Reich (1994).

9. Srinivas (1966).

10. The distinction was first made by Fox (1969, 143) and developed by Laidlaw (1995, 354–345).

11. Agnihotri (2000); see especially chapters 1 and 2.

12. Harriss-White (1999) and Basile and Harriss-White (1999).

13. Athreya (2001).

14. Respectively, Fox (1969), Laidlaw (1995), Ellis (1991), Timberg (1978), Mines (1972), Wright (1981), and Mines (1984).

15. Mines (1972) and Dasgupta (1992).

16. For example, sound services have been pioneered by entrepreneurs from the barber caste (who are also musicians), drycleaning and power laundries by *dhobis*, leather goods and travel agencies by Muslims.

17. Mines (1972, 93–118).

18. Wright (1981, 43); Desai (1984, 22–23); Engineer (1984, 36–41); Deponte (2000); see also Peoples' Union for Civil Liberties (1998) for details of the Coimbatore riots of 1997 in which police were alleged to have destroyed the assets of small-scale Muslim pavement sellers while paid riot-makers wrecked the large Muslim cloth shops.

19. A modern proverb reported by a low-caste trade association leader; see Harriss-White (2003, 192).

20. Beall (1997).

21. Basile and Harriss-White (1999).

22. Gramsci (1971).

23. I have found this form of labor control in organizations "representing" yarn twisters, marketplace porters, and handcart pushers.

24. This is as true for rice as it is for cotton, groundnut and mustard oil, and tobacco (Harriss-White 1996a).

25. Mines (1984).

26. Nadvi (1999) and Schmitz and Nadvi (1999).

27. Kennedy (1999).

28. Ghose (1999).

29. Chibber (2003).

30. Mukherjee Reed (2001).

31. Ghose (1999) for 1994.

32. Nagaraj (1999) and Jayaraj and Subramanian (1999).

33. Omvedt (1993) and Gooptu (2001).

34. Kalecki (1972); Ahmad (1996).

35. To adopt E. O. Wright's term.

36. The phrase is Lenin's in relation to Russia a century ago.

37. See Harriss (1993) for West Bengal, Harriss-White (1996a) for Tamil Nadu, and Harriss (1991) and Basile and Harriss-White (2000) for the long-term study of the market town; see McCartney and Harriss-White (2000) for a detailed critical analysis of the survival capacities of intermediate classes.

38. A reform that directly threatens the intermediate classes is presumptive taxation; see McCartney and Harriss-White (2000).

39. Shariff, Ghosh, and Mondal (2002).

40. Mooij (1999), Wade (1985), and Guhan and Paul (1997).

41. For the case see Bhagwati (1993); for data on regional inequality, see Mohan and Thottan (1992) and Meher (1999).

42. The view of scholars such as Lal (1988) and Panini (1996).

43. Of course, this practice is by no means confined to India; see Joly (2001) on this phenomenon in France.

44. McBarnet and Whelan (1991); see the adverse impact on corporate governance of voluntary codes in Banaji and Mody (2000).

45. See chapter 6.

46. Roy (1996).

47. Capital expenditure as a percentage of GDP declined from 2.8 percent in 1990–1991 to 1.5 percent in 2000–2001, Shariff, Ghosh, and Mondal (2002).

48. Kjellberg and Banik (2000).

49. Harriss-White (1996b).

50. Refer to McCartney and Harriss-White (2000) for details; see also chapter 7.

51. See Myrdal (1973), for instance.

References

Agnihotri, S. 2000. *Sex Ratio Patterns in the Indian Population: A Fresh Exploration.* New Delhi: Sage.

Ahmad, A. 1996. "Fascism and National Culture: Reading Gramsci in the Days of Hindutva." In *Lineages of the Present: Political Essays*, ed. A. Ahmad, 221–266. New Delhi: Tulika.

Athreya, V. 2001. "Census 2001: Some Progress, Some Concern." *Frontline*, April 26.

Banaji, J., and G. Mody. 2000. "Corporate Governance and the Indian Private Sector." Working Paper no. 73, Queen Elizabeth House, Oxford University. Available online at ⟨www2.qeh.ox.ac.uk⟩.

Basile, E., and B. Harriss-White. 1999. "The Politics of Accumulation in Small Town India." *Bulletin of the Institute of Development Studies* 30, no. 4:31–39.

Basile, E., and B. Harriss-White. 2000. "Corporative Capitalism, Civil Society and the Politics of Accumulation in Small Town India." Working Paper no. 38, Queen Elizabeth House, Oxford University. Available online at ⟨www2.qeh.ox.ac.uk⟩.

Beall, J. 1997. "Households, Livelihoods and the Urban Environment: Sociological Perspectives on Solid Waste Management in Pakistan." Ph.D. thesis, London School of Economics.

Béteille, A. 1996. "Caste in Contemporary India." In *Caste Today*, ed. C. Fuller, 150–179. New Delhi: Oxford University Press.

Bhagwati, J. 1993. *India in Transition: Freeing the Economy.* Oxford: Clarendon.

Bhowmik, S. 1998. "The Labour Movement in India: Present Problems and Future Perspectives." *Indian Journal of Social Work* 59, no. 1:147–166.

Carrithers, M., and C. Humphrey. eds. 1991. *The Assembly of Listeners. Jains in Society.* Cambridge: Cambridge University Press.

Chibber, V. 2003. "From Class Compromise to Class Accommodation: the Fate of Labour in Post-colonial India." In *Rethinking Class and Poverty: Social Movements in India in a Transnational Age*, ed. R. Ray and M. Katzenstein, Cambridge: Cambridge University Press.

Corbridge, S., and J. Harriss, 2000. *Reinventing India.* London: Polity.

Dasgupta, N. 1992. *Petty Trading in the Third World.* London: Avebury.

Davala, S., ed. 1992. *Employment and Unionization in Indian Industry.* Delhi: Friedrich Ebert Stiftung.

Deponte, G. 2000. "Desindustrialisation, Précarisation du Travail et Transformation des Réseaux Politiques Urbains: le Cas de la Ville de Kanpur (UP)." Paper presented at the symposium La Ville en Asie du Sud: Quelles specificités? Centre d'Etudes de l'Inde et de l'Asie du Sud, Paris.

Desai, A. R. 1984. "Caste and Communal Violence in the Post-Partition Indian Union." In *Communal Riots in Post-Independence India*, ed. A. A. Engineer, 10–32. Hyderabad: Sangam/Orient Longman.

Ellis, C. C. M. 1991. "The Jain Merchant Castes of Rajasthan: Some Aspects of the Management of Social Identity in a Market Town." In *The Assembly of Listeners. Jains in Society*, ed. M. Carrithers and C. Humphrey, 75–107. Cambridge: Cambridge University Press.

Engineer, A. A., ed. 1984. *Communal Riots in Post-Independence India*. Hyderabad: Sangam/Orient Longman.

Fox, R. 1969. *From Zamindar to Ballot Box*. Ithaca: Cornell University Press.

Fuller, C., ed. 1996. *Caste Today*. New Delhi: Oxford University Press.

Ghose, A. 1999. "Current Issues of Employment Policy in India." *Economic and Political Weekly* 34, no. 36 (September 4):2592–2608.

Gooptu, N. 2001. *The Urban Poor and the Politics of Class, Community and Nation: Uttar Pradesh between the Two World Wars*. Cambridge: Cambridge University Press.

Gordon, D., R. Edwards, and M. Reich. 1982. *Segmented Work, Divided Workers*. Cambridge: Cambridge University Press.

Gramsci, A. 1971. *Prison Notebooks*. New York: International Publishers.

Guhan, S., and S. Paul, eds. 1997. *Corruption in India: Agenda for Action*. New Delhi: Vision.

Harriss, B. 1991. "The Arni Studies: Changes in the Private Sector of a Market Town, 1973–83." In *The Green Revolution Reconsidered*, ed. P. Hazell and C. Ramasamy, 181–213. Baltimore: Johns Hopkins University Press.

Harriss, B. 1993. *Markets, State and Society: Problems of Marketing under Conditions of Smallholder Agriculture in West Bengal*. Report to WIDER. Helsinki: Oxford. 128 pp. (Published in 1993 by The Open University, Development Policy and Practice Group, UK.)

Harriss, B., S. Guhan, and R. Cassen. 1992. *Poverty in India: Research and Policy*. New Delhi: Oxford University Press.

Harriss, J. 1989. "Vulnerable Workers in the Indian Urban Labour Market." In *Urban Poverty and the Labour Market: Access to Jobs and Incomes in Asian and Latin American Cities*, ed. G. Rogers. Geneva: International Labour Office.

Harriss-White, B. 1996a. *A Political Economy of Agricultural Markets in South India: Masters of the Countryside*. New Delhi: Sage.

Harriss-White, B. 1996b. "Liberalisation and Corruption: Resolving the Paradox." *Liberalisation and the New Corruption*, Special Issue, *Bulletin, Institute of Development Studies* 27, no. 2:31–40.

Harriss-White, B. 1999. "Gender-Cleansing: The Paradox of Development and Deteriorating Female Life Chances in Tamil Nadu." In *Signposts: Gender Issues in Post Independence India*, ed. R. Sundar Rajan. New Delhi: Kali for Women.

Harriss-White, B. 2003. *India Working*. Cambridge: Cambridge University Press.

Jayaraj, D., and S. Subramanian. 1999. "Poverty and Discrimination: Measurement and Evidence from Rural India." In *Illfare in India: Essays on India's Social Sector in Honour of S. Guhan*, ed. B. Harriss-White, and S. Subramanian, 196–226. New Delhi: Oxford University Press.

Jayaram, N. 1996. "Caste and Hinduism: Changing Protean Relationship." In *Caste: Its Twentieth Century Avatar*, ed. M. N. Srinivas. Delhi: Viking.

Jha, P. S. 1980. *The Political Economy of Stagnation*. Delhi: Oxford University Press.

Joly, E. 2001. *Notre Affaire à Tous*. Paris: Les Arènes.

Kalecki, M. 1972. *Essays on the Economic Growth of the Socialist and the Mixed Economy*. London: Unwin.

Kennedy, L. 1999. "Cooperating for Survival: Tannery Pollution and Joint Action in the Palar Valley (India)." *World Development* 27, no. 9:1673–1692.

Kjellberg, F., and D. Banik. 2000. "The Paradox of Pollution Control: Regulations and Administration in a South Indian State." Department of Political Science, Research Report no. 2/2000, University of Oslo.

Kotz, D. M., McDonough, T., and Reich, M., eds. 1994. *Social Structures of Accumulation: The Political Economy of Growth and Crisis*. Cambridge: Cambridge University Press.

Laidlaw, J. 1995. *Riches and Renunciation. Religion, Economy, and Society among the Jains*. Oxford: Clarendon Press.

Lal, D. 1988. *The Hindu Equilibrium, Vol. 1: Cultural Stability and Economic Stagnation 1500 BC to 1980*. Oxford: Clarendon Press.

Madan, T. N. 1987. "Secularism in Its Place." *Journal of Asian Studies* 46, no. 4:747–759.

McBarnet, D., and C. Whelan. 1991. "The Elusive Spirit of the Law: Formalism and the Struggle for Legal Control." *Modern Law Review* 54, no. 6:848–873.

McCartney, M., and B. Harriss-White. 2000. "The Intermediate Regime and Intermediate Classes Revisited: A Political Economy of Indian Development from c 1980 to Hindutva." Queen Elizabeth House Website, Working paper no. 34. Available online at ⟨http://www2.qeh.ox.ac.uk⟩.

Meher, R. 1999. "Inter-state Disparities in Levels of Development and the Implications of Economic Liberalization on Regional Economies of India." *Review of Development and Change* 4, no. 2:198–224.

Mendelsohn, O. 1993. "The Transformation of Power in Rural India." *Modern Asian Studies* 27, no. 4:805–842.

Mines, M. 1972. *Muslim Merchants: the Economic Behaviour of an Indian Muslim Community*. New Delhi: Shri Ram Centre for Industrial Relations and Human Resources.

Mines, M. 1984. *The Warrior Merchants: Textiles, Trade and Territory in South India*. Cambridge: Cambridge University Press.

Mohan, R., and Thottan, P. 1992. "The Regional Spread of Urbanisation, Industrialisation and Urban Poverty." In *Poverty in India: Research and Policy*, ed. B. Harriss, S. Guhan, and R. Cassen, 76–141. Delhi: Oxford University Press.

Mooij, J. 1999. *Food Politics and Policy in India. The Public Distribution System in South India*. Delhi: Oxford University Press.

Mukherjee Reed, A., ed. 2000. *Corporate Capitalism in Contemporary South Asia*, Special Issue, *Contemporary South Asia* 9, no. 2.

Myrdal, G. 1968. *Asian Drama. An Inquiry into the Poverty of Nations*. Clinton, MA: Penguin Books.

Myrdal, G. 1973. *Against the Stream: Critical Essays on Economics*. New York: Vintage.

Nadvi, K. 1999. Collective Efficiency and Collective Failure: the response of the Sialkot Surgical Instrument Cluster to Global Quality Pressures. *World Development* 27, no. 9:1105–1126.

Nagaraj, K. 1999. "Labour Market Characteristics and Employment Generation Programmes in India." In *Liberalisation and the New Corruption*, Special Issue, *Bulletin, Institute of Development Studies* 27, no. 2:77–80.

Omvedt, G. 1993. *Reinventing Revolution: New Social Movements and the Socialist Tradition in India*. New York: M. E. Sharpe.

Panini, M. N. 1996. "The Political Economy of Caste." In *Caste: Its Twentieth Century Avatar*, ed. M. N. Srinivas. Delhi: Viking.

Peoples' Union for Civil Liberties. 1998. "Communal Violence in Coimbatore between November 29th and December 1st 1997." *Frontline* 15, no. 5 (March 20):115–119.

Roy, R. 1996. "State Failure: Political-Fiscal Implications of the Black Economy." In *Liberalisation and the New Corruption*, Special Issue, *Bulletin, Institute of Development Studies* 27, no. 2:22–31.

Saberwal, Satish. 1996. *Roots of Crisis: Interpreting Contemporary Indian Society*. New Delhi: Sage Publications.

Schmitz, H., and K. Nadvi. 1999. "Clustering and Industrialisation: Introduction." Special Issue, *Industrial Clusters in Developing Countries, World Development* 27, no. 9:1503–1514.

Shariff, A., P. Ghosh, and S. K. Mondal. 2002. "State Adjusted Public Expenditure on Social Sector and Poverty Alleviation Programmes." *Economic and Political Weekly* (February 23):767–786.

Sinha, A., N. Sangeeta, and K. A. Siddiqui. 1999. "The Impact of Alternative Policies on the Economy with Special Reference to the Informal Sector: A Multisectoral Study." National Council for Applied Economic Research, New Delhi.

Srinivas, M. N. 1966. "A Sociological Study of Okhla Industrial Estate." In *Small Industries and Social Change*, ed. M. N. Srinivas. New Delhi: UNESCO.

Timberg, T. 1978. *The Marwaris: from Traders to Industrialists*. New Delhi: Vikas.

Wade, R. 1985. "The Market for Public Office: Why the Indian State Is Not Better at Development." *World Development* 13, no. 4:476–497.

White, G. 1993. "Towards a Political Analysis of Markets." *Bulletin, Institute of Development Studies* 24, no. 3:4–12.

Wright, T. P., Jr. 1981. "The New Muslim Businessmen of India: A Prospectus for Research." Conference Paper at the 7th European Conference on Modern South Asian Studies, School of Oriental and African Studies, University of London, July.

12

Globalization and Economic Reform as Seen from the Ground: SEWA's Experience in India

Renana Jhabvala and
Ravi Kanbur

12.1 Introduction

Globalization is one of those words that seem to be all things to all people. Some use it in the narrow sense to mean increased trade and capital flows between nations. There is no question that such global integration has proceeded apace since the Second World War, and accelerated dramatically over the last two decades. Spectacular technical change, especially in information and communication, which has facilitated this integration, is also included by some others under the heading of globalization. To yet others, the perceived increase in economic and political power of mobile capital and skilled labor at the global level, vis-à-vis unskilled labor and sovereign governments, is what best characterizes the developments at the end of the twentieth century and the beginning of the twenty-first.

At the same time that discussion of globalization has come to dominate the international discourse, the national discourse is dominated by the issue of "economic reform." In fact, globalization and economic reform are not unrelated because one of the key tenets of economic reform in the last ten years has been the opening up of the national economy to international competition through more openness in trade and in capital flows. The other, and related, key tenet has been the rolling back of the state in major areas of economic and social activity. While the early zeal of globalizers and economic reformers has been curtailed somewhat in the last few years as the result of the financial crises of the late 1990s, and the realization from experience that what is needed is not "downsizing" but "rightsizing" of the state, these two tenets still define the thrust of what "economic reform" means in many developing countries, including in India.

How have globalization and economic reform played themselves out over the last ten years? There has been a furious debate over this question. The perspectives used in the debates have ranged from broadly ideological and theoretical (e.g., "markets versus state"), through the macrolevel empirical (e.g., "does trade openness lead to growth?"), to the microlevel perspectives of poor households and individuals gaining or losing from the global and national level processes (e.g., "exporting creates jobs but increases vulnerability"). The perspective of this chapter is to consider the consequences of globalization and economic reform as seen from the ground level. In particular, we view these global and national phenomena through the lens of the experiences and activities of the Self Employed Women's Association (SEWA) in India.

The plan of the chapter is as follows. Section 12.2 elaborates three key features of globalization and economic reform that are relevant for our discussion, as a way of structuring subsequent discourse. Section 12.3 provides some background to the philosophy and operations of SEWA. Section 12.4, the core of the chapter, provides the ground-level perspective in the context of some specific sectors that SEWA is involved in. Section 12.5 concludes the chapter by drawing the lessons of SEWA's experiences for the globalization and economic reform debate.

12.2   Three Features of Globalization and Economic Reform

As noted earlier, the words *globalization* and *economic reform* are in danger of losing their analytical cutting power because of their wide-ranging use and interpretation. For example, a recent World Bank (2001) report on globalization, while highlighting the conventional "trade and investment" aspects of globalization, also says, "The terrorist attacks on the United States on September 11 were one aspect of globalization," and "The spread of AIDS is part of globalization." At the same time, the "economic reform" moves to more market-oriented economies within countries, and rolling back the role of government and privatizing activities previously in the public sector, are seen by some as also being part and parcel of "globalization."

Moreover, it is argued that this is not the first phase of globalization in the world, nor even the most intense. By some measures, trade and capital flows were more integrated at the end of the last phase, which lasted from the late nineteenth century to the First World War. In this view, the interwar and immediate post–World War II period may well have been an aberration on the long march to global integration. We wish to cut through these definitional issues and focus on three salient features of economic developments in the last two decades that are directly relevant to the poor unskilled women who are members of SEWA—technical change that is biased in favor of capital and skilled labor; increased vulnerability and exposure to economic risks; and a shift of economic power toward more mobile factors of production.

As an introduction to the first of these features, consider the great debate among U.S. analysts on the causes of the widening gap between returns to skilled and unskilled labor in the United States that started in the mid-1970s and has continued to today. This widening is in sharp contrast to a narrowing of the wage gap over three decades follow-ing the Second World War. The debate has raged between "trade" ver-sus "technology" explanations for this widening. Standard economic theory predicts that when an economy opens up to trade, the wages of its abundant factor will be bid up relative to the less abundant factor. Thus, it is argued, if more trade opens up between developed (skill abundant) countries and less developed (unskilled labor abundant) countries, then as a result the gap between skilled and unskilled labor should widen in rich countries and narrow in poor countries. In fact, the latter effect is part of the rationale why some urge developing countries to "globalize."

There have been several critiques of this "trade"-based view. First, in many developing countries, the wage gap between skilled and un-skilled labor has widened, not narrowed. Second, it is argued that even if the trade effect is present, it cannot possibly, in simple quantitative terms, explain the full extent of the widening wage gap in the United States—one commentator has proposed a rule of thumb of "25 percent trade, 75 percent technology." One possible way of combining these two critiques is to give prominence to a global tendency for the returns to skilled labor to increase because of the nature of technical progress in developed countries, and its spillover effects on skilled wages in poor countries through trade and through mobility of skilled labor. For example, the wages of computer programmers in Bangalore, although much lower than those in Silicon Valley, will nevertheless rise with skilled wages in Silicon Valley (the two are linked by skilled labor migration and by trade in services), contributing to the widening gap between skilled and unskilled wages in India. This is in addition to the effects of country-specific technical progress in India itself. Thus we come to what for us is a key consequence of the global forces and national forces of the last two decades—increases in the wages of skilled labor relative to unskilled labor, primarily as the result of technological change, rapidly transmitted through trade and openness.

The second feature of the last twenty years that we wish to highlight is the greater vulnerability of national economies, and components of national economies, to the vagaries of global trade and financial flows. Starting with trade, the standard economic analysis of the gains from trade is well developed and establishes that opening up an economy leads to overall gains in efficiency, even though there may be distributional consequences as some people lose out. However, opening up an economy subjects domestic conditions to global fluctuations in terms of trade and demand for products. The greater efficiency may be purchased at the price of greater risk and vulnerability. In particular, those dependent on their livelihood from selling in global markets or working for those who sell in global markets, even those who gain on average from opening up, may find themselves vulnerable to sharp downturns in demand for their product and their labor, because of global forces beyond their control. To the openness in trade should be added the greater volatility of the global and national economies as the result of capital flows. Whatever the efficiency gains of freer capital movement, the vulnerability side has become all too clear in the last two decades. Liberalization of domestic markets can also, alongside any efficiency gains, produce greater volatility in product and labor markets that impinge directly on unskilled workers.

The third feature we wish to emphasize has become a great bone of contention between what one of the authors (Kanbur 2001) has called the "finance ministry tendency" and the "civil society tendency." Mainstream economics, which undergirds the thinking of the finance ministry tendency, instinctively builds its policy analysis on a basically competitive view of the world, in which no participant in any market has power over any other participant. Many of the policy prescriptions—for example, the advice to developing countries to reduce their import tariffs—are based on such "perfect competition" analysis. It can be readily demonstrated that once we depart from this "first-best" world, and especially if markets have elements of monopoly power in them, then the standard prescriptions no longer hold. In particular, the presence of market power should make us less sanguine about the distributional consequences of moving to a market-oriented economy. Characteristically, there are two interpretations of what the process of greater global trade and capital flows might do to market power. The finance ministry view tends to be that such opening up reduces concentrations of power at the national level—since all participants are now part of a much bigger global market, they are smaller relative to the total market than they were. The civil society view is that, quite to the contrary, allowing capital and skilled labor (but not unskilled labor) to be more mobile increases their relative bargaining power at the national level, vis-à-vis other market players but also vis-à-vis governments. It should not then be surprising that net returns to factors diverge, as governments compete on different dimensions to attract and keep capital and skilled labor.

One of the constant complaints about the managers of the global and national economic systems is that they rarely look down from the global level to see the consequences of global forces for people at the ground level, unless of course these people take to the streets in acts of civil disobedience. But clearly the global forces do have local consequences, especially for the poor who are our main concern. Some of these consequences are good for the poor, and some of these are bad. In this chapter we do not wish to argue that the global forces identified earlier are always and everywhere "evil," as some would have us believe. But a clear-eyed analysis of the chains of causation from the global to the local level, rooted in the actual experience of people on the ground, is needed to inform and alert policymakers and the organizations of the poor to the possible negative effects, and to develop strategies to counteract these effects.

In the rest of the chapter we will follow through the consequences of the three key features of globalization—a lagging behind of the productivity and wages of the unskilled as a result of global and national technical progress; an increased vulnerability and insecurity in the new market- and trade-oriented world, despite significant benefits of these same trends; and a decrease in bargaining power of unskilled workers as a result of the greater mobility of capital and skilled labor. These ground-level impacts will be framed and illustrated in the context of the work of SEWA in India. The observations in this chapter are based on a number of different sources. Some are research studies conducted directly by SEWA while others rely on secondary sources. However, in many cases we have relied on the feedback from SEWA members that are expressed in various SEWA meetings, in observations of SEWA leaders and organizers, and in the experiences of individual women. We begin a discussion of these experiences with a brief introduction to SEWA.

12.3   Background to SEWA

SEWA is a trade union of poor, self-employed women workers. Its roots lie in the organizing of Gujarat textile workers in parallel with the Indian independence movement. SEWA emerged from this base in textile worker's unions, with an initial focus on organizing marginalized self-employed urban women engaged in such trades as street vendors, rag pickers, head loaders, and so forth to give them a voice to address their plight. It now has an all-India membership of around 419,000 women. In Gujarat, two-thirds of its over 284,000 members are from the rural areas. SEWA is now working in five other states in India.

SEWA is primarily a movement of self-employed women workers, a confluence of three movements—the labor movement, cooperative movement, and women's movement based on a Gandhian philosophy. Through this women become strong and visible and their tremendous economic and social contributions are recognized. SEWA's main strength lies in building the capacity of illiterate and barely literate women to manage their own activities. A large part of the SEWA staff is recruited and promoted from among the members, and SEWA is developing its cadre of barefoot professionals, such as barefoot managers, lawyers, engineers, doctors, and researchers, who become "illiterate professionals" by virtue of the practical experience that they gain and the focused capacity building inputs that are provided by SEWA. These members and grassroots organizers constitute the spearhead teams that are formed for each activity and that take the lead in providing direct assistance to members at the village level. They also play a key role in promoting activities in new villages and mobilizing and organizing women to participate. Through this mechanism sustainability and capacity for replication are built-in to the SEWA's organizational structure.

SEWA's philosophy embraces a holistic approach to development—it believes that multiple inputs and interventions are essential for women to emerge from poverty, vulnerability, and years of deprivation. SEWA's integrated approach to poverty alleviation is comprised of (a) organizing for collective strength, (b) capital formation through access to financial services, (c) capacity building, and (d) social security (essentially health care, child care, shelter, and insurance) to enhance women's productivity and to ensure that sudden crises are not a drain on their fragile household economies. SEWA's two main goals are (1) full employment meaning employment that ensures work security, income security, food security, and social security and (2) self-reliance by which SEWA means that women should be autonomous and self-reliant, individually and collectively, both economically and in terms of their decision-making ability.

As a member-based organization, its activities are driven by the needs and demands of its members. A wide range of activities is being implemented covering savings and credit groups, micro-insurance, watershed development, dairy cooperatives and fodder security, agricultural development, forest plantation, drinking water, craft production, salt production and gum collection, health care, child care, functional literacy, mobile ration vans, training and research. Member education in the philosophy of SEWA and basic leadership are provided to all members.

These activities are implemented by the members through a number of different institutions established by SEWA including a total of eighty-six cooperatives (dairy, fodder, grain banks, plantation, ration shops, etc.), of which the largest is SEWA Bank, village committees for integrated watershed development; water users groups for management and operation of village tanks and ponds and piped water supply schemes; handicraft associations; urban community slum organizations; and health workers and child care workers cooperatives. This reflects SEWA's aim to decentralize decision-making powers, including financial responsibility, to the individual institutions and to make members and their organizations self-reliant.

After this brief background on SEWA's philosophy and its operations, we turn to a specific discussion of SEWA's experiences with the consequences of globalization and economic reform in a number of selected sectors.

12.4   SEWA's Experience

12.4.1   The Construction Sector
SEWA has 13,000 members in the construction sector, most of them in Ahmedabad city. These women are mainly "unskilled" construction workers, working as casual labor. A study conducted by SEWA Academy in 1999 (SEWA 1999) found the following:

• Women were engaged in mainly unskilled work, with 92 percent carrying loads of cement, bricks, concrete, etc., and the rest in semi-skilled work like plastering or concrete mixing. In comparison, 36.8 percent of men were engaged in load carrying, the rest being in semi-skilled or skilled work, like masonry, tile laying, centering, etc.

• 64 percent of the women and 60 percent of the men said that they were "traditionally" construction workers, namely, their families did this work before them. Many of them had become construction workers after migrating to the city from the rural areas. The rest joined this work after losing work in other jobs.

• 93.6 percent of the women and 97.6 percent of the men said they were casual laborers; they were engaged on a daily basis from sites where laborers stood every morning and were hired by contractors.

• There were considerable differences between the average earnings of men and women, reflecting their difference in skill levels. The average earnings of women were Rs 60 per day as compared to Rs 128 for the men.

• 88.8 percent of the women and 74.4 percent of the men said that they had physical problems connected with their work; and 51 percent of the women and 13 percent of the men said that they had suffered accidents in the course of their work.

Interviews conducted for the study identified pressure on employment as a key feature of the previous decade in this sector. Here is how the issue appears to Madhuben Maganbhai, a 35-year-old construction worker, in her own words:

I started at the age of fifteen and first carried loads of concrete on my head. Then I learnt to carry twelve bricks at a time. Later, I learnt to lay concrete and then do plastering. When I first started working we were attached to a contractor and would get work everyday. We only had one holiday on *amavas* (no-moon day). However, in the last ten to twelve years, the numbers of workers increased with the closure of the textile mills and the printing factories. Then workers started competing with each other, and we no longer had regular work. We all had to stand at the *kadiya naka* (roadside site for construction workers) and contractors come and hire us by the day. Still, I used to get about twenty days of work a month. However, over the last five years things have become especially bad. I hardly get six to seven days work a month. This is the situation with all of us who stand at the *kadiya naka*. Why? I don't know why. The work seems to have decreased overall. Some say it is due to recession. Other say it is due to new machines, which have come in. In some of the bigger sites now, I have seen that all digging is done by machines, and even carrying bricks that we used to do, is now done by machines, and in some sites whole walls are made elsewhere and brought to the site.

Madhuben clearly identifies technological change as one of the factors affecting her work prospects. This matches many of the institutional trends that we see in this sector in the wake of globalization and economic reform. Under the prevailing WTO regime, the essential requirement of global tendering has facilitated the entry of many multinational corporations on to the Indian construction scene in a big way. The presence of these companies is increasingly visible in many infrastructure development projects being undertaken under government funding as well as under bilateral/multilateral assistance arrangements. Major foreign companies that have already arrived are Bechtel (USA), Hyundai (Japan), Mitsui (Japan), Obayshi (Japan), Savdesa (Sweden), and Traffel House (UK). Many world leaders in construction have already arrived, staking claims on building projects for petrochemical plants, refineries, factories, roads, bridges, and metro rail projects. Highly technology-smart and equipped with the latest machinery and construction methods, these companies are beginning to have far-reaching implications for the domestic construction industry as well as labor.

The trend toward mechanization with the entry of international firms has been responded to by the Indian government—by helping the domestic industry to mechanize as well. The government of India, along with leaders in the construction industry, has set up a new organization called the Construction Industry Development Council. One of its major tasks is to help the Indian industry enter the era of global tendering. In the post-liberalization period, the Indian construction industry is witnessing many structural changes that are going to radically transform the business as well as the construction labor market. With increased mechanization, there would be massive displacement of labor in nearly all construction operations. Clearly, women construction workers are going to be worst affected by this emerging scenario of increasing privatization and mechanization. Female labor might be completely eliminated from the main operations in which they have been traditionally deployed, namely, soil digging and carrying, carrying inputs in concrete mixing and placing, concrete curing, and brick carrying. Although data on labor deployment on construction sites using modern construction methods is not available, it seems that the overall deployment of labor could become one-fiftieth to one-fifth of the earlier numbers (see table 12.1).

In light of this intensifying (un)employment situation in the construction sector, alongside the traditional problems of poor working

Table 12.1
Major construction equipment/accessories being factory-produced

Equipment/accessories	Impact on labor
Excavators	Reduction to 1/20th of present workforce
Ready-mix concrete (RMC) plants	Reduction to 1/20th of present workforce
Concrete pumping machines	Reduction to 1/10th of present workforce
Chemical concrete curing	Reduction to 1/5th of present workforce
Bar-bending machines	Reduction to 1/5th of present workforce
Steel structures with high tension bolts	Reduction to 1/10th of present workforce
Wall panels (made from flyash-based cement)	Reduction to 1/10th of present workforce
Prefabricated segments	Reduction to 1/10th to 1/5th present workforce
Complete prefabricated steel structures	Reduction to 1/20th of present workforce
High-strength concrete ASC slabs of different sizes (made from flyash-based cement)	Reduction to 1/20th of present workforce
Auto-dov wall panels using flyash cement (aerated, lightweight/half of a mud brick weight, low-cost and high heat isolation property; most useful in earthquake prone regions)	Reduction to 1/20th of present workforce
Preengineered buildings	Reduction to 1/50th of present workforce

Source: Information collected from industry sources for CIDC.

conditions, SEWA's response has been multidimensional, but with two main elements—specific programs to help their members, and organization to increase their voice in policy and regulation.

Addressing the problem of unskilled work requires training SEWA's members in new skills. While standard construction work is decreasing on the one hand, there is growth in other types of construction on the other, from large-scale infrastructure projects to urban housing to rural semi-permanent huts. The government has been encouraging low-cost housing. Given the growth of the sector, many new products are coming into the market. As an example, SEWA approached a prominent cement company and a local builder to help the women get better skills. The first training offered was in masonry, where the women trainees had to face a great deal of ridicule—who had ever heard of women masons! However, after the training, about one-third of the trainees improved their earnings from Rs 60 to Rs 130 per day. After that a large number of women wanted to take the training and this is an ongoing activity, ranging across other construction skills as well.

But training is not enough. What is also needed is to influence the councils of policymaking and regulation that make decisions that affect the daily lives of poor women. In this regard, SEWA's first action was to organize the workers, make them members, and enlist their demands. These demands included the issuance of identity cards and attendance cards for construction workers, key documents for accessing local public services, insurance coverage and payment of medical expenses, and payment of minimum wages. As a result of broad-based pressure, the government of India has passed the Construction Workers Protection and Welfare Act (1996). However, the government of Gujarat has not yet implemented this act. The main demand of the SEWA in Gujarat was that the government of Gujarat implement the Construction Workers Act. Thus construction workers now do have some voice through the SEWA. However, the major decisions to deal with globalization are not made in Ahmedabad, but in New Delhi. The SEWA has now become a member of the Construction Industry Development Council and through this channel, among others, is making the needs of the workers felt at the level of government policy.

12.4.2   The Garment Industry

In the wake of liberalization, during the 1990s the garment sector in Ahmedabad grew rapidly: Output grew by 18 percent and retail trade grew by 12 percent (Singh 1999). A recent study of over one hundred small factories and workshops found that well over half were under five years old and over one-third were under two years old (Singh 1999). Because the garment industry in Ahmedabad is fast growing and changing, it is difficult to capture in official statistics or otherwise. To begin with, the garment labor market is highly segmented by product, market, location of work, employment status, and, across or within each of these niches, by gender. Second, many garment workers are not factory-based but home based—both own-account and subcontract— and are not adequately captured in official statistics (SEWA 1998). Third, the garment sector is highly volatile, experiencing rapid changes in the domestic market and rapid (but fluctuating) expansion of the export market.

A SEWA survey found that 50 percent of workers in all registered firms did not have written contracts and about 10 percent did not receive any benefits. Another study found that many large factories hire workers on both a piece rate basis (whereby wages vary according to output) and a time rate basis (whereby wages are fixed by the week or month). This study also found that women are typically hired on a piece rate basis, whether or not they are permanent workers and whether they stitch or do ancillary tasks (Unni, Bali, and Vyas 1999).

Small factories and workshops tend to hire workers without written contracts and below minimum wages (Kantor 2000). One recent study found that only 34 percent of female workers and 40 percent of male workers in small garment workshops are paid a regular monthly salary. The rest are paid by the day or piece, depending on their output (Unni, Bali, and Vyas 1999). Moreover, workers typically do not get worker benefits such as paid leave, severance notice, or bonuses. Only 15 percent receive employer contributions to a pension or provident fund; only about 5 percent are covered by accident insurance. Subcontract workers are paid per piece or per dozen pieces produced. The rate per dozen pieces varies by the type of garment. Whatever the item, dependent home-based garment makers earn only a small percentage of the selling price—as low as 2 to 5 percent—while the employer-trader (the *seth*) and his contractor (if any) earn a far higher percentage—as high as 40 percent (Singh 1999).

Most workers—both dependent and independent—experience fluctuating earnings and income. What a person earns is not just a function of her wages but also of the number of days she gets work. There are seasonal fluctuations in the garment industry. The season when most festivals and weddings take place—from September to February—is the peak season for garment production. During the peak season, the volume production that is "put out" to small manufacturing units and home-based producers increases to help meet demand. During the other six months of the year—March through August—the volume of subcontracting declines. During those months, if they do not get or expect work orders, some dependent producers shift to other occupations: for instance, rolling *bidis* or incense sticks.

The products in the market have been changing rapidly. A decade ago, women were making mainly petticoats and children's wear for the local market. Now, the demand is for more sophisticated items in the national and international market, which they do not know how to stitch. Earlier, cotton cloth was the main raw material, but now there is a variety of synthetic materials including satin and velvet. These materials do not stitch well on the older sewing machines owned by the women. Most women have the simplest types of sewing machines, and although many women have fitted these machines with motors, they still remain low in productivity. They would like to move to the next level of sewing machines but cannot afford the capital to do so. In addition, many types of work, which used to be done by hand such as making buttonholes and hemming, now are done by machines, or by add-ons to existing machines.

One of the major problems of the garment workers is the lack of capital to expand their business if they are self-employed, or to upgrade the quality of their sewing machines. The SEWA Bank has a special emphasis on asset creation, on buying new machines. Every month about three hundred garment workers take loans from SEWA Bank ranging from Rs 5000 to Rs 25,000. But many are unable to afford them. Also, some women claim that when they bought the special add-ons they were able to earn a lot, but soon the market changed and they were left to repay the loan with greatly reduced income from the machine.

SEWA's efforts on behalf of its members in the garment industry have been directed to increasing their access to employment opportunities, to capital, to skills, and to markets. For example, while there has been a growth of small factories of all types including garment factories in Ahmedabad city, there does not exist any system by which workers can get to know of vacancies or opportunities in these factories, or for the factory owners to find good workers. The existing employment exchanges only cater to formal-sector jobs. SEWA has set up its own employment center, where SEWA members register themselves, their qualifications and skills, and the kind of the work they are willing to do. The center keeps in touch with potential employers through direct visits and through other forums such as the Chamber of Commerce, and attempts to place workers as well as negotiate a good wage and working conditions for them. About 150 workers are placed every month.

Since most garment workers can only stitch one type of garment, as the market changes they lose work. SEWA has been running classes where workers learn to stitch twenty-five different types of garments, which are most popular in the market. The courses are part-time for three months and about one hundred workers are trained at one time. The women say that learning these new skills has increased their work opportunities by about 50 percent. Moreover, SEWA members are generally at the low end of the scale of products. The government has set up a number of institutes of fashion technology to promote the garment industry and exports, and there are many private institutes also training people in fashion and design. SEWA has an agreement with the most prominent such institute—the National Institute of Fashion Technology—that they will accept about fifty SEWA members for training every year. The skills taught in this institute enable the workers to enter the market directly, or to work for exporters.

A final example is the SEWA Trade Facilitation Center (STFC). A significant number of SEWA members are embroidery workers, mainly in rural areas. In the last ten years they have been hit by repeated disasters such as droughts and cyclones, and at these times embroidery is the only livelihood they can sustain. The objectives of SFTC are to link artisan rural micro-enterprises with the national, international, global, and virtual marketplace, thereby offering access to both domestic and external trade opportunities and increased sustainable employment opportunities for the disaster-affected poor artisans. In order to achieve its goals, STFC uses the latest management tools and information technology to realize the true potential of the products produced by the artisans and to connect them with the targeted market arenas and segments globally. In its brief one and half year period it helped to realize an annual growth of 62 percent in overall sales and 311 percent growth in exports in 2001 over the preceding year. The plan is that in five years the STFC, which is incorporated as a company, will have developed into a profitable institution, which is totally dedicated to assisting the poorest women to market their own products locally, nationally, regionally, and internationally. This unique business model for poverty alleviation operates via a unique principle whereby the majority of shareholders are the disaster-affected artisans themselves.

12.4.3   The Forestry Sector

About 90 percent of India's 64 million hectares of forests are under state ownership; the rest are community and private forests. Altogether there are an estimated 100 million forest dwellers in the country living in and around forests and another 275 million for whom forests constitute an important source of livelihood support. Women's economic dependence on forests extends far beyond their involvement as wage labor in forestry operations and forest-based industry. Women interact with forests at multiple levels, and this complex relationship needs to be understood in its entirety before any effort is made to trace the impact of macroeconomic and policy changes on their lives and livelihood (Nanavati 1996).

A large number of SEWA members earn their livelihood from the forests. For example, in the drought-prone villages of Banaskantha,

Gujarat, gum is a product collected from the trunks of *babul* (proposis julifera) trees. It is used as an input into a variety of manufacturing processes such as glues, dyes, firecrackers, and certain eatables. Owing to lack of irrigation, the agriculture in this area is very meager and most people pick gum as a means of supplementing their livelihood, often as their only source of livelihood. According to a survey conducted by SEWA in 1997:

• 92 percent of the women said that gum collection was their main occupation

• 68 percent of families earn Rs 500 or less and 25 percent earn Rs 500– Rs 1,000 per month

• 77 percent of the children help their parents, and most do not go to school

• 38 percent of the women and their families have to migrate to other districts during the summer in search of work

• 70 percent of the families have mortgaged their land

SEWA's actions in the forestry sector confound any simple characterization of its general stance as pro- or anti-market, or pro- or anti-state. It is well recognized that state intervention in the forestry sector in India has been pervasive and government policies have had a decisive influence on the management and health of forests in the country. A number of studies (e.g., Bajaj 1994) have established that these policies have been detrimental in their economic, environmental, and distributional effects and made the case for a smaller and more focused government presence in the forestry sector.

In the last decade, the sector has seen a number of changes in the wake of the economic reform process. The most salient change has been the lowering of import barriers for wood and wood products. Timber in log or sawn form and pulp have been included under Open General License and private entrepreneurs can now import. There has been a quantum jump in the import of timber with imported quantities reaching about 50 percent of recorded timber production from forests land. An estimated 50 percent of pulp consumption is also currently imported. The liberalization of imports has helped to conserve forest resources among other benefits.

Overall, SEWA would argue that the impact of the reforms on forest-based communities and particularly women has been positive, although the import of pulp has adversely affected some farmers who had undertaken block plantation of eucalyptus and other such species.

International participation and influence on forest management has been positive to the extent that greater stakeholder participation and community-based management are now widely accepted within the forest bureaucracy. With the institutionalization of Joint Forest Management a great conceptual breakthrough has been made in sharing ownership with local communities. However, JFM covers only a miniscule proportion of the country's forests, and even here the literature suggests that women's interests may have been adversely impacted upon in the initial stages.

In SEWA's view, by far the greatest failing of the reform process, which also has the greatest impact on women collectors, is that of the continued state control and monopoly of the nontimber forest produce (NTFP) trade, across different states in the country. Gum collection by SEWA members is a leading example of this phenomenon. Almost all of the important NTFPs are nationalized and can be sold only to government agencies. Most state Forest Development Corporations are defunct agencies confronted with mounting liabilities. Huge and redundant manpower and capital enhance operating costs and huge markups are needed to break even. Very often subcontractors are deployed and the collectors' margins further squeezed. The extensive literature on the subject almost unanimously points toward decontrolling the trade and reducing the government role in it (Bajaj 2001).

In response, SEWA organized the gum collecting women into groups, which got licenses from the forest department to collect gum (SEWA 2000). Due to the forest laws, the groups were not allowed to sell the gum in the market but had to sell it to the forest department at prices determined by the latter. The forest department began reducing its price from Rs 12 per kilo to Rs 10 and in one year even as low as Rs 6, further impoverishing an already impoverished community. One of the reasons cited for this decrease of prices, was a large-scale import of gum from Sudan. However, the prices in the market were much higher than forest department prices, remaining around Rs 20 to Rs 26. SEWA began a dialogue with the government asking for special permission to sell gum directly in the market. This permission was reluctantly granted for a year, during which the earnings of the women went up considerably. However, the permission has not been renewed. Meanwhile SEWA is exploring ways of processing the gum in the villages. At the same time, SEWA is working with the agriculture university to upgrade the quality of the trees and make them more productive.

With annual production of over 2.5 million standard bags (each bag containing 1,000 bundles of 50 leaves each), Madhya Pradesh is one of the largest producers of *tendu* leaf in the country. The state has a system whereby the leaves are collected by collector cooperatives set up by the government. More than 3 million workers are involved in the *tendu* leaf collection. The entire family gets up at four in the morning and walks five to six kilometers in the forest for the collection of *tendu patta*. They come back by noon and then make bundles from leaves and deposit it at *fudh* by four in the evening. For 100 bundles they get Rs 40.

In both Gujarat and Madhya Pradesh, SEWA has helped the women form collector groups and sell to the forest department. In Madhya Pradesh SEWA found that the cooperatives were in name only. The tendu pluckers have nothing to do with the governance of the tendu business. The business is clearly run by the forest department hierarchy. Tendu pluckers who are supposedly the "members" of primary societies have not been issued membership certificates even after a decade. For all practical purposes, the tendu pluckers who are supposed to be members of cooperatives are treated as casual workers. In fact, many forest department officials don't even know what a cooperative is and how it should be run. They think they are providing employment to tendu pluckers for which they should be grateful to them. In response, SEWA's campaigns have focused on empowering the tendu pickers to organize and claim their rights via-à-vis the forestry department, including the right to sell to private traders.

12.4.4 Insurance

SEWA's poor women members have always faced tremendous vulnerabilities in their lives—the risks of accidents and illness, fire and theft, and periodic unemployment and loss of income through the vagaries of product and labor markets. As documented in the previous sections, this last factor has increased in the last decade of liberalization. SEWA found that poor women want support to tackle as many risks as possible at a time, thereby reducing their vulnerability, and that they are willing to pay premiums for insurance. In 1992, SEWA set up its insurance program, implemented by SEWA Bank. Women paid a small premium and in exchange were covered for death, hospitalization, and asset loss. The premium had to be paid every year, so to simplify payment, SEWA Bank linked it with saving and the interest on a fixed deposit amount covered the premium.

In the early 1990s only the Public Sector firms were allowed in the insurance sector, and so the insurance schemes were worked with the Public Sector, Life Insurance Company, and General Insurance companies. It was very difficult working with these companies, because first, all the work of collecting premiums, convincing the women, identifying claims and following up with the insurance company was done by SEWA, at its own cost. Second, the insurance company rules and regulations required procedures that were very difficult for poor women with limited resources to comply with for example they were required to get a certificate from the weather bureau about speed of winds, if their houses were destroyed by a storm. Third, the companies were very slow in checking out claims: for example, assessors would not reach the site of house damage by flood or riots for weeks afterward. This slowness also resulted in the women going to moneylenders and into debt.

In the late 1990s the Indian Parliament passed an act allowing private insurance companies into the sector. SEWA's stand was that a provision should be introduced into the act, that a certain percentage of the insured of each insurance company should be from the informal sector and the poor, and this clause was indeed introduced into the act. Once the act was passed, SEWA was keen to launch its own insurance company in the form of a cooperative. However, it was not allowed to do so because the act seemed to be only promoting very large companies. The minimum capital required to register a company under the act was Rs 100 crores for life insurance and for general insurance. SEWA argued with the government that an insurance company for the poor did not require such a large capital base and that Rs 30 crores would guarantee the safety and stability of such a company. However, this argument is not being heard and so far only the very large companies are being allowed to enter the market.

Meanwhile SEWA has being building up its own insurance program for its members (Chatterjee 2002). By 2001 over 92,000 people had been insured, including about 72,000 women and 20,000 men (husbands of SEWA members). Three packages are being offered to the members, all of which include benefits for death, illness, asset loss, and maternity. With privatization, SEWA has been able to get better deals for its members, as there is more competition among the insurance companies.

As in the forestry sector, therefore, SEWA's position on liberalization is a nuanced one. The support of state-owned insurance companies to the poor was not great, and the privatization has allowed SEWA to get better deals for its members. However, the dream of starting its own insurance company is unfulfilled, as the regulatory framework in the newly privatized sector seems more suited to the needs of large insurance companies than to organizations of the poor. SEWA's needs are greater representation and clout at the councils where these issues are discussed and decided, so that it can better make the case for the needs of its members.

12.5   Conclusion

What do we learn from SEWA's ground-level perspective on the consequences of the global and national forces that go under the labels of "globalization" and "economic reform"? We draw the following five lessons:

1. The effects of globalization and economic reforms on poor women are highly differentiated and nuanced, so a blanket analysis or stance is not justified (Jhabvala 1995). Some features of the economic reform process, such as reducing the role of the state in forestry, and some consequences of greater openness, such as the easier access to international markets for poor women's products, are beneficial to poor women. But other features are not.

2. Despite the benefits of globalization and economic reform, the three troubling features identified from first principles—relative decline in unskilled wages, increased risk and vulnerability, and a declining bargaining power of unskilled labor—are indeed seen in SEWA's ground-level experience.

3. Maximizing the benefits and minimizing the costs requires active management of the process of globalization and economic reform with the outcomes for poor in mind. A hands-off policy is not an option. Strategies for management should be developed by listening to the experiences of the poor and to their representatives.

4. Managing and mitigating the negative consequences of liberalization will require direct interventions to enhance the skills of the poor, and developing insurance tools to manage the risks they face will be crucial. These interventions need to combine government action and action by organizations of the poor.

5. The poor, especially unskilled poor women, need organization to counteract the growing economic power of capital and skilled labor as a result of their greater national and global mobility. Organization is also the sine qua non for representation of the interests of poor

women in local, national, and global policymaking councils, a point also emphasized in World Bank (2000). Public policy can help by developing an enabling legal and regulatory environment in which membership-based organizations of the poor can represent their interests and provide them with services they need.

References

Bajaj, Manjul. 1994. "Public Policy and the Sustainable Use of Forest Resources: A Study of the Indian Experience of State Intervention in the Forestry Sector." MSc diss., MSc Environmental Managment, Wye College, University of London, October.

Bajaj, Manjul. 2001. "The Impact of Globalization on the Forestry Sector in India with Special Reference to Women's Employment." Paper commissioned by the Study group on Women Workers and Child Labour, National Commission on Labour, Government of India.

Chatterjee, Mirai. 2002. "Strength in Solidarity: Some Experiences of SEWA Insurance (VimoSEWA)." SEWA Academy, Ahmedabad.

Jhabvala, Renana. 1995. "Liberalising for the Poor." SEWA Academy, Ahmedabad.

Kanbur, Ravi. 2001. "Economic Policy, Distribution, Poverty: the Nature of Disagreements." *World Development* 29, no. 6:1083–1094.

Kantor, Paula. 2000. "Home-Based Workers." SEWA Academy, Ahmedabad.

Nanavati, Reema. 1996. "Feminize Our Forests." SEWA Academy, Ahmedabad.

SEWA. 1998. "SEWA-NCAER Project on Contribution of the Informal Sector to National Income." SEWA Academy, Ahmedabad.

SEWA. 1999. "Labouring Brick by Brick: Study of Construction Workers." SEWA Academy, Ahmedabad.

SEWA. 2000. "The Gum Collectors: Struggling to Survive in the Dry Areas of Banaskantha." SEWA Academy, Ahmedabad.

Singh, Pratima. 1999. "A Report on Subcontracted units and Women Workers in the Garment Industry." SEWA Academy, Ahmedabad.

Unni, Jeemol, Namrata Bali, and Jignasa Vyas. 1999. "Subcontracted Women Workers in the Global Economy: Case Study of Garment Industry in India." SEWA Academy, Ahmedabad.

World Bank. 2000. *World Development Report 2000/2001: Attacking Poverty.* New York: Oxford University Press.

World Bank. 2001. *Globalization, Growth and Poverty: Building an Inclusive World Economy.* New York: Oxford University Press.

Index